MIRFIELD ESSAYS
IN
CHRISTIAN BELIEF

MIRFIELD ESSAYS IN CHRISTIAN BELIEF

by members of the
Community of the Resurrection

WIPF & STOCK · Eugene, Oregon

Wipf and Stock Publishers
199 W 8th Ave, Suite 3
Eugene, OR 97401

Mirfield Essays in Christian Belief
By Community of the Resurrection,
Copyright©1962 Community of the Resurrection
ISBN 13: 978-1-61097-958-0
Publication date 2/15/2012
Previously published by The Faith Press, 1962

CONTENTS

ACKNOWLEDGMENTS   *page* 6

GENERAL INTRODUCTION   7
by the Revd. Fr. Jonathan Graham, C.R. (Superior)

PART I
  I. *The Preparation.* Fr. Jonathan Graham   11
 II. *The Incarnation.* Fr. Godfrey Pawson   32
III. *The Crucifixion.* Fr. Jonathan Graham   49
IV. *The Resurrection.* Fr. Nicolas Graham   65

PART II
INTRODUCTION TO PART II
  I. *Dialogue on the Existence of God*
     Fr. M. Jarrett-Kerr   85
 II. *The Living God.* Fr. William Wheeldon   100
III. *Creation and the Fall.* Br. Dunstan Jones   119
IV. *The Holy Spirit.* Fr. Nicolas Graham   139

PART III
INTRODUCTION TO PART III
  I. *The Apostolic Church.* Fr. Andrew Blair   157
 II. *The Worship of the Body.* Fr. Mark Tweedy   170
III. *Baptism and the Quest of Unity*
     Fr. Geoffrey Curtis   191
IV. *Prayer in the Body of Christ*
     Fr. Mark Tweedy   211
 V. *The Christian Attitude to Suffering*
     Fr. Hugh Bishop   223

PART IV
INTRODUCTION TO PART IV
  I. *This is our World.* ✝Trevor Huddleston   241
 II. *Witness of the Church in an Expanding World.* Fr. M. Jarrett-Kerr   249
III. *Vocation and Response.* ✝Victor Shearburn   266
IV. *All in All.* Fr. Aelred Stubbs   281

NOTES   296
INDEX OF BIBLICAL PASSAGES   300
INDEX OF PROPER NAMES   306

ACKNOWLEDGMENTS

Thanks are due to the following publishers for permission to quote from their books:

Messrs. Harvill: Eliade, *Myths, Dreams and Mysteries*.
Messrs. Collins: Teilhard de Chardin: *The Phenomenon of Man*.
Messrs. Nisbet: Tillich, *The Protestant Era*.

Thanks are also due to:

The Revd. E. Leshnick for his help in preparing the MS. for the press; to Mr. C. Cherriman for compiling the Biblical Index and the Index of Names; and to Miss B. M. G. Smith for help in typing.

THE REVD. FR. SUPERIOR

GENERAL INTRODUCTION

'HELP one another, serve one another, for the times are urgent, and the days are evil' : so the Archbishop of Canterbury called on all who heard him on his enthronement day. This book, planned before that summons, has no other ambition.

It is the product of a common life, worked out and lived out by ordinary men who, in the ups and downs of cheek-by-jowl experience, share the conviction that the resurrection of Jesus Christ is the fact of facts. The aim of the religious community in which they have found their vocation is to reproduce the life of the first Christians of whom it is recorded that they had in common a belief which made them of one heart and soul, and a worship in which all shared with gladness and singleness of heart.

A common life with such ideals keeps its flavour only by giving itself away. Not to share what God has given is to lose the gift. Hence this book. Its authors, taken by their work into the world which has grown away from the fact of facts, long to share what they have been given, a unity springing from the truth and holiness of God.

There is a characteristic gaiety of spirit in the life of the first Christians; Christ has died and is alive again for ever. So all human life is of immense potentiality; and simultaneously of laughable insignificance; an obscure Ethiopian *must* receive baptism, while one of the chosen three among the apostles is killed with the sword without a word of comment or regret. There is every reason to care intensely, no reason whatever to worry; in the life of the expanding Church there is a sense of compelling urgency yet one must wait upon God to work out his purpose. 'The times are urgent and the days are evil'; but that is no reason for panic. It is impossible to imagine any disaster from which the glorified Christ will not emerge victorious, crying 'I am risen and am still with thee.'

In the Old Testament writers there is a delightful phrase used to describe the moment of truth when the word of God grips a man and claims his allegiance; they spoke of God 'Uncovering the ears' of a man. If this collection of essays should be used by him to remove that invisible barrier which makes ears dull of hearing; so that men should hear with their ears and understand with their heart, and he should turn again and heal them; if it could be that, in any degree, then it will have been worth the writing and will justify the hope with which it is published.

PART I

CHAPTER I

FR. JONATHAN GRAHAM, C.R.

THE PREPARATION

THE official genealogy of the family of Jesus of Nazareth, which Matthew saw fit to place at the beginning of his gospel, contains the names of four women: Tamar, Rahab, Ruth and Uriah's wife, Bathsheba. Tamar was incestuous, Rahab was a harlot, Ruth was an alien, and Bathsheba committed adultery and connived at the murder of her husband by her lover. Many of the ancestors whose names figure in the family tree were morally respectable, most of them monogamous; it is startling therefore that the ancestresses selected are designed to shock. It would occasion no great surprise to find that a twentieth century novelist had provided his readers with heroines whose sexual lives were irregular; he would be showing his emancipation from the stuffy notions of biblical morality! What is remarkable is to find that the Church's first official account of the life and ministry of the Son of God should go out of its way to include the unsavoury skeletons lurking in the cupboard of his human family.

Jesus has been visible for so long only through the haze of his halo; believers and opponents alike have detached him from his setting and found themselves overwhelmed or exasperated by his supreme genius; but detach any character from his setting and he becomes distorted and out of proportion. Matthew, well aware of the danger of presenting Jesus to his readers as a demi-god, deliberately prefaces his gospel with a genealogy, and a scandalous genealogy at that, in order to rivet our attention to the fact that Jesus is a branch of a family tree, a chip off an old block, rooted, embedded in human history and identified with our human frailty.

Matthew is careful to tell us that this genealogy is that of Joseph, the husband of Mary, but not the father of Jesus, whose birth was miraculous. In any case, the word 'son' is very loosely used in Hebrew genealogies to mean 'heir,' not necessarily offspring. The original readers of the gospel believed in the Godhead of Jesus; what Matthew was concerned to do was to emphasize his human background and preserve the truth that Jesus was God *and* man. So he helps his readers to see him in proportion, a paradoxical person, miraculously conceived but bound up with the history of a particular racial group in a corner of the Mediterranean over a period of two thousand years. He was the 'heir of David, the heir of Abraham' (Matt. 1 : 1).

Abraham was a barbarous, heartless and polygamous sheikh of Mesopotamian extraction, whose religious and social beliefs and behaviour were to a great extent dictated by taboos and fertility rites. So much is obvious to any moderately educated reader of the Book of Genesis; and it was certainly obvious to Matthew, to whom polygamy was abhorrent and taboos pagan nonsense. Then why did he claim Abraham as an ancestor for Jesus? That's the first puzzle : what was the point of linking up the two? Biographers don't normally mention any but the honourable ancestry of their heroes.

As soon as one begins to brood on that question, other strange problems begin to emerge. For instance, in the course of an argument recorded by John in the Fourth Gospel, a group of Jews protested to Jesus, who was speaking to them of truth and freedom, 'we be Abraham's seed, and have never yet been in bondage to any man' (John 8 : 33). What could they have meant by that claim? Apart from one short period of freedom, the race of Abraham had been in continuous bondage for six hundred years and largely dependent on neighbouring empires long before that. What did the contemporaries of Jesus mean by claiming a long history of liberty? The political facts proved so patently that the claim was untrue; was it then some strange liberty of mind or spirit, some freedom beyond the reach of a conqueror that the Jews reckoned as a necessary consequence of being 'Abraham's seed'?

Or again, consider for a moment the well-known but inexplicable characteristic of 'Abraham's seed' in preserving their identity in every civilization and country on the earth, except their own. There is no other racial group that has shown such a vigorous power of refusing assimilation, while thriving spiritually and materially in a hundred different lands, only to meet and patiently suffer time and again the bitterest of persecutions. When Frederick the Great asked Voltaire the most effective proof of the truth of Christianity and was given the reply: 'The Jews, Your Majesty,' the conundrum was simply being posed in a fresh context. There is a strange stubborn fact for the social historian to account for.

Here is a nation that has scarcely ever known freedom, never at any period claiming for its homeland more than a narrow strip of mountain country, its capital with no road or river to bring it wealth or culture, without harbour and without natural resources, uniquely free and powerful and indomitable.

The only explanation which begins to account for the facts is that which led Matthew to link Jesus with Abraham, the explanation enshrined in the literature of the Old Testament, that Abraham and his race were chosen by the One Eternal God for the purpose of preparing for and receiving the Eternal Son of God when he came to this earth to redeem it.

The history which Jesus was taught as a child began with the remote ancestors of his race, who had lived and died two thousand years before; their names were Abraham, Isaac, Jacob and Joseph, known collectively as the fathers or the patriarchs. Next there followed a period of four hundred years—the Dark Ages of dependence and slavery in the neighbouring empire of Egypt. The third era was one of liberation, freedom and conquest under the leadership of Moses; this the Jewish child must master in the greatest detail. The fourth period or 'Middle Ages' saw the development of a kingdom, which reached its peak of prosperity early—about the year 1000—and declined gradually to complete disaster and deportation four hundred years later. The last five or six hundred years had been, with one bright interval of freedom, squalid and uneventful, ending in the Roman conquest of his land about seventy years before his birth. Such a sequence of legendary origins, periods of success and periods of decline is at first sight as dull and ordinary a record as many another; what makes it utterly unlike any other national history is the persistent belief, maintained without a break for two thousand years, that it was the history of a Divine purpose consistently worked out and due to culminate in some glorious display of Divine power. In the earliest strands of the tradition this future event is conceived in the vaguest of terms: in thee 'and in thy seed shall all the nations of the earth be blessed' (cp. Gen. 12 : 3); in the time of Jesus, his people were keyed up to the expectation of a divine conquering hero who would inaugurate a Reign of God. But from start to finish they believed in a purpose.

Many nations have believed from time to time in a divine destiny; Greece under Alexander, Rome under Augustus, Germany under Hitler and Britain in the full tide of imperialistic expansion, summing up her blasphemous creed in the immortal lines :

God that made thee mighty
Make thee mightier yet.

But such beliefs never last long because they are based on shifting foundations, personalities, conquests, empires. The seed of Abraham, Jews, Hebrews, Israelites—they were called by many names—have kept their belief in a purpose, a destiny, a mission for the best part of four thousand years, and show no signs of relinquishing it. Conquests and empires are nothing to them; of course they have had grandiose dreams of expansion 'from one sea to the other' and they fell a prey to the vulgar mistake of admiring Solomon in all his glory, though his empire was never much larger than Wales. Personalities they have certainly produced in profusion; but to the greatest of them all, Moses, they rejoiced to apply the epithet 'meek'—not a tribute that would have been paid to Alexander, Augustus, Hitler or, let us say, to Kitchener of Khartoum.

The Hebrews' conviction of purpose, of election, of divine guidance was based on the constant experience that a personal God was forever interfering in their national life in a peculiarly characteristic way which can fairly be called 'The Reversal of the Expected.' There is no doubt that the most formative of all these experiences was their deliverance after four hundred years of slavery in Egypt, an event which can be dated about 1300 B.C., when a whole series of startling 'Reversals of the Expected' welded them together in allegiance to this peculiar, interfering God. But the same theme is to be found in the traditions of their earliest beginnings; and it is to be found, like the theme of a symphony, repeated in a variety of recognizably related ways. The very origin of the chosen race is a reversal of the expected; a childless couple in old age found themselves presented with a son. This precious child, whose descendants Abraham was told would be as innumerable as the stars, was named Isaac, and Isaac means 'a good joke'; and what is the essence of a good joke, but the reversal of the expected? The good joke, however, was swiftly succeeded by an extremely grim joke, for Abraham heard the same voice of God which had promised him a son in his old age and descendants unnumbered now command him to kill the son as a sacrificial victim. Blindly obedient, Abraham lifts his knife to plunge it into the boy's heart, and at that instant is interrupted again by the same voice and told to spare the victim's life. What strange, supernatural game of hide and seek is this? It is uncanny, unaccountable, unexpected. In the succeeding generations it is prolonged: Isaac's wife was barren, as his mother had been, but she bore twins of whom the one to become the heir to God's promises was the younger. That is strange enough, but what an heir! Crafty, mean, obstinate and avaricious, Jacob. He too was within a hair's breadth of being killed by his elder brother, but escaped and married two sisters. The elder sister and the slaves gave him hordes of children, but the younger, whom alone he loved, was barren. At last she bore a child, Joseph, who after two narrow escapes from death rose beyond the wildest dreams of even his expectations to be Viceroy of Egypt. No sooner has the story reached this high peak of destiny for a descendant of Abraham, than it collapses like a pack of cards; and Abraham's race are slaves.

In all these strange reversals of the normal and predictable: three generations of long barrenness before childbirth, three generations of the older brother or brothers serving the younger, three generations in which the heir had narrowly escaped from death; in all these the Jews saw the hand of a purposeful God at work directing and interfering for the promotion of his own plans. And they coined a word for these characteristic acts, a word that means 'acts too hard for mortal man to do'; acts incomprehensible, amazing, challenging man to look outside himself: a word translated in our version as 'wonderful works.'

When Matthew called Jesus a Son of Abraham, he was drawing attention to this heritage; he was heir to generations of Israelites whose whole life was bound up with the characteristic wondrous works of God: whose strange sense of freedom and power of pertinacity was nourished by an unconquerable faith in a God who revealed himself by 'reversing the expected.' When Matthew proceeded to tell the story of Jesus the Son of God, he expected his Jewish readers to find the proofs of this unbelievable proposition in his birth, life, death and resurrection as supreme examples of the wondrous works of God. Where Abraham's immediate descendants were born of once-barren mothers, Jesus was born of that which is by definition unfruitful —a virgin's womb; where they each narrowly escaped death and rose beyond all expectation to high position and power, Jesus himself did actually die and then rose again to sit on the right hand of the Majesty of his Father. We begin to see Jesus in perspective; he is the long-prepared-for heir of all the self-revealing activity of God. Thus seen, he makes sense.

But do not let us imagine that Matthew's conviction that Jesus was God—or any one else's—rests on the real or fancied correspondence between a few stories of ancient tribal history and the tradition about Jesus. There was a great deal more than the early patriarchal legends for the child Jesus to learn as a schoolboy: the centre of his nation's creed was a Reversal of the Expected on an earth-shaking scale, when every natural phenomenon, earthquake, volcano, landslide, plague, pestilence and terror all combined and coincided to reverse their hopeless destiny as slaves in Egypt and to liberate and revive a corpselike rabble and build them into a conquering nation. This never to be forgotten fact, they called the Exodus. And it haunts their literature as the Cross haunts Wesley's hymns.

Turn up the word 'Egypt' in a Concordance of the Bible, and you will see that there is scarcely a book in the whole series from Genesis to Malachi in which there is not a reference to the deliverance 'out of Egypt'.; add all those countless allusions where the country's name is not actually mentioned, and any reader with his eyes open will have it forced on his attention that this deliverance was the fact of facts, the one unshakable certainty, the one supreme proof of the Living God's activity, this Exodus.

THE PREPARATION

This was the core of the faith in which the young Jesus was nourished and drilled and trained. Realize that, and his whole strange career makes better sense than ever; for you can perceive, however dimly, the master idea which led him deliberately to choose to be crucified.

It is easy for the casual reader of the Gospels to receive a hazy impression that Jesus wandered rather aimlessly about the country-side performing miracles, teaching, telling stories, annoying the authorities and finally dying for not too clearly defined a cause. No doubt that assumes a most superficial attitude, but it is commoner than it might be among those who take real trouble to understand the education and psychological processes of other heroes of mankind; and it largely results from not trying to see Jesus in his setting. If one once recollects that the first article of his belief was this, learnt and repeated from earliest infancy, 'I am the Lord thy God which brought thee out of the land of Egypt' (Exod. 20 : 2), then one can understand something of the purpose of his inner mind, which blazed out in the great spiritual experience we call the Transfiguration.

Taking three witnesses to the top of a mountain, he was transfigured by a dazzling radiance; that is a relatively common experience in the history of the spiritually advanced. The witnesses were aware of his being joined in this state of radiance by two saints and heroes of the race. This, too, has its parallels. But the unaccountable thing, unless it is true, is the subject of the conversation between them. These visitants were talking to Jesus about an Exodus, but not the Exodus that was the centre of their creed, but they spoke of *his* Exodus which he was about to accomplish at Jerusalem. In this conversation he received a confirmation of the whole scope and method and purpose of his life; he was to be a second Moses, delivering his people out of a death more deadly than the slavery in Egypt, the death of sin into a life more glorious than that of the promised land, life eternal. He then deliberately set his face toward Jerusalem in order to accomplish his exodus. For those who shared in the apparently wasteful tragedy of his death there was reserved the most catastrophic of all Reversals of the Expected, his resurrection. This was all of a piece with the crude hints in the lives and careers of the patriarchs; it was a fulfilment of the hopes of a race

B

nurtured in the Creed of the Exodus. It also inaugurated the Kingdom of God.

The Royal Lineage of Matthew's gospel insists on 'Son of David' as well as 'Son of Abraham.' But, again, 'Son of David' is not an honorific or snobbish title; it means far more than 'the royal blood ran coursing through his veins' or 'of course his people came over with the Conqueror'; it is a pointer to a Kingship of which David's was but a pale shadow, a Kingship revealing finally the nature and character of God's relation to his people, as partially and dimly they had been revealed in the wonderful works surrounding the reign of David. For when we turn to the story of David we find that 'reversal of the expected' is the very stuff of it, all through. The eighth and youngest son of his father, and born in a different tribe from that of the reigning King Saul, he nevertheless was chosen King by one of those interferences in the normal course of events which the pagan historian finds so baffling. The greatest single stroke of genius in his career was the conquest of a fortress town which despite its entire lack of communications and water-supply he turned into the capital city, the centre of the political and religious life of his people. But the feat which most endeared him to all generations of his descendants was his singular courage as a lad in accepting the challenge of the enemy champion, Goliath the Philistine, to single combat and defeating him not by force of arms but by the sleight of hand which any boy might achieve with a catapult. The astonished ranks of Saul's army, petrified for weeks by the giant's challenge, watched aghast the sturdy little fellow stride out to meet him unarmed. Before they had time to gasp, David made one swift skilful contortion with his sling and the giant toppled and fell. 'So David prevailed over the Philistine with a sling and with a stone . . . but there was no sword in the hand of David. Then David ran, and stood over the Philistine, and took his sword, and drew it out of the sheath thereof and slew him, and cut off his head therewith' (1 Sam. 17 : 50).

Now, watch how this popular story, this nursery tale which never fails to elicit storms of applause at every performance of Jack the Giantkiller, this story of the big bully laid low by the junior fag, watch how it finds its place in the thinking and teaching and passion of Christ, the Son of David: 'When the strong man fully armed guardeth his own court, his goods are in peace: but when a stronger than he shall come upon him, and overcome him, he taketh from him his whole armour wherein he trusted, and divideth his spoils' (Luke 11 : 21f.).

Taken by itself, and robbed of the archaisms of language, such a statement is obvious to the verge of the commonplace; any one with the most rudimentary reasoning powers knows that the stronger of two combatants will win and then disarm his victim. But read in its context, it is seen to be the Son of David's proclamation that he will destroy the enemy of the human race, the devil, and wrest from his grasp the very weapons by which he exerts his power. There could be no shorter or clearer summary of what Jesus saw to be the purpose of his life and death; the defeat of the devil not by force of arms but by reversal of the expected. At every turn he is seen defeating the devil's weapons of disease, madness, loss of faculties, even death; all the weapons which he employs to make men doubt the love of God; and finally destroying the power of death itself by accepting it in his own person and rising from the grave.

The witness to the divine preparation for the coming of Christ, as foreshadowed in the person and career of David, is by no means exhausted by the story of David and Goliath. David was according to the tradition and despite his gross failings a king after God's own heart; he was a shepherd with intrepid care for his sheep; and a loyal member of his family at Bethlehem. He was many other things besides, a poet, a soldier, a general, with a genius for friendship and a quixotic gift for pardoning his enemies, a man of strong passions, great loves and great griefs, a magnetic leader of men, a man of profound spiritual insight and a penitent. All these characteristics may be traced, purified and enhanced, supernaturalized and perfected in the character of the Son of God. In David they are broken half-lights, hints, half-revealed mysterious glances into the character of Perfect Man. Let us select but the first three of the titles of David and see the Christ in the context of them : King, shepherd, Bethlehemite.

Christ deliberately entered David's city of Jerusalem to face his death, riding on an ass, to make sure that there was no doubt whatever of his claim to be King. The frenzy of excitement which greeted him from the crowds was due precisely to that choice of his; for he knew and they knew that a divinely inspired oracle had said:

> *Behold, thy King cometh unto thee,*
> *Meek, and riding upon an ass*
> (Matt. 21 : 5; cp. Zech. 9 : 9)

He knew and they knew that David in his old age had nominated his son Solomon to succeed him and told his courtiers to cause him to ride on the King's mule and bring him to the place of enthronement; so no wonder that they cried out: 'Hosanna to the son of David.' And when the chief priests and scribes saw the wonderful things that he did (note that technical phrase, 'the wonderful things') and the children crying out 'Hosanna to the son of David,' they protested against the claim, only to be crushed by the reply: 'Yea: did ye never read, Out of the mouth of babes and sucklings thou hast perfected praise?' (Matt. 21 : 16). But the enthronement was a bitter and pathetic reversal; a crown of thorns and a cross, and on it a title written, David's title, the King of the Jews.

'I am the good shepherd'—probably the most popular and certainly the most sentimentalized of all the titles which Jesus gave himself. But shepherding was no sentimental or idyllic pastime for a Hebrew; that picture comes from the lesser Greek and Latin poets. David had said to Saul, 'Thy servant kept his father's sheep; and when there came a lion, or a bear, and took a lamb out of the flock, I went out after him, and smote him, and delivered it out of his mouth: and when he arose against me, I caught him by his beard, and smote him, and slew him' (1 Sam. 17 : 34f.). That was the ideal of the Shepherd—Son of David; and he went far beyond him, for the good shepherd 'layeth down his life for the sheep' (John 10 : 11). Such was the cost to him of our being able to take on our lips the words of David's song: 'The Lord is my shepherd.'

'Christ was born in Bethlehem'; that much every one knows who has heard a Christmas carol sung. And Bethlehem means the Home of Bread. Let no one imagine that place-names or personal names were as unimportant to the Hebrew as they are to us: the most casual reader of the Old Testament cannot fail to notice, and perhaps be bored by, the constant interest in names and the meaning attached to them. In the New Testament, too, John the Baptist and Jesus himself are named with a purpose; Simon is surnamed Peter, James and John Boanerges, the name of Nazareth is called attention to by a pun, Saul changes his name to Paul: great significance is attached to naming; it was part of the mental furniture of the race, which loved puns and plays upon words. In the context of this Hebrew trait, it would not be surprising to discover that any person born in the Home of Bread might give himself a nickname which referred to the place of his birth. What is quite certain is that Jesus did specifically call himself the Bread, just as seriously as he called himself the Shepherd. It appears on reflection that this image was one of the most prominent in which he pictured his life and work. It would certainly add great point to the first of his temptations if he who had long meditated on himself as the son of the Home of Bread heard the devil's urgent whisper: 'If thou art the Son of God, command that these stones become bread' (Matt. 4 : 3). The one miracle which all four evangelists relate is the feeding of the five thousand and it is succeeded in St. John's Gospel by a long discourse in which he speaks of himself as living bread and as the bread of God. Most natural, then, that when he came to sum up his whole ministry present and future, it was bread that he took, saying to his disciples, 'Take, eat; this is my body' (Matt. 26 : 26); that after his resurrection he should be recognized in the breaking of the bread; that after his ascension his disciples should continue steadfast in the breaking of the bread; and that St. Paul should be saying to his converts thirty years later: 'we, who are many, are one bread, one body: for we all partake of the one bread' (1 Cor. 10 : 17). The one shatteringly simple focus of unity with God himself is bread, which is the body of the Son of God, Son of David, of the Home of Bread.

At his trial before the Roman court, Pilate asked Jesus: 'Art thou a King then?' to receive the considered answer of the Son of David:

To this end have I been born,
and to this end am I come into the world,
that I should bear witness unto the truth
(John 18 : 37)

In all that he thought, said, did and was, he bore witness to the true nature of God's dealings with his world, revealed in the history of his chosen people, seen in their finest flower in his own brief life, heard in the very words he spoke. For he added the heart-searching challenge:

Every one that is of the truth, heareth my voice
(John 18: 37)

Pilate dismissed that challenge with a world-weary cry, echoed by all the philosophy schools before and after him: What is truth? How could he argue about a subtle philosophical question with a Jewish trouble-maker? What could this illiterate provincial know about truth? So, not for the last time, a great misunderstanding arose because two men were using the same word with entirely different meanings. To Pilate, truth was something you could 'know about,' if indeed you could know anything about anything; a matter for speculation and argument and definition; to a Jew, speculation and argument about metaphysics were either unknown or despised: final truth, to a Jew, was the character of God, expressed either in his historical revelation of himself or through the words of inspired men of insight, and truth among human beings was the bringing of one's own character into line with that of God. It was ethical, not intellectual; a virtue, not a concept.

This truth of God was to be seen primarily in his characteristic way of working; he made promises and he kept them; he alone was faithful and true. This certainty was enshrined in the history of his chosen people; it was expounded by his inspired prophets. To them also Jesus was heir. If you turn from Matthew's gospel to Mark's you will see that he dispenses with a genealogy and after his title-heading, 'The beginning of the gospel of Jesus Christ, the Son of God,' he writes abruptly: 'Even as it is written in Isaiah the prophet' (Mark 1: 1f.).

Jesus is not only in the succession of Abraham and David; he is the heir also of the prophets. As another writer, the author of the Epistle to the Hebrews, was to say later: 'God, having of old time spoken unto the fathers in the prophets . . . hath at the end of these days spoken unto us in his Son' (Hebrews 1: 1).

And in so saying, this writer was claiming divine inspiration for a particular class called 'prophets' and drawing a parallel between this class and Jesus. He was not the first to do this; Jesus had done so unmistakably himself.

In one of the parables by which he forced his claim on contemporary authority, he spoke of himself as the heir to a vineyard whom the lessees killed after they had arrested the owner's servants and 'beat one, and killed another, and stoned another' (Matt. 21 : 35). These servants clearly represent the prophets; in Jesus's lament over the city to which he went to meet his death, he apostrophized it: 'O Jerusalem, Jerusalem, which killeth the prophets, and stoneth them that are sent unto her!' (Matt. 23 : 37). The climax of the parable describing the murder of the owner's son and heir points as clearly to himself and the murder already brewing in the minds of the listening authorities. They saw it in a flash: 'And when the chief priests and the Pharisees heard his parables, they perceived that he spake of them' (Matt. 21 : 45).

Jesus claimed this unique relation to the prophets: it is therefore indispensable for any one who would weigh his whole claim to understand who they were. Bishop Gore states unequivocally: 'no representation of the teaching of Jesus Christ can make any pretence to truth which fails to recognize that he stood upon the foundation of the prophets.' Yet how absurdly lightly have critics dogmatized about Jesus and his teaching, dismissing the Hebrew prophets merely as a mixture of dervish and neurotic in whose works occasional flashes of insight are hidden among mountains of unrelenting, harsh denunciation. If that were all, Jesus's own claim to treat them as his spiritual ancestry is nonsense. Let us rather approach them from the position we have reached by considering Jesus as the heir of Abraham, Moses and David: that is, that the Eternal God was dropping hints about his character for several centuries before he revealed himself in person. These hints were worked out in a tribal history; his characteristic method of reversing the expected, of interfering in human affairs to bring life out of death, was seen and experienced in the adventures of the patriarchs, the supreme intervention of the Exodus and the establishment of a kingdom. But there were still inferences to be drawn, generalizations to be made, relationships to be clarified; it had yet to be made clear that the God of the Hebrews was different from all the crowd of local deities by whom they were magnetized, as different as chalk from cheese, or rather as different as solid chalk from the smell of cheese. It had yet to be made clear that behind all the traditional wonderful works there lived a personality, with attributes and characteristics, with purposes and longings and demands that he must make upon men.

This was done by a unique series of teachers over a period of at least four hundred years; who have but one thing in common, an intense personal experience of God forcing them to speak about Him against natural inclination and without reference to the unpopularity of what they have to say. There is nothing the least like this in any other national history; there have indeed been dervishes, subject to trances in the same kind of way as were a few of the Hebrew prophets; there have also been prophets of disaster and unpopular counsellors, in the records of many races. But never over a period of some hundreds of years has there been a succession of teachers, consistent yet independent, advanced as well as primitive, with an intense devotion to God and an intense conviction that He is speaking to them and they must in turn speak to their generation. These form the 'goodly fellowship' of the prophets; the foundation upon which Jesus stood.

Foundation is St. Paul's word—the church 'being built upon the foundation of the apostles and prophets,' and its aptness is shown by the succeeding phrase, 'Christ Jesus himself being the chief cornerstone' (Eph. 2 : 20). He is the summit, the apex, the perfectly fitting complement which gives meaning and shape to the whole.

Any great teacher has to build on his predecessors. If the life and teaching and passion of Jesus were to make any sense whatever, it had to be the very heart and soul of his hearers' convictions that there was only one God. It has so long been obvious to us that if God exists he must by definition be the one and only God that it is not easy to recollect that this has not always been self-evident. It is improbable that Abraham, Moses or David (and they cover a period of a thousand years) doubted of the existence of other gods besides the one they worshipped. It was not until eight hundred and fifty years before Christ that the first great showdown took place on Mount Carmel, between four hundred passionate believers in a Tyrian god and Elijah, a prophet of the God of the Hebrews. The story is too good to abbreviate; it starts with the prophet issuing a challenge:

> *if the Lord be God, follow him:*
> *but if Baal, then follow him*

and it ends with the shout of acclamation:

> *The Lord, he is God;*
> *The Lord, he is God*
> (1 Kings 18: 21, 39)

However little those who shouted may have realized what they were saying, they were, under Elijah's inspiration, laying the first foundation stone for the Son of God to build on nine hundred years later. Four and five hundred years before the great Greek philosophers argued their way by the application of pure reason to tentative conclusions about the nature of ultimate reality; and at least a hundred years before the first primitive foundations of the city of Rome were laid, the Rome which was to crucify God when he came to earth, a solitary and arresting figure braved the murderous hostility of an unscrupulous queen and a barbarous and bloodthirsty crowd, to proclaim that there is only one God.

But a solitary God might be cold, aloof, distant, separate, unapproachable; like Aristotle's god, contemplating his own perfection. Does he care? Or is he neutral?

The generations of Abraham's seed who had been nurtured in the tribal traditions, and had learnt that Jacob the father of the twelve tribes had cheated his way into his inheritance and yet remained the favoured and chosen instrument of God might well have been excused for believing that God had strange standards, strange likes and dislikes. It had to be made clear beyond all cavil that God passionately hates and passionately loves conduct of certain kinds; that he is not neutral or amoral or indifferent. It is another prophet, Amos, who lays this foundation; not because he had reached his conclusion at the end of a train of reasoning, but because he was gripped by an irresistible conviction: 'I was an herdman . . . and the Lord took me . . . and the Lord said unto me, Go, prophesy unto my people Israel.' 'The lion hath roared, who will not fear? the Lord God hath spoken, who can but prophesy?' (Amos 7 : 14f.; 3 : 8). So he declared God's hatred of oppression and lust and cruelty, not least when the perpetrators were maintaining a cult of piety, and cried out:

> *Seek good, and not evil.*
> *Hate the evil, and love the good.*
> *Let judgement roll down as waters,*
> *And righteousness as a mighty stream*
> (Amos 5 : 14f., 24)

Those words were uttered the best part of eight hundred years before these others:

> *Blessed are they that hunger and thirst after righteousness*
> (Matt. 5 : 6)

The Son of God can express himself with that metaphor, because he and his hearers know in their very bones that righteousness is a mighty stream from God himself. The foundation had been laid by the prophet Amos.

Elijah, Amos, the list can be extended through Hosea, Isaiah, Micah, Jeremiah, Ezekiel and the great successor of Isaiah (whose work is to be found in the final chapters of the book ascribed to Isaiah himself) down through a number of minor figures to that of John Baptist. Often incomprehensible and intolerably verbose, some of them writing incomparable poetry, others turgid, commonplace, complicated and obscure, these are the prophets: not to be dismissed lightly as psychopathic dervishes. Those who attempt to read them must face a real horde of difficulties; but ask one question only, burrow away for one treasure: 'What has he got to say about God?' and the effort is rewarded.

> *Elijah, God's uniqueness*
> *Amos, God's righteousness*
> *Hosea, God's mercy*
> *Isaiah, God's holiness*
> *Micah, God's humility*
> *Jeremiah, God's willingness to suffer*
> *Ezekiel, God's omnipresence*
> *'Second Isaiah,' God's incomparable majesty*

Printed like that, one can perhaps obtain a glimpse of the stones that build the foundation; but each stone is a precious stone, reflecting the Light of God's glory and shedding its rays on the whole of human life and conduct. No mere list does justice to the subtleties and riches of the prophets who prepared the way of Christ.

However, the very slightest acquaintance with the prophets will help one to see that their writings contain a great deal more than direct foretellings of the future; and that they were to be a storehouse of the wisdom and truth of God from which Jesus was to draw, not a collection of proof texts for those who wished to prove that Jesus had been foretold. It is an impossible labour to decide what sentences in any given prophet 'foretell' the coming of the Son of God; we have the authority of the gospel writers for some texts which they believed to be direct 'prophecies' in the 'Old Moore' sense of the word. The Church has refused always to define the manner of the inspiration of the biblical writers; and it is wise not to close the mind to any well-authenticated theory, yet to keep a clear hold of the central truth: that the prophets can only be explained as men inspired in different ways and ages to bring aspects of God's character vividly to the light, which are to be found revealed, unified, fulfilled in Jesus Christ, the Son of God. For he said himself: 'Think not that I came to destroy the law or the prophets: I came not to destroy, but to fulfil' (Matt. 5 : 17).

We have tried to demonstrate two of the elements of the context of the life of Jesus; he was heir to a history, and heir to the interpreters of that history, the prophets. There is a third element of equal importance; and we may well take as a starting point for its consideration the opening words of St. Luke's Gospel narrative: 'There was in the days of Herod, king of Judæa, a certain priest' (Luke 1 : 5). This priest, named Zacharias, was the father of John the Baptist, the last of the prophets, and had married a cousin of Mary the mother of Jesus. Jesus therefore was born and brought up in a priestly family; he was closely connected to a cult; his religion was a highly organized institutional affair, regulated by a priestly caste, focused in a central shrine in Jerusalem, controlled by a vast body of rules and ordinances, and culminating in sacrificial worship. The pious family to which he belonged made frequent pilgrimages to the feasts at the central shrine; their day by day practice of worship and meeting for instruction was conducted at the local synagogue.

Jesus was steeped in this atmosphere of institutional religion; he had drawn it in with his mother's milk. The first faint inkling of his approaching birth was made to the priest Zacharias in the temple, as an infant he was formally presented to God in the temple, as a boy of twelve he was taken to the passover feast and found, after three days' anxious search, in the temple; he taught in the temple, he healed the blind and the lame in it, he drove out the traders from it, he wept over it, so intensely did his lifelong devotion to it affect him. He is recorded as having gone out of his way to attend the temple feasts; and in the course of the country part of his ministry he was always in the synagogues, preaching and teaching and observing the lovers of the chief seats and the dramatic postures of hypocrites at prayer. The humours and hypocrisies and incongruities of churchgoing no one has ever crystallized more skilfully than he; just because he was a devotee of institutional religion, with a compelling sense of obligation.

There is a verse in a popular hymn by Whittier, which reads:

> *O sabbath rest by Galilee!*
> *O calm of hills above!*
> *Where Jesus knelt to share with thee*
> *The secrets of Eternity*
> *Interpreted by love*

However beautiful the sentiment may be, there is no evidence to support the picture drawn. On the Sabbath Jesus went to the synagogue; that was the normal and accepted thing. If on the way he passed through the cornfields, it was only to find himself arguing with Pharisees about the significance of the Sabbath; and he appears deliberately to have chosen this day for public healings, not to have treated it as an opportunity for private prayer. That opportunity, the hours for long converse with his Father, had to be wrung by main force out of sleep-time. The first obligation was to public worship.

This means that for him, on any showing the greatest religious genius of all time, the cult had a deep and enduring significance. It was part of the heritage that he had come to fulfil, that is, to sum up and reform and re-establish in his own person. He was in himself the perfect king and the perfect prophet; he was also the perfect priest.

In the tradition of his people the priest was one who was set apart and supported by almsgiving in order that he might be the means of offering their common worship to God and of conveying God's blessing to them. No race could have held so tenaciously to their sense of God's purpose for them, had they not been able to express in some way, however unworthily, their dependence upon Him and to receive in some tangible and accessible form the assurance of his continuing blessing. No society can live long on a historical tradition or on the verbal interpretation of it; no club, regiment or school, valuing as they do an ancient tradition and sharing an interpretation of it, can survive without a festival, a celebration, a function of some kind which is a communal expression of loyalty and thankfulness. At a much profounder level, the Hebrew race found the deepest expression of their unique vocation in the offering of sacrifice by priests on their behalf.

Much has been conjectured and written on the quite obvious parallels between Jewish and pagan sacrifice; and Jewish sacrifice has been belittled because its origins have been traced by conjecture to crude and superstitious beginnings. But to lay bare the origins of anything is to say very little about its meaning; to trace the origin of man back to the amoeba or of Shakespeare back to an embryo does nothing to explain civilization or the composition of *Hamlet*. There can be no greater fallacy than to dismiss any achievement as *merely* the consequence of its origins. The marvel of the achievement lies in what is achieved. In considering Hebrew history, it is absurd to dismiss Abraham as merely a sheikh, or David as merely an oriental despot, or Elijah as merely a dervish; it is equally absurd to dismiss the Passover as merely an animal sacrifice. For the Passover we may take as the supreme expression of Hebrew priestly sacrifice.

In the tradition in which Jesus was educated, the Passover was the central sacrifice of institutional religion, the memorial of the central wonderful work of God, the Exodus from Egypt and the central means by which the whole family of Abraham's descendants expressed their dependence upon God and received, by eating a share of the sacrificial lamb duly offered, an assurance of his blessing and renewed union with him in will and purpose. Yet it was crude and imperfect and ineffective; the priests who offered it were indeed ceremonially purified beforehand, but they were frail and sinful men not worthy to offer any gift to the Holy and Terrible God; the lamb they offered was but a token offering of the lives and wills of men, will-less and unintelligent; the result of it, who could say? It was at best only the renewal of an old covenant or agreement between God and man, made long ago with the ancestors of the race and so often by them broken and despised and ignored.

Jesus, as we saw, accepted the obligations of this crude and imperfect worship; and then reformed and remodelled and reinstituted a full, perfect and sufficient sacrifice in his own person. He was himself perfect man, holy, harmless, undefiled; the offering he presented to God on man's behalf was himself; and its effect was to inaugurate a new covenant, to provide for a new meeting place between God and man. Deliberately he chose for his death and resurrection the very feast of the Passover, and the night before his Exodus, took bread and brake it and gave it to his disciples, saying, 'Take, eat, this is my Body which is given for you.' Likewise after supper he took the cup and when he had given thanks he gave it to them saying, 'Drink ye all of this; for this is the new Covenant in my Blood. Do this, as oft as ye shall drink it, in remembrance of me.'

There, then, at that sacrificial offering and feast, the people of God find the focus for their thankful recollection of his death, the Exodus he accomplished at Jerusalem; offer, not themselves primarily, but the perfect sacrifice of their Saviour; and receive him and nothing less.

It is perhaps true that the New Testament writers fought shy of describing Jesus in terms of priesthood, possibly because it was the leaders of the Jewish cult who had been responsible for his death; possibly because priesthood among the pagans to whom the Gospel was first preached was a gross distortion of reality; but the title comes into its own in the Epistle to the Hebrews, where the priesthood of Christ is expounded and described as the fulfilment of the priesthood of the Old Testament. And the author of that treatise—for it is more a treatise than a letter—discovered yet another tradition in the scriptures, the tradition of a supernatural priesthood, that of Melchisedek, in which he finds a pattern of the perfect priesthood of Jesus. The neglect of this book by those who attempt to assess the meaning of his life and death can only lead to a very partial and incomplete estimate.

We have seen how the Gospels of Matthew, Mark and Luke each arrest us at the very beginning by forcing us back to consider Jesus in the context of his heritage. He is the descendant of Abraham and of David and of all the purposeful history of their race; he is the cornerstone of that building whose foundation is the prophets; he is the perfection of sacrificial priesthood. He is in himself the purpose for which Abraham was called, for which Moses lived, for which David reigned, for which the prophets suffered, for which the priests offered their sacrifices; he is the promise of God, made to prophets, priests and kings by the word of God spoken to them in their generations.

It was left to John, author of the fourth gospel, to sum up all this and infinitely more in the majestic prologue with which he prefaces his portrait of Jesus. 'In the beginning,' he writes, 'was the Word, and the Word was with God, and the Word was God' (John 1 : 1). Whatever light may be shed on this supremely simple and unfathomable statement by the use of 'the Word' in contemporary philosophers, for a Jew 'the Word' was the promise, given by the Eternal God to Abraham, burning its way into the souls of the prophets, enshrined in the law which governed the sacrificial priesthood. And it was this Word, existing before all time, with God in timelessness, yes, God himself, it was this Word which 'became flesh . . . and we beheld his glory' (John 1 : 14). The glory was the glory of the only begotten from the Father, full of grace and truth. That was to see Jesus in his context; and only so does he make sense.

CHAPTER II

FR. GODFREY PAWSON, C.R.
THE INCARNATION

I

WHAT do Christians *mean* when they say that Jesus is God? I have put the word 'mean' in italics. Christians are being asked to-day not to *prove* their credal statements but to explain them. The demand may be ironical and derisive; it may on the other hand be a puzzled request for information. In either case it cannot be rejected. Whether this question can be answered in such a way as to give entire satisfaction to the inquirer is, frankly, very doubtful; whether it can be answered so as to satisfy ourselves—even that remains to be seen. But apologetics have seldom had direct results in converting unbelievers; their value lies in clarifying, and so strengthening, the apologist's own faith.

The question of the divinity of Jesus is *the* fundamental question for the apologist of our generation. In St. Paul's day it was the proclaiming of a crucified Messiah which to the Jews was the stumbling-block, to the Greeks folly. But now for a hundred years and more it is the incarnation which has been and is, to those who stand outside the Christian tradition, either completely baffling or matter for derision. And yet of the millions of professing Christians in the world none but the members of a few small groups, such as the Unitarians, would surrender this article of their creed, for they consider it to be its master-link. In the last section of this essay I shall try to show how the Christian view of the world and the distinctively Christian way of life both depend on the doctrine of the incarnation; but for the moment it is sufficient to point to a simple fact—the fact that one of the things that invariably strikes a chance visitor to a Catholic church is the custom of kneeling at the words of the Creed, 'and was incarnate . . . and was made man.' And this acknowledgment by Catholics of the centrality of the doctrine of the God-manhood of Jesus is further emphasized by the ringing of the churchbell at early morning, midday and evening for the recitation of the Angelus, a memorial of the Incarnation.

'Jesus is God'—what does this mean? One way of answering the question might be to offer definitions of the three words: 'God,' 'Jesus,' 'is.' But that way seems unpromising. There is, to begin with, no definition of the word 'God' which Christians would accept as expressing all they would want to convey by it. A famous anthropologist, for instance, tried to explain the origin of the concept of God as arising simply from primitive man's desire for a universal provider. If that were all, the hypothesis of God would tend to become less and less necessary in proportion to man's increasing mastery of his environment, until we reached the point where all but a few obscurantists would look to science rather than to a mysterious supernatural power to satisfy their needs and their wants. But even in the most primitive societies we know about, is it likely that the concept of deity sprang from a single source, and one so simple? Certainly the Christian believer to-day would emphatically claim that the word 'God' means to him something much more than one who could satisfy his natural necessities. Otherwise prayer would be a synonym for asking, and the Lord's Prayer might have consisted of a single clause: 'give us this day our daily bread.' The fact is that the concept of God is a complex one; God certainly to modern man, and probably more inchoately to his earliest ancestors, is also the goal of moral effort—the Challenger; also the worshipful and adorable—the Unutterable Beauty.

II

We must note that the concept of God is prior to any recorded revelation. Of course you can say that a knowledge of God presupposes a divine self-revelation; but in fact the purpose and result of revelation as recorded in the Old Testament is not to demonstrate God's existence. That is assumed. The purpose of revelation is to make known God's will. Take for example the first revelation to Abraham: 'the Lord said unto Abram, Get thee out of thy country, and from thy kindred, and from thy father's house, unto the land that I will shew thee' (Gen. 12 : 1).

Or take the message which accompanied the first appearance of God to Moses; it began with the words: 'I am the God of thy father, the God of Abraham, the God of Isaac and the God of Jacob'; and then followed the delivery of a mandate (Exod. 3 : 6).

The Old Testament provides the indispensable background for understanding the New Testament, and therefore for understanding the Christian faith with its central dogma, the incarnation. If we are asked what sort of a divine being Christians have in mind when they say that Jesus is 'divine,' it is no good our sheltering behind the tautology, 'Jesus is God, God is Jesus'—though there are Christian apologists who deliberately do just this—we must base our answer on the teaching of the Old Testament. There, behind many crudely primitive expressions, we find stories and statements which combine to show that God is apprehended as both transcendent and immanent (indwelling). Jehovah stands over against men in a number of relationships which contrast Him with them : as Creator to creature, as Judge to sinner, and so forth. 'All flesh (human kind) is grass. . . . The grass withereth, the flower fadeth ; but the word of our God shall stand for ever' (Isa. 40 : 7ff.). So much for his transcendence. But at the same time God is, to use a very un-Hebraic expression, the archetype of human nature, man being made 'in the image, after the likeness' of God. And God dwells in the midst of—nay, more mysteriously, 'in'—his people, so that Israel may be conceived of as his ambulatory and abode (2 Cor. 6 : 16, quoting Lev. 26 : 12 and Exod. 29 : 45). It is now recognized that, as the idea of God develops in the course of Israel's history, the emphasis of her prophets and teachers upon the transcendent attributes of deity increases. Theophanies (appearances of God), for instance, give way to angelophanies; for God is not now one who prefers to hide himself, he is by nature invisible. He is the God of all the earth and not locatable. He who in Genesis 'walked in the garden in the cool of the day' (Gen. 3 : 8) has become in the later parts of the book of Isaiah 'the high and lofty One that inhabiteth eternity, whose name is Holy' (Isa. 57 : 15). This shift of emphasis does not contradict or supersede previous ideas; indeed it is a shift that is mostly unperceived and unacknowledged. Nevertheless the total conception of God that we

THE INCARNATION 35

can gather if we read the Old Testament as a whole, and with a knowledge of the history of its formation, could be summarized as follows: he is the creator and source of all that exists; he is the director of events, inexorably working out the purpose for which he created all things; he is holy and righteous in all his ways, requiring holiness from his people; above all, he is one, supreme and unique, majestic, worshipful.

Now such a background of theistic thought does not seem to be the soil from which a doctrine of divine incarnation would be likely to spring. There is indeed from beginning to end of the Old Testament an unfailing, inescapable note of expectancy. It is heard first in what has been called the *protevangelium,* the prophecy that the seed of Eve will bruise the Serpent's head (Gen. 3 : 15); it is still heard in the last book of all, in Malachi's prophecy that God will send his messenger to prepare the way before him (Mal. 3 : 1). There is after David's time the repeated promise of a restored kingdom and of a second David. But, if we discount an unconscious tendentiousness in the familiar English translations, we shall not find anywhere in the Old Testament an identification of the Promised One with God Himself. And had there been in the first days of Christian preaching a blatant proclamation of God made flesh we can be sure that Jewish opposition to the infant Church would have been less hesitant than the early chapters of Acts show it to have been.

III

And so we have arrived at the New Testament. It is generally agreed that the earliest New Testament writings are the earlier epistles of St. Paul; that Mark is the earliest gospel, written very shortly before St. Paul's death at Rome; that Luke and Matthew made use of Mark, embodying other material (which may or may not have been collected together earlier than Mark's); that the writings attributed to St. John, including the fourth gospel, are among the latest in the New Testament. We need not go more deeply into the assured results of New Testament criticism, nor into the continuing uncertainties. But dates, i.e. approximate dates, are important; for when we are asking what Christians mean when they say that Jesus is God we need to ask when they began making this affirmation explicitly, and whether what they had previously been used to say implied his divinity. Though St. Paul's letters were written before any of the gospels, let us start with the Synoptic Gospels. These three works assumed their present form not less than thirty years, even in the case of the earliest of them, after the events which they describe. An honest historian would feel bound to allow for the possibility, one might almost say the inevitability, of a development in understanding those events, so much time having elapsed since they took place. I can remember several things which happened to my brothers and sisters, as well as to myself, in my very early childhood; but I should not at the time have described those happenings in the way that I do describe them now. And the reason for that is not simply that I have acquired a larger vocabulary; the events remain whatever they were when they happened, but they *seem* different now. And so it looks at first as if we shall have two questions to answer: (1) What did his disciples think of Jesus *at the time*—'all the time that the Lord Jesus went in and went out among us, beginning from the baptism of John, unto the day that he was received up from us' (Acts 1: 21f.)? (2) What did the Evangelists think as they sat and wrote thirty and more years later?

Now, I want to show that these two questions cannot, in the nature of things, be answered precisely as they stand; that, if we are to get anywhere at all, we must reformulate them. Students of the Gospels have been trying for very many years to abolish or, failing that, to bridge the gap between, on the one hand, the deeds and the words of Jesus and, on the other hand, the recorded accounts of his words and deeds. They have succeeded to this extent: most of them now think that stories and blocks of teaching from the mouth of Jesus were circulating piecemeal from a time perhaps not very much later than the birth of the Christian Church at Pentecost, and that a principal task of the Synoptic Evangelists was to assemble this material *substantially as it stood* in some sort of a pattern. This means that these Evangelists were not, for the most part, imposing their own very late-in-the-day interpretations upon events of which they themselves had not (with the possible exception of St. Matthew) been eye-witnesses. No, they were reproducing what they, and other Christian believers, had received from the Apostles and first preachers of the gospel, much in the form that they had originally received it. There is still a gap between events and records; but it is not such a long gap. We shall never in this life be able to do more than guess what the constant companions of our Lord were thinking as they walked and talked with him in Galilee and Judæa. At the same time we do not have to rely on the faded memories and titillated imaginations of 'forty years on.' What the Gospels present us with is, substantially, the Jesus of history as seen in retrospect by His closest associates, *after* their eyes had been enlightened by a profound spiritual experience (Pentecost), which befell them some two months after he had disappeared from their sight. Their record is, admittedly, not the detached account of disinterested observers. It is *testimony;* for they were ardent believers. But it is *apostolic,* not merely evangelistic, testimony. And all this means that the two questions to be answered are not the two we first suggested, but these: (1) What precisely was that testimony? Was it a direct affirmation of the divinity of Jesus, or was it at any rate such as to imply that? (2) What were the facts on which the faith that underlay the testimony was grounded?

To take the second of these questions first: whether or not the words and works of Jesus have been accurately recorded, *some* facts—some actions, utterances, experiences of his—are required to account for their estimate of him. And we could reasonably add that if, as we suppose, the gospel was preached to create, and the gospels were written to sustain, faith in others, the preachers and writers would not have relied on lavish embellishment or sheer invention; they would naturally rely on those facts which had engendered their own faith in order to assist others to attain a like faith. Of course we must allow the careful historian to go on examining each item of the gospel story; it is his duty to do this. But there is surely an *a priori* probability for the general trustworthiness of that story. The 'Jesus' in our assertion, 'Jesus is God,' is the Jesus in whom the Apostles believed, whom the Evangelists have depicted.

As regards the first of our two questions (concerning the substance of the apostolic testimony, rather than the facts on which it was based), recent New Testament investigations have made several things clear. Among others that there was a large degree of unanimity among the earliest Christian preachers and teachers, including St. Paul who was the first to write, as to what had to be proclaimed and taught concerning Jesus. It is true that between St. Paul, the Apostle 'born out of due time' (1 Cor. 15 : 8), and 'them which were apostles before' him (Gal. 1 : 17) there were temporary differences as to policy. But there is nowhere any hint that the other apostles took exception to St. Paul's *teaching about Christ,* or he to theirs. What Paul had originally preached—and he sometimes had occasion to remind his converts of his initial message—was substantially the same gospel as that which Peter, John and Stephen, according to St. Luke in Acts, had preached a decade or two before. So St. Paul's writings are directly relevant here.

And what was this gospel on which they were all agreed? It was not in so many words that Jesus was God come down from heaven. (In fact Jesus is not called 'God' either in the Pauline epistles or in the synoptic gospels or in any but the latest New Testament books.[1] But this we should hardly expect at this stage.) It was this: (1) The expected Messiah has come; he is Jesus. (2) This Jesus is Lord and Master.

A great deal has been written on the connotation of the titles given to our Lord—Christ, Son of God, Lord. The first of these is the really definitive one. The gospel was the confident and triumphant proclamation that the Expected One had come, that in him the promises of God had all been fulfilled in a manner exceeding expectation. 'Let all the house of Israel therefore know assuredly, that God hath made him both Lord and Christ, this Jesus whom ye crucified' (Acts 2 : 36), says St. Peter on the day of Pentecost. And St. Paul sums up his own early teaching when he writes: 'how many soever be the promises of God, in him is the yea' (2 Cor. 1 : 20).

I have already pointed out that in the Old Testament there is no identification of the Promised One with God himself. An incarnation was no part of Jewish expectation. 'Lord' was certainly not an exclusively divine title, even though in the Greek version of the Old Testament it was substituted for the Name that might never (except by the High Priest once a year on the Day of Atonement; and then the sound of it was drowned by trumpet-blasts) be uttered. 'Lord' was the title, for instance, by which the Greeks who wished to see Jesus addressed Philip (John 12 : 21—the Revised Version translates it 'Sir'). 'Son of God' could mean little more than Messiah or Christ, for was not Israel Jahweh's son, and the Messiah the recapitulation of the faithful remnant of Israel? Most certainly to those who first heard it the title 'Son of God' would not have implied eternal generation, a doctrine first taught by Origen in the third century, or what was later still to be called 'consubstantiality' ('of one substance with'). To Jewish ears the title 'Son of God' would connote 'Messiah' with special emphasis on filial obedience and faithfulness to God. The title is once used by a Gentile. But it is noteworthy that, whereas Mark, followed by Matthew, attributes to the centurion at the foot of the Cross the words, 'truly this man was a Son of God' (Mark 15 : 39—not *the* Son of God' : see footnote), Luke paraphrases the saying to bring out its correct meaning thus : 'certainly this was a righteous man.'

Must we say then that the earliest faith in Jesus was a belief that he was Messiah and that this developed later into belief in his divinity? The matter is not so simple as that. Let us return to St. Paul. He certainly avoids in his earlier epistles (Galatians, 1 and 2 Thessalonians, 1 and 2 Corinthians) any downright assertion of the divinity of the Lord; he hardly suggests the pre-existence of him who was 'born of a woman' (Gal. 4 : 4), except perhaps in 'one Lord, Jesus Christ, through whom are all things' (1 Cor. 8 : 6). But he couples 'our Lord Jesus Christ' with 'God the Father' in the salutations with which his epistles usually open (e.g. Gal. 1 : 1) as well as in other statements. (These collocations more often than not do not include the Holy Spirit, but that raises other questions with which we cannot deal here.) He speaks of Christ not as a dead hero and exemplar but as a living reality, in whom the radically new life of baptized Christians is grounded and centred. And when we turn to the later Pauline epistles—Colossians, Ephesians, Philippians—we meet with a profounder christology. 'Jesus is Lord,' not 'Jesus is God,' might still be the formal confession of faith; but he is 'the image of the invisible God,' 'in him (or by him) were all things created' (Col. 1 : 15f.); 'in him dwelleth all the fulness of the Godhead bodily (i.e. substantially)' (Col. 2 : 9); and finally, he 'being in the form of God counted it not a prize to be on an equality with

God, but emptied himself, taking the form of a servant, being made in the likeness of men' (Phil. 2: 5–7).

In this last passage, written about A.D. 60, we have the earliest explicit statement of a divine incarnation. It is earlier than the synoptic gospels; and these have no real parallel to it; for it is only fair to point out that, if it were not for the influence on our minds of this passage of St. Paul's, or of the passage about the Word 'becoming flesh' in the prologue to St. John's Gospel, we could take the Birth stories of Matthew and Luke as implying less than a divine incarnation. Are we to say then that St. Paul's understanding of Christ had grown? The question is not of real importance and is anyway perhaps unanswerable. Some would assert that the doctrine of Philippians is already implicit in such an earlier passage as Rom. 1: 3–4. At least we can say that the false teaching rife at Colosse was the occasion of more explicit teaching by the Apostle, first in Colossians, then in Ephesians and finally in Philippians, on the relation of Christ to creation and the created world—to 'all things visible and invisible'—and so to the divine Creator. The kind of christological teaching to be found in these later epistles of St. Paul is paralleled in the Epistle to the Hebrews (a work of unknown authorship and uncertain date) and in the Fourth Gospel.

So we can sum up thus: the Apostles, including St. Paul, were united in and by a common faith. The brief, formal expression of that faith was 'Jesus is Christ' or 'Jesus is Lord.' Whatever the minimum meaning of these formulas may have been, they were pregnant. Paul, the author of Hebrews and the Johannine writer (about whom, more presently) all taught explicitly that Jesus, before he identified himself with our humanity and participated in it, belonged to the sphere which we can call 'Creatorship' as contrasted with 'creature-hood.'

IV

But what about the facts upon which this faith relied and from which it was generated? The chief of them was the Resurrection. We have only to look at the speeches and other passages in the first half of Acts, and at St. Paul's epistles (see especially 1 Cor. 15: 1ff.) and other New Testament epistles (especially 1 Peter 1: 3ff.), to see how strongly the early preachers emphasized this

THE INCARNATION 41

event. Before the Resurrection the high-point in the story of the association of the chosen disciples with Jesus, a token of how far their apprehension of their Master had developed, had come when, towards the close of his active ministry, Peter as spokesman of the others had confessed his messiahship (Mark 8 : 29). That faith was rudely shaken by the Crucifixion—'Christ crucified, unto Jews a stumbling-block' (cf. Luke 24 : 21a). But as a result of the appearances of the Lord after the Resurrection it re-emerged stronger and deeper. Deeper, certainly: Matthew (28 : 17) has the significant words, 'and when they saw him they worshipped' (cf. 28 : 9). And the latest of the Evangelists attributes to St. Thomas the words, 'My Lord and my God' (John 20 : 28).

But the Resurrection did not have this effect as if it were just a stunning but independent and unrelated miracle—something 'out of the blue.' Indeed St. Paul (in 1 Cor. 15) uses the fact of Christ's resurrection not to prove his divinity but to prove that resurrection from death is a human possibility: 'if there is no resurrection of the dead'—i.e. of dead *men*—'neither hath Christ been raised.' It was the Resurrection as the concluding item in a series of events which proved Jesus to be the Promised One foretold in Scripture; this was what had its effect.

I am not at the moment trying to prove Christ's divinity; frankly, I fight shy of that word 'prove.' I am trying to explain the origin, and thereby the meaning, of the Church's faith in Christ as God. Actually, no facts, no miracles, could prove the divinity of the Person of Jesus of Nazareth. People once thought they could, but we can no longer think so. The miracles of healing performed by our Lord can be paralleled both in modern and ancient times, both within and without the circles of believers. In Scripture itself others besides Jesus are said to have been instruments of divine power in raising the dead. A Sunday newspaper a few years ago published some statements which, if credited, would show that Jesus' birth of a virgin was not a unique event. However this may be, remember that we Christians, though required to assert in the Creed that he was 'born of the Virgin Mary,' are not required to assert (or to deny) that he could not have been born in the ordinary way. Some of the miracles of the Gospels remain mysterious and without parallels;

e.g. what happened at the Feeding of the Multitude? Was it the unbroken loaves or the divided fragments that were multiplied—or magnified? Or what did happen? The Evangelists are indifferent to our curiosity; their purpose in recording this event is not to demonstrate the supernatural nature of Christ. (If any one wishes to discover what that purpose was let him carefully study John 6.) Indeed these Evangelists lead us to believe that any merely human being might, if endowed with divine Spirit, and if God should so will, be the agent of similar 'mighty works.' Our Lord himself promised, 'he that believeth on me, the works that I do shall he do also; and greater works than these shall he do' (John 14 : 12). There is, however, one of these—largely out-moded—'proofs' of our Lord's divinity which is still persuasive: *'aut Deus aut homo non bonus'* (either God or not good)—meaning that he who could say, for example, 'come unto me all ye that labour and are heavy-laden, and I will give you rest. Take my yoke upon you and learn of me; for I am meek and lowly in heart' (Matt. 11 : 28f.), was either a liar and a braggart or else the One who alone can be adored without idolatry.

There were events in the life of our Lord of special luminosity. Foremost among these were his transfiguration, his passion, death and resurrection. But it was not just an accumulation of events in themselves which begot the faith of the Apostles. Some of the things that Jesus said and did seem indeed to have caused a temporary set-back in the growing trust and reverence of his followers. Their faith came finally to rest in the Person who acted, spoke and endured, though his actions, words and experiences, while sometimes illuminating, seemed at other times obscuring. Thus they came to accept, and finally to understand, the events because they were *his,* rather than accepting *him* because of the events. Events in themselves, especially when they fulfilled predictions or common expectations, might convince them of his messiahship. But underlying the events was something more than the events; and that surplus of significance was not fully expressed by the unsatisfying titles, 'Christ' or even 'Lord.'

The Fourth Gospel appeared in the last, or last but one, decade of the first century A.D. It is the product of a mind nurtured on the same facts, but a mind that had learned to see those facts more clearly and to express their meaning more boldly:

'The Word was God . . . the Word became flesh'; 'My Lord and my God.'

V

More than two hundred years separate the age of the Apostles from the first world-wide council of bishops, the Council of Nicæa (A.D. 325), which issued a common creed to supplement the many local baptismal creeds. (This ecumenical creed was a first edition of what we call 'the Nicene Creed.') During those centuries there were many theological controversies, all of which either centred on or touched on christology in its broad sense. Christianity had sprung from Judaism, a staunchly monotheistic religion. 'Marcionism,' a heresy which arose in the middle of the second century, tried to jettison the Old Testament; but the Church rejected Marcionism. Yet if Jesus was God, how could the doctrine of the divine unity and indivisibility—let alone such other unquestioned attributes of God as his invisibility, ubiquity, eternity—still be maintained? In the earlier part of this period there were some in Christian circles who were still so close to Jewish ways of thought that they spoke of Christ as the last and greatest of the Prophets—a man, though one endowed with divine grace in fullest measure. An attitude similar to this reappears among the 'Adoptionists' of the third century: Jesus, they taught, being pre-eminent among the sons of men in virtue and holiness, was 'adopted' by God to be his son and given divine status. These teachers could support their doctrine, if not by appeal to the general sense of Scripture, at least by a varied anthology of biblical quotations. At the other extreme were some, influenced by a non-Jewish, pluralistic conception of deity, who had little regard for the Gospel facts and even denied the reality of the Lord's manhood. There were also some in the third century who wanted to obliterate any but a temporal distinction between the Son and the Father.

But midway between these mutually contradictory aberrations we can discern, as we study early Church history, a succession of writers and teachers whose exposition of the Faith was more firmly rooted in tradition and Scripture. Their teaching was not always verbally consistent with what later emerged as orthodoxy, but we can see in retrospect that it was tending—and tending, broadly speaking, progressively—towards orthodoxy. These writers of the middle path follow the scent like a pack of hounds with noses quick to detect false trails. The earliest of them, the Catholic 'Apologists' of the second century, seem now to have been too much in love with the *Logos* conception (*Logos* could mean either 'word' or 'reason'), and therefore too intent on relating Christ to the Father in terms of revelation only. Such giants as St. Irenaeus (*c.* A.D. 180), Tertullian (A.D. 160–240) and Origen (third century) had a wider sweep; but it was St. Athanasius, hero-champion of orthodoxy in the fourth century, who decisively shifted the emphasis in christology from the idea of revealing to that of redeeming. The coming of the Son of God into the world meant an irruption from on high not only of light but also of re-creative and redeeming power. It was to *restore* our nature that Christ asumed it. The human race, depraved and debilitated, needed God himself to save it not only from blindness but from death.

Theology had not completed its christological task when the formula 'of one substance with the Father' had been hammered out, laboriously explained and finally accepted. There was still the question how the divinity of the Eternal Son made man is related to his human nature. Three further ecumenical councils met at long intervals, the last of them in 451. The formula finally adopted, 'two natures in one Person,' has been attacked and defended up to our own day. In a short essay like this there is insufficient space to discuss it; we can only say that it has been accepted by the wide consent of central and traditional Christendom.

We must see the development of dogma, that is to say of definitive doctrinal formulas, as a slow groping for the right mode of expression. Liturgical formulas took fixed shape long before credal formulas and must have played a big part in keeping the writers of what has been called 'the Catholic centre' from straying over the verges of their path either to right or left. Dr. H. E. W. Turner has written: 'In order of time there is no question of the priority of the *lex orandi*. The Church lived Trinitarianly before she evolved a satisfactory doctrine of the Trinity, while her devotion to Christ as God preceded by a still larger time-span the achievement of a *theologia Christi*.' [2]

VI

Why should so much of this essay be spent on the historical development of the Church's formulas of faith? We began by considering how those primitive ideas of God with which the Children of Israel had started gradually expanded. We went on to consider the difficulty the first Christians found in combining their knowledge of God with their belief in Jesus Christ. At last, by the middle of the fifth century, they had agreed upon certain formulas to express their faith. Our method of procedure was necessary for answering the question we started from. That question was: what do Christians mean when they say that Jesus is God? And we can now see two things:

(1) *That the formula was the result of an evolutionary process and can only be properly understood by reference to the growth through which it has come to be what it is.*

(2) *That this formula incapsulates the essence of a common faith;* that is to say, it is not the outcome of a process of reasoning undertaken by a number of individuals in isolation, and cannot yield sense to any one who tries to analyse it as if it were just this.

(1) In the historical evolution of the formula two factors were continually interacting—facts and faith. The outstanding facts that form the basis of the full Christian faith are, of course, the earthly life, death, resurrection and ascension of Jesus. But the events of Israel's history too were an indispensable preparation for the Gospel and an integral element in its significance, since these had gradually given shape to an originally nebulous and incoherent conception of God. There is thus a logical sequence of *facts, faith, formula* in which faith feeds on facts (and in doing so transforms not its substance but its appearance), while the final formula is a superstructure built upon previous formulas which one by one have been seen to be inadequate.

A fuller study, if space had allowed it, of the process which culminated in the formula would have ruled out many possible misunderstandings of the doctrine of the Incarnation. In becoming man God has never ceased to be God. Nor did he on earth merely act the part of a man, as an actor acts a part in a play; he *became* man. Moreover he has never henceforth ceased to be man. If we start by defining what we mean by 'God' and what we mean by 'man,' we seem to arrive at a hopeless paradox. Is that paradox just nonsense? Only a study of Church history —and ecclesiastical historiography begins in the New Testament —can obviate such a conclusion. You cannot arrive at faith in the incarnation merely through a step-by-step train of argument. Religious faith, in the last analysis, rests on an intuition. The sort of study here briefly outlined is the best preparation for receiving the light—the Light which is Christ.

(2) The affirmation of the divinity of Jesus links the believer, not only with contemporary adherents to the same faith, but also with a tradition which has welded together individuals and groups, within and across racial boundaries, through many centuries. Why should we conceal from ourselves or others that the unitive value of this shared belief has influenced, and does influence, us in first accepting and then clinging to it? Christian philosophy has never tried to conceal that there is a 'volitional' as well as a 'cognitive' element in faith. The volitional aspect of believing is very complex. To deride it wholesale as 'wishful thinking' is superficial and unfair. No one, admittedly, should assent to a proposition which seems to him manifestly untrue. And yet, to believe is more than to assent, though it includes assent. The 'venture of faith' does not involve 'wishful thinking,' but it does require the 'will to believe.' Some remain outside the Christian family not because they *cannot*, for intellectual reasons, accept Christian doctrines, but because they have no strong desire, no incentive for believing. They remain shivering on the edge of the water and cannot bring themselves to take the plunge. And perhaps there are many who deceive themselves when they plead 'intellectual difficulties' for agnosticism. The catholic-minded Christian, certainly, can freely concede that in his case the desire for incorporation into a great company of men and women, living and departed, has been and remains a strong incentive to belief; also, that by sharing in the common life and worship he has deepened his understanding, as well as his hold, of the *common* faith.

To say, then, that Jesus is God is to say that, in and through the events which the Apostles proclaimed and interpreted, God has both revealed the Truth—his nature, his creative purpose, and his will for man—and also poured forth saving and perfecting grace. But it is to say more than that; for Jesus is, to the Christian, more than a divine instrument of revelation and redemption. He is God himself, unchanged and undiluted, giving himself to men, from the moment of his conception in the womb of Mary to the present time, to be heard, seen and handled (1 John 1 : 1). No other language can do justice to the experience which the Apostles tried to describe so that their hearers might share it too (1 John 1 : 3). We cannot rest content with saying, for instance, 'He has the value of God'; we say 'He *is* God.'

So the incarnation is not one of a number of isolated tenets of faith. It is an integral part, indeed the very hinge, of the Christian creed. Jesus incarnate recapitulates all divine revelation, summing up and crowning what has been made known before, so that in him the very connotation of the word 'God' has become transfigured for the believer. 'I found,' said St. Paul at Athens, 'an altar with this inscription, To an unknown God. What therefore ye worship in ignorance, this set I forth unto you' (Acts 17 : 23). But in Jesus we see also, and for the first time, human nature no longer unrecognizably disfigured by self-centredness and all that results from that, but as it essentially is, and as, dynamized by his grace, God intends it to be. And since man is the crown, and therefore the meaningful key, of God's created handiwork, in Christ we see all nature in principle renovated. God has, by entering the world, taken it up into himself in an indestructible unity. In this way 'the mystery of his will' is made known. *Sub specie aeternitate* the restoration is already achieved, but in time it is seen as a process. The process begins with mankind; men and women, 'wounded and divided by sin,' are being drawn into the Body of Christ. The consummation of the process is symbolically envisaged in those passages of Scripture which picture a restored Paradise (such as that in which 'the wolf shall dwell with the lamb' (Isa. 11 : 6–9)). Jesus is God because this redemptive work is creative work. He is the Lord of creation, the Lord of history. To man, the first-fruits of the harvest, he addresses the absolute command which only God can pronounce; his word comes to us as a challenge, and his authority is final and unquestionable.

I have devoted much of this essay to discussing the beliefs of Christians who lived during the first three or four centuries A.D.; but it will be appropriate to end with the belief of a Christian much nearer to our own time. Here is something that John Ruskin wrote:

'I find numbers, even of the most intelligent and amiable people, not knowing what the word (*sc.* "Christianity") means; because they are always asking how much is true, and how much they like, and never ask, first, what *was* the total meaning of it, whether they like it or not. The total meaning was, and is, that the God who made earth and its creatures, took at a certain time upon the earth, the flesh and form of man; in that flesh sustained the pain and died the death of the creature he had made; rose again after death into glorious human life, and when the date of the human race is ended, will return in visible human form, and render to every man according to his work. Christianity is the belief in, and love of, God thus manifested. Anything less than this, the mere acceptance of the sayings of Christ, or assertion of any less than divine power in his Being, may be, for aught I know, enough for virtue, peace and safety; but they do not make people Christians, or enable them to understand the heart of the simplest believer in the old doctrine. One verse more of George Herbert will put the height of that doctrine into less debatable, though figurative, picture than any longer talk of mine:

> *Hast thou not heard that my Lord Jesus died?*
> *Then let me tell thee a strange story.*
> *The God of power, as he did ride*
> *In his majestic robes of glory,*
> *Resolved to light: and so, one day*
> *He did descend, undressing all the way.*
>
> *The stars his tire of light, and rings, obtained,*
> *The cloud his bow, the fire his spear,*
> *The heavens his azure mantle gained,*
> *And when they asked what he would wear,*
> *He smiled, and said as he did go,*
> *'He had new clothes a-making, here, below!'* [3]

CHAPTER III

FR. JONATHAN GRAHAM, C.R.
THE CRUCIFIXION

On Maundy Thursday 1960 the Evening Paper vans were rushing through the London streets, surmounted by a yellow placard, 'CRIME before CALVARY.' It is significant that those words swell the sales of the *Standard*; it is the height of improbability that a paper whose function it is to provide news should be able to arrest attention by advertising a news story nearly 2,000 years out of date. One can hardly imagine the average Londoner making sure of buying his paper, if the placard read 'TREACHERY at TRAFALGAR' or 'ARMADA ALLEGATIONS'; both events are remote. But Calvary is not. Calvary is news.

Calvary is news: and that, not only in the opinion of some earnest young clergyman teaching a class of children that 'gospel' means 'good news,' but news in the sense that the word is employed by ruthless sub-editors, advertising agents and sales managers. Of course there is no reason for supposing that the facts supplied in the evening papers are true; or that the copywriter has got hold of the right end of the stick or that his readers are in the least interested to learn the truth about the trial and crucifixion of Christ. But it does mean that a historical event which took place centuries before Trafalgar, the Armada or the first beginnings of English history, is surrounded with enough popular interest to make it sell. However ignorant of Calvary the twentieth century may be, however little we accept the dogmatic statements of the Church about it, however irrelevant theories of atonement or salvation or vicarious sacrifice may appear to be, however feebly Christians maintain the standards of Christ, however wide the gulf between the Church and the people, yet one thing is clear. The twentieth century and Calvary can at least understand one another's language at the level of violence and crime.

To read the Gospel accounts of the passion and death of Christ is to tread familiar ground. We are familiar with a world of horrors, brutality, scourgings, blood-lust, denials, suicide, women mourning and men breaking down, soldiers at their coarsest, judges at their most corrupt, religion denying itself, darkness and blood, horror and despair. A world that has got out of control; yes, we know all about that.

Yet Calvary is not just another crime story, not just another example of intolerable cruelty or miscarriage of justice. If it were merely that, it would of course be recognizably twentieth century in tone and content, but it would not be news, arresting, gripping, holding and in some sense satisfying the reader. There is something more to it, something which does not belong to any other judicial murder or innocent suffering, be it Socrates or Savonarola, John Huss or Joan of Arc, none of whom would arouse the mildest interest in the strap-hanging commuter of the 1960s. This 'something' is the character, the history, the person of the sufferer.

The Christian Gospel lies precisely there, in the character, the history and the person of him whose gibbet was placarded with this label: 'Jesus of Nazareth the King of the Jews.' Here, proclaims the Christian, in this innocent victim of man's brutality, murdered on a certain day by the authority of a certain Roman Governor, here, in the very thick of it all, is God. Here, where we suppose religion to have failed, is God; here, where the unpardonable crime is committed, is God; here, where the world is out of control, is God; here is God accepting the worst that devils and darkness can do, here is God sharing to the bitterest and ghastliest limit the storm and onslaught of the basest devices of man. Here is God, saving the world from itself.

Such is our Gospel; we need saving from ourselves, who can live in our age and doubt it? We need a Saviour, and thank God we've got one. For here on Calvary is no neat little formula for living, no tidy little guide to life, no elaborate technique of deep-breathing, muscular control and vegetable diet; here is no 'simple gospel' of kindness to men and domestic animals. This Gospel is not sanctified commonsense or moderation in all things; at Calvary there is no rubbish about being 'in tune with the Infinite,' no sympathy with integration of personality or fullness of self-expression. Here is God-man suffering like hell, suffering hell, in fact. God-man in the heart of reality, supported by angels, fighting against devils and the power of darkness, with the only weapon that can win—suffering love.

It has been said that modern scientific technique has led man up the garden path of progress, faced him with nuclear energy and left him helpless, in a cul-de-sac. Man's helplessness has come home to him with new and unexampled force since Hiroshima; but the state of helplessness in itself is nothing new. The very earliest traces that survive of the life and thought and history of man show him, for all his pride in achievement, at the mercy of three enemies, hemmed in by three dark curtains, baffled in turn by each of three culs-de-sac.

The first and most obvious cul-de-sac in man's existence is death; his earliest literature reflects the bitterness of death's blank finality and silence. Homer makes Achilles among the shades of the departed say he would rather be:

> *A slave to some poor hind that toils for bread*
> *Than reign the sceptred monarch of the dead*

and this is echoed by Ecclesiastes:

> *A living dog is better than a dead lion.*
> *For the living know that they shall die;*
> *But the dead know not any thing*
> (Ecclesiastes 9 : 4f.)

And behind the literature is the evidence of inscription, wall painting and pyramid, testifying to the obsession with death and the unwillingness of man to admit that all his pride and achievement comes to dust.

Less obvious and less easy to describe, but no less paralysing and humiliating, is man's insignificance in a world of forces too strong for him, spiritual as well as material. Fate and vengeance and fury are on his track; pitfalls open at his feet, immensity threatens to crush his puny strength; tragedy is the Greek word for this blind-alley in the life of men; yet sometimes it is more meaningless and more distorted than any tragedy of the poets, a void yet not a void, a waste howling wilderness, with the howling elusive and mocking yet real with the reality of panic. The earliest traces of religion are obsessed with the need to placate and pacify and come to terms with the hideous unfamiliar heights and depths which surround us as we strut or cower on our little tract of earth.

And the third cul-de-sac is sin. Seldom called by so short and crude a name, except by those who have the courage to face it and recognize its real nature; but all through human literature and the other traces that man leaves of himself from century to century, there runs the stream of man's disillusionment and disappointment with himself. He means so well and does so badly, he excuses himself and pretends that all is well, but he cannot deceive himself. He knows he ought, yet he does not; he knows he ought not and he does. Who is to rid him of this unceasing failure to be himself, of which he knows he can never rid himself?

Every one of the two million who bought an evening paper in London on April 14th 1960 is afflicted, baffled, limited by these three culs-de-sac, death, the void, sin; some with full consciousness and recognition of them for what they are, some entirely careless or entirely ignorant, others with every degree of knowledge and ignorance in differing proportion and variety. Some crushed by a recent bereavement, some in the toils of mental delusion, some under the dominion of vice; others helpful, sane and penitent; yet all sharing the common limitation, and all being confronted with Calvary. Look, if you will, at the shattering simplicity of its relevance.

Here, on any reckoning, human nature shows up at its worst—'Crime before Calvary'; and the crucifixion portrays precisely the baffling, infuriating, insoluble nature of that failure which the Christian faith calls sin. Those responsible for the crime hadn't *meant* to do such an appalling thing; one of them, Judas, when he saw what he had done went away and hanged himself; Pilate the Governor had meant to represent Roman justice at its best; the priests had meant to further the interests of true religion, yet they had all failed miserably to be true to themselves, they had all sinned. The crucified Jesus, with superb insight and even more superb disregard of his own intense suffering at every level, goes straight as an arrow to the very core of their need: 'Father, forgive them; for they know not what they do' (Luke 23: 34).

They do not know—that's exactly it; they had not meant; they were baffled, blinded, hemmed in; they need salvation, they need light, they need forgiveness. To him the need and the remedy are alike quite simple and quite clear; and in the calm assurance of his prayer and its address at this moment of moments with unhesitating faith to the Father, there comes the conviction —even if we knew no more of him than this one sentence, that he can in fact assure us of the remedy to meet the need. These first recorded words of Jesus from the Cross—eight short words in Greek to provide us with the solution of one of man's three great agelong problems—authenticate themselves. The man himself is so immediately, astoundingly and penetratingly relevant and assured that we hardly need a theology or a rationale; as we let the weight of the words tell, we realize it is the man himself who is the reality, the way, the truth, the life, beside which any poor human theory of atonement must seem complex, pale, ineffectual. Yet such a rationale must be attempted; but not until we have looked at Calvary in the light of those other two enemies of human life and achievement, death and the void.

No sooner had the prayer for men's forgiveness been offered, than it was answered by the conversion of an incorrigible, a gangster hanging by his side. Here is the dialogue from St. Luke (23: 39–43):

And one of the malefactors which were hanged railed on him, saying, Art not thou the Christ? save thyself and us.

But the other answered, and rebuking him said, Dost thou not even fear God, seeing thou art in the same condemnation? And we indeed justly; for we receive the due reward of our deeds: but this man hath done nothing amiss.

And he said, Jesus, remember me when thou comest in thy Kingdom.

And he said unto him, Verily I say unto thee, To-day shalt thou be with me in Paradise.

Ten words, this time, this supreme genius needs to solve the problem of all problems, death. It is not easy to assign any clear meaning to the gangster's prayer; what kingdom he could conceivably have pictured as the destiny of his fellow condemned victim it is impossible to guess. But it is clear that Jesus was listening not to his words but to the doubts and fears and horrors that were filling an inarticulate soul at the prospect of lingering torture and death that very day. 'To-day'—yes to-day, when your body and mine will be thrown out mangled into a common grave, the real you and the real me will be with each other in a state of innocence and joy. Death, the common enemy, is robbed of all its poison by the promise that he will share its inevitable loneliness; and will be in control of the state to which we go. Once again, the assurance of his authority is crystal clear; and on this, the last occasion in his life, it is given in the characteristic phrase, 'Verily I say unto you,' which had so constantly been used to precede statements and claims that only God or a madman could have made.

'And it was now about the sixth hour, and a darkness came over the whole land until the ninth hour, the sun's light failing' (Luke 23 : 44f.). There could be no better description in nature of 'the void'; uncanny, eerie, sinister, diabolical, when the very sun on whose light and heat every living thing depends, fails; when reason fails and all is confusion and horror and gloom, without meaning and without end. The void is so pathetically and increasingly common now, when the pace and insecurity of our existence multiply beyond all precedent the number of those suffering from aberration and mental confusion and madness. This is hell 'with the lid off,' an emptiness full of all that appals and revolts, monstrous and unclean; the state of which the first great Christian visionary John wrote as that in which 'men shall desire to die and death fleeth from them' (Rev. 9 : 4ff.) and then went on to picture a great abyss swarming with fantastic half-human monstrosities. Into this darkness worse than darkness Jesus plunged during those long three hours, emerging with that strange cry, compounded of despair and victory: 'My God, my God, why didst thou forsake me?' (Matt. 27 : 46; Mark 15 : 34).

Unfathomable despair, yes: he has been through the deep waters of separation from the God of whom he had said: 'I and the Father are one' (John 10 : 30), but he has come through them with his will unbroken, assured of God and triumphant. Of that there can be no doubt, as he uses his dying energies to proclaim the completion of his life's work and to commend himself to the unfailing love of his Father. Those few words, spoken from the cross by Jesus, in response to human needs as they arose, unstudied and unbelievably simple and satisfying, are in themselves the assurance that he possessed the key to unlock the chains of sin, to open the gates of death and to lock the gates of hell. Years after his death and resurrection, the same visionary, John, wrote of him as he that 'loosed us from our sins by his blood' (Rev. 1 : 5) and heard him proclaim : 'I was dead, and behold, I am alive for evermore, and I have the keys of death and of Hades' (Rev. 1 : 18).

That is all very fine and grand, but what exactly do we mean by this reference to 'Blood' ? Keys we can understand, for the keys are clearly metaphorical; but is blood metaphorical too? We can grasp that a man must suffer and die if he is to share the depths of human pain, failure and despair; but what are we with our culture, our materialism, our analytical science, what are we to make of the traditional language that surrounds the Cross? How can we attach meaning to the

Blood of Jesus (which)
for our pardon cries?

Saints wash their robes and make them white in the blood of the Lamb; we are told to drink a cup containing the blood of Christ; we are to address Jesus in our worship, as the Lamb of God; we get caught up in technical terms like redemption, atonement, oblation and propitiation; in short, we find the Church forcing upon us the traditional language of animal sacrifice in which no one believes and by which our intelligence is amused or revolted. What meaning can we extract from such a phrase as the 'sacrifice of the death of Christ' ? What is its history, what is its relevance?

It is only fair to recall, before trying to provide the materials for a reply to that question, that, as we said, there is something more to the death of Christ than there is to any other story of martyrdom, a something which poses a question to the historian as he takes into account that Calvary is 'news' to the century in which we live. This crucifixion has had and continues to have incomparable power over men's lives, a power not lightly to be dismissed by the student of comparative religion. So strange and pervasive and universal is this power that one might reasonably expect that one might need a peculiar vocabulary with which to attempt to describe and define it.

The key word of the vocabulary is *sacrifice* and our generation is unfamiliar with it, except on war memorials and the advertisements of bargain sales. Neither of these has much to do with Christian theology; we must dig deeper into the meaning of life itself if we are to find out why Christ died on a Cross, the full perfect and sufficient sacrifice for the sins of the whole world.

Few thinking people would deny that creative partnership in love is the highest characteristic of human life; that procreation is the noblest of man's privileges. To bring into life a free and separate human being, to create on behalf of the Creator the fruit of mutual love, this cannot but reflect the original creative love of God himself. All that God has revealed to us of Creation is in the poetry and picture language of Genesis, for Creation is indescribable; our experience of procreation is at best an analogy, removed at incalculable distance from that which it reflects. Yet the poetry of Genesis lets us into the pure delight and joy with which God regarded the new life, free and endowed with separate existence, as it responded to him in harmony and loving obedience. And we can infer too that man, alone of all that creation endowed with reason and intelligence and choice, found his whole joy and life and meaning in seeing that he is not his own, self-sufficient and independent, but entirely and absolutely the offspring and possession of God his Creator. The whole meaning of man's life is just that; he was created innocent, free, but blissfully dependent, and true life consists in recognizing this utter dependence upon Creative love. In the life of the innocent, religion is life and life is religion; it is one long act of homage, of dedication, of sacrifice.

This is the intensest joy, to realize the fact that 'I am not my own, but thine' and to go on offering back to God who made me all that I am and all that I have because he gave it to me. That is sacrifice, making holy all that I know and have and am; that is man's privilege; that is his joyful and exultant duty. That is what life is meant to be, innocent, natural, loving, glad sacrifice.

Some tiny glimpse of what such life on earth might be we can obtain by thinking of mankind as one vast orchestra, the player of each instrument totally surrendered to the will of the Conductor and finding in his own self-surrender and the giving of his particular faculty the highest satisfaction.

But experience and revelation alike teach us that man's life is not perfect homage, self-dedication, sacrifice. Every race and culture of which we can learn in prehistory and history gropes after this ideal; sacrifices of corn and wine and oil, of lamb or goat, yes, even of son or daughter, sacrifice permeates history; universally mankind is saying by these strange rites: 'I am not my own but thine; all that I am, all that I have is thine: accept this offering of mine as a token of my homage.' This universal instinctive practice (universal until Science 'did away' with the need for God) bears witness to the truth that man's present state is fallen; he knows inside himself that he is not innocent and free and unspoilt, he knows that sin is a blunder, a catastrophe; he knows that cakes and rams and human sacrifice are no substitute for the glad homage of himself. Yet he can do no better, for he is in the grip of sin and tragedy and death; somehow his life has been spoilt and poisoned very near the source, somehow his inheritance has been tainted, so his homage is tainted too. But in his bitterness of soul, man is not alone; the spoiling and poisoning of the beautiful creative work of God must cause him too exquisite grief. And so he decides to act. He—God in Three Persons, always co-operating in perfect love from eternity to eternity—he acts; he resolves to restore man to his former innocence and beauty and joy by entering deep into our fallen condition and himself offering the perfect homage, the perfect sacrifice on our behalf.

Language of that kind, when used about God, is always in danger of appearing unreal, because God is by definition incapable of description or definition in human terms, he is outside time and cannot change or be changed; it is obviously inaccurate to speak of him making decisions or resolutions, grieving or acting. Yet human language is the only medium we have got, and it is the appropriate medium for those who believe that God became man in time and space and was seen and touched and handled by men of flesh and blood. Another danger that creeps into any attempt to provide a rationale for the sacrifice of Christ, to explain why he got on to the Cross and how he got there, is that of elaboration and consequent unreality. The simple sinner who knows himself freed of sin by the love of Christ has the reasons in his heart, reasons of which the mind cannot know; to him the theology of salvation is irrelevant. He just knows, whereas he was blind, he now sees and the technical description of the state of his optic nerves is a matter of indifference. This is the concern of the optician, a matter of debate, perhaps, for those who do not share his experience. He simply knows. So long as we stand outside the experience of salvation through the blood of Christ, the language is likely—one would almost say is bound—to appear unreal and to describe some kind of mysterious legal fiction on the part of God, unworthy even of that God whose existence can be proved by pure reason.

But the attempt must be made to understand with the mind that which in the last resort can only be apprehended by the whole man in his experience. And the surest guide is the analogy from human life, activity, instinct and behaviour, procreative co-operation in perfect harmony between man and woman acclaimed by poets and philosophers alike as the supreme function of human life, and the new, free yet dependent child finding its completest joy and fulfilment in loving obedience. When this is lost and spoilt, there can be no restoration of confidence until repentance on one side and forgiveness on the other have brought about reconciliation. So far the parallel is easy to follow; man the created must repent, God the Creator must forgive. But suppose he can't! After all, he has an absolute right over all his creation, a right to total homage and worship, whereas a human father has only a limited right to honour and respect from his children. And to rebel against the absolute rights of the Creator is plainly incalculably more heinous than to rebel against the limited rights of a parent. How can the Creator possibly forgive? He cannot pretend that his rights don't matter; the glad homage which he created man to give must be rendered. For God to forgo it would mean that all the purpose of creation— the mutual joy of Creator and created in perfect harmony—must be cancelled and written off as failure. The homage must be paid and must be paid perfectly; God cannot abolish the demand, or forgo the sacrifice. The demand must be fulfilled by man, by perfect man, who alone can fulfil it; so God must find a different way for accomplishing the demand. He must find a perfect man to offer the perfect sacrifice. Where can he find one? There is only one way: he must become man himself.

Jesus was the name he chose; the meaning of the name is Saviour. He came to save creation from the appalling cul-de-sac in which it had landed itself; he came to offer to God the Father his perfect sacrifice; he came to restore to our human nature the possibility of offering the perfect sacrifice which was the purpose of our creation; he came, in short, to save us from our sins. And this involved the Cross.

Speculation has ranged from time to time over the necessity of God becoming man, had there never been sin; and some theologians have held that it was from the beginning in the eternal counsels of God that his Son should come to this created earth to lead the perfect homage of man, to reign and to rejoice as the perfect high priest, offering the perfect homage and sacrifice. Such a beautiful speculation lends great poignancy to the changed character of the perfect sacrifice which he in fact offered on Calvary. The sacrifice of Calvary was indeed perfect, but at what hideous cost was it offered!

To take our human nature upon himself and to offer perfect homage to God involved for Jesus lifelong perfect obedience: by this obedience, consistently practised out of love for God to the end, he restored the havoc worked in our relationship with God by man's disobedience. For disobedience is the root of all that theology means by the Fall of man. We are not concerned here to elaborate this doctrine; common sense and experience teach us every day that there are faults and taints and corruptions in human nature that no amount of education or common sense will ever cure; and revelation has added its poetry in the story of Eden. This story makes quite plain that what ruins man's life is failure in allegiance; man who alone is free to reason, to speak and to praise, has been deceived into thinking that his freedom is freedom to do his own will, instead of freedom to do freely the will of his Creator. That deception cuts right into the heart and meaning of his existence; for allegiance to God was man's sole life, the deception means separation from God, and separation from the Creator is death.

Into the whole of this predicament, sin, separation from God, death, a Saviour must somehow enter, or his sympathy with our race would be incomplete. Yet somehow he must enter into it sinless, innocent and at one with God, or his offering will be less than perfect. Such was the obedience of the Son of God from his first recorded words as a child in the temple of Jerusalem: 'Wist ye not that I must be about my Father's business?' to his last recorded words on the cross 'Father, into thy hands I commend my spirit' (Luke 2 : 49; 23 : 46).

He would suffer anything rather than break allegiance to the will of God. Every possible display of evil, disease, insanity, immorality, is thrust upon him during his ministry—every known reason for not believing in a God of love; every possible argument that human nature is incorrigible is acted out against him in his passion—deceit, betrayal, denial, injustice, cruelty; every temptation to curse God and die adds to the strain of his allegiance; the full pressure of sin, death and the void is brought to bear on his exhausted and crucified body; but all in vain. He is obedient, totally and absolutely. And that meant the Cross, it meant the shedding of his blood.

Otherwise his sacrifice would not have been complete, it would not have been a satisfaction to God the Father; and it certainly would not have satisfied the deep inarticulate longings of the human heart. Just suppose that the Son of God appeared on earth in the manner of a Greek god, exquisitely beautiful and immaculate, and calmly and with perfect poise had passed in stately procession to some High Altar shrine and there performed his priestly rites in radiant beauty. What sort of kinship could we have had with that kind of perfection? None. The poor, soiled and baffled human heart demands a Saviour who has borne the ghastly effects of sin and entered the hideous void and shed his blood and been torn in bits by death; that sacrifice we know instinctively to be effective, even had we never known that the Victim could not be retained by death, but rose in triumph to proclaim his victory.

But what sort of a victory is this? How can we honestly use language about Christ 'reigning from the tree'? Does not experience belie the exorbitant claims made in his Name? Two thousand years have passed since that great saving sacrifice; and where is the world now? We might well long to believe that all Christ said and promised is true; we may well protest and proclaim and preach that he is Saviour of the world, because we see the beauty of the scheme and know it answers the desire of our heart. But where is the evidence of the victory? Where, on Maundy Thursday 1960, is the reader of the evening paper to see evidence of the saving power of Christ? Jostled by a tight-packed rush-hour crowd he sways strap-hanging in a clattering, swaying prison cell, elbow to elbow with a hundred more, hurtling from an office in which he would rather not work to a suburb in which he would rather not live. This is his life, and all his eyes and ears take in all day is money, prestige, evil suggestion, fumes and dirt; the day's sole relief, perhaps, being the smiles of his children or the scent of a rose at his journey's end. Where is the doctrine of Creation, Redemption and Sanctification in all this? Does God really exist or care? Is it really true that he is to be found in that quaint contemporary hangar along the road? What if he did live and die and rise again as perhaps one in fifty of our generation believe? What if he did? Where is the fruit? If Christ did go through the cosmic and shattering experience, God and man, to save us from sin, where is the fruit of it now?

In the 'Ring and the Book' Browning puts these lines into the mouth of the aged Pope:

> *And is this little all there was to be?*
> *Where is the gloriously decisive change*
> *Metamorphosis immeasurable*
> *Of human clay to divine gold, we looked*
> *Should, in some poor sort, justify its price?*
> *... Well, is the thing we see, salvation? I*
> *Put no such dreadful question to myself,*
> *Within whose circle of experience burns*
> *The central Faith, Power, Wisdom, Goodness—God*
> (X, 1614 *et seq.*)

If the central truth of God burns within the circle of a man's experience, he will not be tormented for long, though he may from time to time be haunted by doubts. But the intellect demands an answer . . . 'is the thing we see, salvation?'

We must return to the first premiss of all rational and therefore of all Christian thought, that the dignity of man consists in his freedom to think and reason and choose and praise. That freedom is of the very essence of God's love in creation, as it is of man's love in procreation; no human couple would prefer slot-machines to children, however infallible the former, however self-willed, tiresome and disobedient the latter. The Salvation of God could never turn us into automatically sinless entities; that would be to destroy the whole purpose of creation and redemption alike. There is therefore no reason in logic any more than there is reason in history to suppose that the conquest of sin by Christ for us should involve our being relieved of the dread responsibilities of choice. Certainly there is no hint in the New Testament that this was to be expected; in fact no other religious teacher has ever laid down so frequently or categorically that his followers are to expect temptation, persecution and suffering: and the history of the first years of the Church shows all the old vices at work among the redeemed. St. Paul's first Epistle to the Corinthians is addressed by that most exacting of pastors to those who are 'sanctified in Christ Jesus' and goes on to reveal that they were guilty of partisanship, disunity, incest, litigiousness, fornication, idolatry, disorder in public worship, spiritual pride and infidelity to the central doctrines of the faith! Well might he have asked: 'Is this thing we see salvation?' or doubted the total victory of Christ over sin and death. Yet he did not hesitate to proclaim the victory of Christ and our need to assimilate its fruits by our free allegiance, or faith, and by our obedience in showing his perfect sacrifice. His converts were to 'proclaim the Lord's death till he come' (1 Cor. 11 : 26) by eating his body and drinking his blood, a participation in the body and blood of Christ. The fruits of the victory of Christ will be found in those who accept him in faith and obedience; and each of those is the result of the free choice of an individual. There were to be no mass conversions, no waves of conviction sweeping souls into the Church, but free men making free choice and freely maintaining it by obedience.

The real answer to those who question the effectiveness of the salvation of Christ is to be found not in the kind of statistical evidence which might satisfy a manufacturer of soap-powder that his brand was more effective than those of his competitors, but in the quality of those who take him at his word and share in his victory by faith and obedience. Life of a particular quality that the world has agreed to set on a pedestal and call sanctity is the real reply to the doubters and cynics. Here is a strange and humanly unaccountable army, comprising every variety of human being in every century of our era, ignorant and learned, stupid and clever, king and beggar, men, women, children all with a family likeness shining out of their portraits from Stephen the first martyr to the most recently tortured Christian in the Congo. And that likeness consists of conformity to the Cross, in faith and obedience. In other words, the saints share his sacrifice and they share also its cost; this is how they bear witness to the victory of Christ.

When in 1945 the British armies moved into areas of South Eastern Asia, which had recently been occupied by the Japanese, there were discovered some verses scribbled by an unknown British soldier on the walls of his prison cell:

> *If I must face the firing squad,*
> *Though harm I did nobody,*
> *Help me to love them still, my God,*
> *As bullets strike my body.*
>
> *If I must die a lowly spy,*
> *Though spying did I never,*
> *Stay in my heart, O God, and I*
> *Will love thee more than ever.*
>
> *Forgive them all the tortures done,*
> *My thirst and my starvation;*
> *For who could suffer more than One*
> *Who died for our salvation?*

There rings the authentic note, the note of total self-offering to God in glad homage and sacrifice, the note of victory. For such a saint is victorious; there is nothing that can possibly defeat him; there is no power which can master him, whether physical or spiritual. He is crucified with Christ and is beyond the reach of sin, death and the void; he is, in fact, saved, saved by the blood of Christ.

Perhaps we may still feel that there is an element of the dramatic—firing squads and tortures—in the life of this unknown poet and saint, which has passed our humdrum life by. All very well to be united to Christ's passion and to triumph over evil, when we are keyed up to the crisis and ready for the blow; but how are we, whose lives are ordinary, drab, monotonous, domesticated, to make real to ourselves this homage and this triumph? Experience will at least teach us that the moment of dramatic sacrifice or heroic virtue, if it comes and offers itself to any man, will only be accepted and grasped by him who has trained himself by life-long discipline; this is the principle which lies behind all military drill and all athletic training. We know that the *Tale of Two Cities* is melodrama, not real life; the dissolute habits of Sidney Carton are no preparation for sacrificial death, calculated, planned and perfected. The sacrifice of Calvary was the fruit of years of self-disciplined faith and obedience in the least exciting or heroic sphere, village life. That, minding the shop, mending the table, fetching the water, hunting for the lost coin, that was the stuff of which the full perfect and sufficient sacrifice was compounded. So it will have to serve for all who want to share the sacrifice and the victory; the acceptance of hard facts, wood and nails, the offering of our body with all that may happen to it, through it and in it in thankful homage to our Creator.

A line of an old hymn describes the paradox of our relationship to Christ quite simply:

To the Cross we look, and live.

What appears to be the place of death is the source of life; what appears to be the triumph of sin is the place of its defeat and forgiveness; what appears to be tragedy is high triumph. There is no other explanation which fits the facts; here is God in the thick of human corruption, transforming the worst into the best, avenging our sin by making reconciliation possible, atoning for all the insults we have offered God in denying the sole purpose of our existence. Here and here only is rest and satisfaction for twentieth century man; here and here only is life given adequate meaning. It is this that makes Calvary news.

CHAPTER IV

FR. NICOLAS GRAHAM, C.R.

THE RESURRECTION

'JESUS ... shewed himself to the Apostles alive after his passion by many proofs.'

The phrase has a strange ring to the ear which is accustomed to the language of the Bible; strange, because the Bible does not generally deal in scientific terms like 'proof' and 'evidence.' In fact the word 'proofs' used here by St. Luke in the preface to his second volume, The Acts of the Apostles (Acts 1 : 3), occurs nowhere else in the New Testament. It is a strong word, so strong that the translators of the Authorized Version felt justified in translating it, 'infallible proofs.' It means 'demonstrative evidence,' such as is presented directly to the senses; just the kind of evidence that the Gospels in fact record of the Risen Christ: 'See my hands and my feet, that it is I myself : handle me, and see; for a spirit hath not flesh and bones, as ye behold me having. ... And they gave him a piece of a broiled fish. And he took it, and did eat before them' (Luke 24 : 39ff.) or 'Reach hither thy finger, and see my hands; and reach hither thy hand, and put it into my side : and be not faithless, but believing' (John 20 : 27).

But St. Luke is more like a scientific historian than any other Bible writer; the preface to his Gospel insists on method and reliable evidence even more strongly than the preface to Acts. He has consulted eyewitnesses (again a unique word in the New Testament); he himself has 'a thorough firsthand familiarity' with the facts; he will write 'in order' (again the word is used by no other New Testament author); he wishes to establish 'certainty,' to present the title-deeds of Christianity. Such are his claims as an historian; whether they are justified is a proper question for scholars, but no ordinary reader of his books can have any doubt of his intention.

Now when a man of good will sets out to write an account, first of a man's life and then of the events immediately following from the circumstances of that life; when, moreover, he has been in touch with eye-witnesses of the life and is himself an eyewitness of subsequent events, and when he is writing of a person whose influence has changed the whole course and orientation, not only of his own life, but also of the lives of thousands of his contemporaries; when, finally, that life and those events have the deepest and most sacred significance for him, he is likely to tell the truth.

But perhaps it may be thought that an ardent disciple is the very last person to be trusted with a biography of his master? Such an author, of all people, is likely, even if unconsciously, to falsify, to tone down, to evade awkward facts? That depends, of course, on the integrity of the writer. But if one thing emerges from a reading of the Gospels and Acts more clearly than another, it is that the most awkward fact of all is not only not evaded, but described with a wealth of detail and positively gloried in. It is, indeed, made the pivotal event of the whole narrative—the Resurrection of Jesus Christ from the dead, complete with flesh, bones and digestive processes.

Why Christ's resurrection was held by the earliest Christian writers and preachers to be of central importance both to the understanding of his life and to the living out of Christianity in the world, we shall consider later. At present we are concerned with the evidence.

And here it must be said that you cannot extract all references to the Resurrection from the New Testament writings without damaging the whole structure. Even if the actual narratives in the Gospels (which are later documents than most of the New Testament) were written off as a spurious 'happy ending'; if we were left with Christ in the tomb at the end of the Gospels, we should find him already risen in the Epistles. Whole tracts of the New Testament would make nonsense 'if Christ hath not been raised' (1 Cor. 15: 14) and documents just cannot be treated like that.

The actual evidence, as far as it is contained in the New Testament, is, then, as good as we can expect from written sources and far better than the evidence for a vast number of historical facts which we all take for granted. The difficulty lies, not so much in the evidence, as in the event. On an ordinary view of the world, men who have been killed simply do not rise from the dead. The Evangelists themselves tell us that Christ's most intimate friends, despite what he himself had often told them, did not really expect the Resurrection to happen. Who shall blame them? Resurrections don't happen. They did not really expect him to die—certainly not in the way he did; and if that sounds odd or superstitious, just ask yourself whether you really consciously allow yourself to contemplate as probable the death of a healthy man of thirty or so. (He will die some time of course, but you do not really expect it or think about it.) The manner and occasion of Christ's death, then, was a hideous shock to his friends. It appeared to put an end to all their highest hopes, however ill-defined those hopes may have been. Whatever they were, they could hardly have come to fruition on a Roman cross.

The death an accomplished fact, the undreamed-of event having unmistakably and horribly happened, they certainly did not expect a resurrection. Dazed with disappointment and sorrow as they were, any hint of such a thing would have seemed a mockery of their grief. So when the first hint came, from the women who had gone early to the tomb, and found it (so they said) empty, their story was dismissed as an idle tale—mere hysteria. Even when one or two of them went to see for themselves and found that the tomb was indeed empty, they only went away again, wondering. A week later, when the rest were convinced that Christ had truly risen, one of the intimate circle still stuck out for 'infallible proof': 'Except I shall see in his hands the print of the nails, and put my finger into the print of the nails, and put my hand into his side, I will not believe' (John 20 : 25). He was given it.

To find a friend's grave empty two days after his burial was as much of a shock and an enigma then as it would be to-day, especially if (a vivid detail not likely to have been invented) the shroud and head bandage were lying undisturbed at the bottom of the grave.

The most obvious explanation was that which occurred to the most devoted of Christ's women friends: 'They have taken away the Lord' (John 20 : 2). Who? His enemies? But why should they have destroyed the best evidence of his death, which they had gone to such trouble to bring about? His friends? Again why? The only possible reason would seem to be, in order to put about the story that he had miraculously risen. The arguments against this seem psychologically overwhelming. Physically, perhaps, it could have been done, though the disposal of the body would have been a problem. But consider the psychological difficulties. Here is a group of men, devoted disciples who have seen something if not all of the nobility of Christ's character. They have been overwhelmed by his sudden and terrible death on a trumped up charge of treason. They are living behind locked doors for fear of implication in their master's so-called crime. They are disorganized and demoralized. Their natural leader, Peter, is more deeply sunk in remorse and misery than the rest. Nowhere in any description of them has there been the slightest hint that they were the kind of men who would readily either conceive or practise deceit. Yet on this theory, they must have planned and carried out, within not much more than twenty-four hours of their initial grief and shock, a dangerous, difficult and repugnant act of body-snatching, so efficiently that no trace of their activities could be discovered. On top of this, these men who locked themselves in for fear of the Jews, were, six weeks later, in the same city, under the same High Priest and the same Governor who had brought about the death of Jesus, openly, vigorously and joyously proclaiming his resurrection.

The stories of the appearances of Christ after his death would also have had to be concocted, agreed upon and foisted upon posterity. In such circumstances one would have supposed the invention of a consistent story, whereas in fact the stories we have are not easy to harmonize at all points. There is certainly nothing in them which suggests the too neat and tidy result of collusion. They just do not read like fiction. Nor do they read like ghost stories.

All this is on the assumption that the tomb was really empty. What if *that* was not true? It is only fair to say that there is no mention of the empty tomb in the earliest records (i.e. in St. Paul's letters), but there is abundant mention of resurrection—a raising or rising from death—and the plain sense of this in ordinary usage is physical resurrection. We commonly associate a person with his body and if you buried someone's body on Friday and were told on Sunday that he had risen from the dead, you would expect to find his grave empty.

If, however, Jesus's body simply lay and corrupted in the tomb, we are again faced with the necessity of supposing a great deal of deceit on the part of the Evangelists and of their informants. Though there are discrepancies in the accounts of the appearances, the one thing all the Gospels agree on is the empty tomb. And again, it would have been unwise, to say the least, to preach the physical resurrection of Christ in Jerusalem, where he had been executed and buried only a few weeks earlier. The Jewish authorities could have silenced the Apostles once for all, by simply opening the tomb.

Yet there are still those who will ask, 'Was it not a spiritual resurrection? Surely it is far more fitting and beautiful to believe that the spirit of Christ lived on in the hearts of his disciples?' But if that means anything at all (as perhaps it may) it does not mean Resurrection. At most it might mean the survival of a real immortal spirit after physical death, a spirit which had some means of uniting itself with other human spirits, presumably stronger means than by simply dwelling in men's memories. That this is true of the Spirit of Christ all Christians believe. But they believe that this is a *result* of his Resurrection, not that it *is* his Resurrection. You might as well say that the existence of your children and their resemblance in some respects to their parents *are* your marriage.

Whatever difficulties there may be in the evidence (and there are difficulties) yet, to put it at its lowest, the least incredible theory is that which Scripture teaches and the Church believes, namely that, on the third day after his crucifixion, Jesus Christ rose again, body and soul, never again to be subject to death.

There is also another kind of evidence, which, because it is living and tangible, is really more compelling than anything written. This is the existence of Christians, of Christianity, of the Church, to-day. As St. Paul said long ago: 'If Christ hath not been raised, then is our preaching vain, your faith also is vain. Yea, and we are found false witnesses of God; because we witnessed of God that he raised up Christ' (1 Cor. 15: 14f.).

This is not the place to write at length about the nature of the Church. The only point we are here concerned with is, that one of the principal functions of the Church is to witness to the Resurrection of Christ; that is, to the Resurrection as an abiding reality, not simply as an event, though of course dependent on that event. To have been literally a witness of the Risen Christ was, in the first generation, a necessary qualification for Apostleship (Acts 1 : 22). That is what an Apostle primarily was. The Gospel of these, the first preachers of Christianity, precisely was: 'This Jesus did God raise up,' and their warrant for so preaching, 'whereof we all are witnesses' (Acts 2 : 32—the first Christian sermon).

To have been literally a witness of the risen Christ was a qualification which in course of time must cease to operate. All future generations of Christians must of necessity be those who 'have not seen, and yet have believed' (John 20 : 29) and it was possible for St. Peter (who had seen) to write to his converts of Jesus Christ, 'whom not having seen, ye love' (1 Peter 1 : 8). How could one be said to love or believe in an invisible person, unless he were believed to be fully alive and personal?

A reader of Dickens could say 'I love Mr. Pickwick' (who never existed at all); he might say, 'I love Dickens' (who is dead); he might even say, 'I believe in Dickens.' By the first statement he would mean that he is sure he would love a man of Mr. Pickwick's character if such a man existed; by the second, that he enjoys reading Dickens and feels that he must have been a lovable person; and by the third, either that he agrees with what he takes to have been Dickens' opinions or that he finds the reading of his novels a remedy for boredom or melancholy.

No doubt there are people who might say that they love and believe in Jesus Christ in one or other of these ways. They generally use slightly different language, saying wistfully, 'Of course it's a wonderful story, but it isn't true,' or, 'Jesus Christ was a great man,' or, 'Jesus Christ was a great teacher,' or, 'The example and teaching of Jesus Christ has helped me.' But this is not how Christians talk about Jesus Christ. They speak of him as a living person, both human and divine whom, by various means, they really know and love and trust. They speak, in fact, as witnesses of his Resurrection. Millions have so thought and spoken and still do. It would be possible, but temerarious, to write them all off as deluded. Can history anywhere parallel a delusion so persistent, so widespread or so strange? The fact that large numbers of men and women are going about saying openly that they know, love and trust someone who died twenty centuries ago, calls surely for investigation? There must be some very strange and very powerful force abroad in the world to have produced a phenomenon so improbable.

Well, there is. It is a force which was generated in a garden in the suburbs of Jerusalem on what we now call the first Easter morning, when Perfect Man, perfectly united to God in the Person of Jesus Christ, burst through the barrier of death and by that act, released into the world of men the power of an indestructible life. 'Generate,' a word which by courtesy is used of the production of impersonal forces, is here used literally and precisely. This is how a New Testament writer speaks of the Resurrection and its effect upon human beings: 'Blessed be the God and Father of our Lord Jesus Christ, who according to his great mercy begat us again unto a living hope by the resurrection of Jesus Christ from the dead' (1 Peter 1 : 3).

To become a Christian is to be reborn, to receive a new life, to be begotten of God the Father by the Resurrection of Christ. This rebirth is actually effected in each individual by baptism, with its accompanying acts of faith and repentance. Like St. Peter, St. Paul connects this rebirth closely with the Resurrection: 'We who were baptized into Christ Jesus were baptized into his death. We were buried therefore with him through baptism into death: that like as Christ was raised from the dead through the glory of the Father, so we also might walk in newness of life' (Rom. 6 : 3f.).

New life here and now; life of an eternal and indestructible quality, which therefore must survive physical death; new men; a new creation—this is the New Testament language about the Resurrection. And very incomprehensible and mysterious language too, it may well be thought. What, after all, have we here but a repetition of those images which have so long and so widely haunted the minds of men; images which are so easily (and so drearily) explained as mere projections of our unsatisfied desires? New life; immortal life painfully achieved by means of purificatory and initiatory rites; union with a god who died and rose again: these ideas can be paralleled at perhaps a dozen or more points in man's religious history. Is Christianity, after all, just one more Mystery Religion?

Christianity certainly is a Mystery Religion, but with this all important difference from all others, that it claims historicity for its 'myths.' Call Christ a Corn King if you like; the god who typifies the rhythm of the seasons, dying and rising again, feeding his people on his flesh (identified with bread) and his blood (identified with wine). When Greeks asked to see him, he sent them a message in the kind of language they understood: 'Except a grain of wheat fall into the earth and die, it abideth by itself alone; but if it die, it beareth much fruit' (John 12 : 24). It is the language of the fertility cult. Call him a Corn King if you like, but you must not call him merely a Corn King, or just one more Corn King, for against the shadowy background of the pagan myths he stands out in bold historical relief. No one ever claimed to have touched or handled Osiris in the reign of an identifiable King of Egypt, or to have had dinner with Adonis in Byblus, or to have rowed Attis across the Hellespont.

The historicity of the Founder of Christianity gives also unique reality to its rites. In the rite of Holy Communion, Christians may finally and truly do what their pagan forefathers were dimly groping for; that is, they can indeed eat the flesh and drink the blood of the sacrificial victim, because the Victim himself instituted the rite at a particular time and place, among chosen witnesses. Similarly, the Catholic ceremonies for preparing the font for use in Baptism have unmistakable features of a fertility rite. The significance of dipping a lighted candle into a bowl of water can hardly escape an untoward and Freudian generation. But then the Founder actually said we should be born again and instituted the rite of Baptism to effect it, not just to mime it.

It is all the more remarkable to find Jesus Christ so clothing himself in the images of natural religion, in a race and tradition so strictly and spiritually monotheistic, so rigidly anti-pagan and a-syncretistic as Judaism.

Moreover the very word 'mystery' has a new significance in Christian language and thought. A Christian mystery is not something which is hidden, but something which has been or is being revealed. The images are fused in The Image, for Jesus of Nazareth is the image of the invisible God (Col. 1 : 15; 2 Cor. 4 : 4) and the pagan yearnings after a new, purified and immortal life through union with a slain and risen god are but broken reflections in the cloudy, troubled waters of men's minds, of the truth which is in Christ Jesus.

It may be seen, then, that the truth of the Resurrection of Jesus Christ is pivotal to Christian belief. The entry into Christian life is by means of the Sacrament of Baptism, which, as we have seen, the New Testament declares to be the means of new life. The quality of this new life may be apprehended from the various ways in which it is described. It is Sonship of God the Father; the Christian becomes a joint-heir with Christ; he becomes a member of Christ; he becomes a new creature—even a new creation. All these attributes of the Christian life are dependent on the Resurrection which in turn is, of course, dependent on the sacrificial death and perfect human life which precede it in time. This sonship is not the natural state of man. Man is, by nature, God's creature, but only by grace, by supernature, has he the privilege of sharing in the sonship which is primarily and properly unique to the Son, the second Person of the Holy Trinity. That privilege of sonship, of joint heredity with Christ, implies also immortality—for the full life of the Son is Eternal Life and, that eternal life can be extended to the sons of men, is demonstrated in the Resurrection of the Son of Man.

Again, membership in Christ—and notice, it is membership in a person, not simply (though it is this too) in a society—whatever it means, must be actually meaningless if Jesus Christ is not still fully alive in his human as well as in his divine nature. For membership means an intimate sharing in a living organism. It is difficult enough to see how one human person can be said to be a member of another human person (though marriage and friendship, parenthood and sonhood give us some glimpses)—but it is downright impossible for one kind of nature to share in the life of an entirely different kind of being. So a man cannot become a member of God, any more than he can become a son of God, unless God chooses to share his nature. To share that nature completely involves sharing the experience of death and it is just here that the Son of God, united to human nature, takes the momentous new step and carries manhood with him. The Resurrection of the Son of Man does more than assure us of life after death; it points to an altogether new direction, one might say a new dimension, for the lives of men here and now. 'If any man is in Christ, he is a new creature' (the words can be even more dramatically translated 'there is a new creation') 'the old things are passed away; behold, they are become new' (2 Cor. 5 : 17).

If we are looking for the 'next step in evolution,' we need not fascinate ourselves with the picture of super-brains bred in test-tubes. Such nightmares, or worse, may already be lurking in our laboratories. But whether or not a few human beings are ultimately permitted so to manipulate the nature of man, it will not be the next step in evolution. Rather it will be an aberration leading to a dead end. For though the result might be, in popular language, 'a new creature,' it would be a creature diminished rather than increased in humanity. The next (and final) step in evolution has already taken place. If any man be in Christ, he is a new creature. The Risen Christ, who is the prototype (or what the New Testament, in more homely terms, calls the firstfruits) of the New Man, is not less, but more, more gloriously, more—but comparatives will no longer serve. He is wholly, completely and finally human.

A new creation must be an act of God. Man, though he has what are, by courtesy, described as creative powers, is in fact no more than pro-creative. God alone is truly original, truly creative. So it is that the Resurrection is described in Christian writing, not as an isolated instance of 'survival,' a kind of biological freak as if, by some moral or spiritual quality of his own, Jesus had somehow managed to circumvent the natural results of his death; nor is it a recalling of the dead to an earthly life as it had previously been lived. Still less does it appear as a kind of desperate divine expedient for saving at the last minute a situation which had got out of hand. Rather it is one of the mighty acts, one of the 'wonderful works' of the God of Israel, such as the Hebrews loved to rehearse and glory in. It was a deliberately prepared and planned intervention in the life of the world; the first event of its kind in cosmic history.

'God raised him from the dead, and gave him glory; so that your faith and hope might be in God' (1 Peter 1 : 21). Here St. Peter closely connects the Resurrection with belief in God, as does also St. Paul: 'If thou shalt confess with thy mouth Jesus as Lord, and shalt believe in thy heart that God raised him from the dead, thou shalt be saved' (Rom. 10 : 9). Belief in the Resurrection is thus seen to be integral to Christian faith, to a full understanding of the significance of the life and death of Jesus Christ and to the living out of Christianity in the world, here and now.

What of life after death? Does the Resurrection of Christ 'prove survival'? Is it evidence for the immortality of the soul? It is not used as an argument for these things in the New Testament. In St. Paul, indeed, the argument is reversed. He has heard of some Christians at Corinth who are saying that there is no such thing as resurrection of the dead.

'If that is the case,' he argues, 'then Christ did not rise from the dead' (1 Cor. 15 : 15). The doctrine of resurrection was in fact a bone of contention between the two most prominent sects in Judaism, the Pharisees who affirmed it and the Sadducees who denied it (see Acts 23 : 7ff.). Certainly St. Paul taught that Christ's resurrection had a unique character and was unique in its consequences, but as a Pharisee, he believed in a resurrection of the dead before he ever heard of Jesus Christ. Even so, the questions at issue were not those of mere survival of death, or of the immortality of the soul.

That human beings in some sense survive death has been widely held and closely associated with religious belief and practice throughout world history. If this belief, as materialists would have us think, is merely a projection of an almost universal human desire for survival, it is strange that the after-life has so often been represented as a poor thin shadowy affair, as, in fact, not really desirable at all. Concentrating on the tradition in which Christianity was born, we find in the Old Testament but few intimations of an after life which held any promise of a richer or freer life than the present one. The Hebrew Sheol (variously translated in our Bibles as 'the pit,' 'the grave' or 'hell') is not dissimilar from the Greek Hades. It was a place of departed spirits, who are sometimes thought of as asleep or in darkness or at best as enjoying (if that is the right word) an attenuated existence as wraiths or ghosts. Immortality was to be sought in length of days and children's children. Earthly prosperity, including a numerous and strong posterity, are the dominant signs of God's favour in the Old Testament. Some verses of

Psalm 115 give, compactly, the main outlines of the picture:

> *He will bless them that fear the Lord, both small and great.*
> *The Lord increase you more and more, you and your children ...*
> *The heavens are the heavens of the Lord;*
> *But the earth hath he given to the children of men.*
> *The dead praise not the Lord, neither any that go down into silence.*
>
> (verses 13ff.)

In later Judaism, and especially in the period between the Old and New Testaments, a greater sense of the reality of the future life developed, partly through reflection on the mystery of suffering (here Job, a late book of the Old Testament shows some advance on earlier ideas) and partly from an ardent desire for abiding communion with God. Outside Palestine too, later Judaism is much coloured by Greek thought and in e.g. the Book of Wisdom (which probably belongs to the first or second century B.C.), the doctrine of immortality has a strongly Platonic flavour.

In this development the believing ear discerns one of the many signs of preparation for the Gospel. It is as if what were first heard as a number of fragmentary musical phrases (as in a symphony of Sibelius) were being blended and built up by the sure hand of the Master, until at last they emerge in the statement of one noble and triumphant theme. The attentive listener is rewarded: 'So that is what we have been waiting for. Of course we see it now, though we could never have guessed at anything so totally right and satisfying.' It is the Risen Christ who announces that master theme. The thin broken phrases are caught up and transmuted in the new strong statement: The Resurrection of the Flesh.

In plainer prose it may be said that the Resurrection of Christ gave a new and characteristic shape to the doctrine of the immortality of the soul. Man's highest destiny is more than the survival of an immortal soul (indeed, as we have seen, survival in early Jewish tradition was not thought of as an even moderately high destiny). It is to be a life of abiding union with the Risen Christ, begun in the baptized in this life and reaching its completion in the reunion of body and soul hereafter. The full redeemed life of heaven must include a restoration of the whole psycho-physical organism, because man was created by God to be and to remain an embodied spirit or, as is perhaps a preferable expression, an ensouled body.

'But some one will say . . .' St. Paul was moderate. To-day we should have to write: 'But practically every one will say: "How are the dead raised? and with what manner of body do they come?"' (1 Cor. 15: 35). St. Paul, however, was no velvet-gloved apologist for Christian doctrine. 'Thou fool,' he exclaims impatiently, and the verses which follow might be summarized: 'That is God's business.'

St. Paul was not troubled, nor probably have the vast majority of Christians been troubled by the problem of the literal resurrection of the particles which belonged to the body at the time of death: It is quite true that the general resurrection has been crudely represented as an opening of graves and a giving up of their dead by earth and sea alike. This may be crude, but it is defensible. In less atom-conscious ages than our own, the sheerly impossible chemistry of the thing was not considered, and at least the Christian doctrine was retained, not spiritualized away. But our Christian ancestors were not fools. They did not suppose that a man who had the misfortune to be eaten and digested by a lion thereby lost his chance of resurrection at the last day. As for St. Paul, he never even suggests a literal resurrection of the body, but plunges into a series of analogies all designed to show that the resurrection body will be quite different in kind from the earthly body, though recognizably continuous with it, as the ear of corn is recognizably continuous with the seed which 'died' to produce it. 'Flesh and blood,' he says emphatically, meaning the physically (not morally) corruptible matter of which we partake on earth, 'cannot inherit the kingdom of God' (1 Cor. 15: 50). But equally emphatically this does not mean that the life of heaven is a life of disembodied spirits. It may even be doubted whether there are such things as disembodied human spirits. It is certainly impossible to form a mental image of such a thing (though this of course does not prove that it cannot exist). Try to imagine a disembodied spirit and you will find that you have given it a body, however gaseous and refined.

At all events the Risen Christ was at great pains to convince the disciples that he was not a spirit or ghost. It is true that his risen body had properties which ordinary human bodies have not. But it is here contended that these properties made it not less, but more, truly human. This may appear, at first, a startling and perverse contention. It may be approached as follows.

The role of the human spirit has always been to become master of the flesh which it informs. This principle is common to all high philosophies, both eastern and western. Like other lofty human aims, it has known many aberrations and corruptions. In the East it has on the whole, led to a despising of the flesh; at many different times and places it has sought for morally impermissible short cuts, by way of sorcery, witchcraft and magic. In the earthly life of Christ himself we are allowed to overhear the agonizing struggle for mastery: 'The spirit indeed is willing, but the flesh is weak' (Matt. 26: 41; Mark 14: 38). The Christian life has often been represented as a combat, one phase of which is the battle between flesh and spirit, and none have felt this more acutely than St. Paul: 'for not what I would, that do I practise; but what I hate, that I do . . . for the good which I would I do not: but the evil which I would not, that I practise' (Rom. 7: 15, 19). One can hear the agony of the struggle in the tortuous repetitive phrases. The moral struggle is common experience and not, of course, confined to Christians and in the end it may be said, in this life, the flesh always appears to win. The forces of decay and decline at last issue in death and, to all appearances, 'quite o'ercrow the spirit.' Or alternatively, if you hold a doctrine of survival and of the immortality of the soul, death may appear a victory for the hitherto imprisoned spirit.

The Christian moral law demands as rigidly as any that the spirit should have the mastery, but not that the flesh should thereby perish. There is no true mastery if the thing mastered ceases to exist. A better analogy can be found in the taming of a horse or the mastery of a musical instrument. The good rider has so mastered his mount that it obeys his lightest touch or softest whisper; the good rider can be felt and seen to be 'one with his horse.' The higher nature has indeed subdued the lower to its will, but the result is a harmonious relationship, wherein the higher is confident to command and the lower glad to obey.

Something similar may be seen in the player who has (as we say) mastered his instrument.

The flesh, then, of the Risen Christ will never again be weak. His spirit and body are now conjoined in a glad partnership, so that, for instance, he can at will be visible or invisible, disguised or recognizable. In him the control of the flesh by the spirit was always perfect, but under the earthly conditions of the Incarnation he shared the moral struggle with the rest of the human race. In the Risen Christ, that struggle is over: he is one with his body. Thus it may be said that what seems to us the non-human properties of his risen body are in reality an index of his full and true humanity. Those who saw the Risen Christ saw a real Human Being for the first and only time in their lives.

But what is the relationship of the resurrection of Christians to the Resurrection of Christ? Does it follow the same pattern? In literal detail evidently not. The bodies of Christians, like those of other folk, lie in their graves and rot. Nor is it surprising that the Resurrection of him who is God-made-Man should be, in earthly experience, unique.

It was necessary for what we now call 'apologetic purposes,' that Christ should demonstrate the fact of his Resurrection to his disciples, but the Resurrection appearances were not necessary in themselves. Christ had no need, in himself, to remain on earth for forty days (if, indeed, 'remain' is the right word) after his Resurrection. His work was accomplished with the great triumphant cry from the cross 'Tetelestai' (weakly translated 'It is finished': better, 'the goal is achieved'). He knew that death could not hold him; the limit of human experience, namely death, had been suffered. Seeing that he is God, the wonder is that he was able to die, rather than that he was able to rise again. He speaks of these things in the tones of one who is master of life and death: 'I lay down my life, that I may take it again. No one takes it away from me, but I lay it down of myself. I have a right to lay it down, and I have a right to take it again' (John 10: 17f.).

These are the rights of the Lord of Life and as such they are not shared by mortal men. But as always, he is willing to lay aside his rights and stoop to the needs of men. The Resurrection must be demonstrated to his disciples in such a way as to convince them that the whole man, body and soul, has risen from death, and yet in such a way as to make it clear that he is no longer confined by earthly conditions and must, before long, withdraw his physical presence from the earth. What they saw at the last of his appearances (which we call the Ascension) was not the human Christ becoming divine or returning to divinity, but the whole Christ, ceasing to be earthly and becoming heavenly. There they saw finally what three of them had glimpsed momentarily at the Transfiguration. And it is recorded that so far from this being a sad occasion, they returned to Jerusalem with great joy.

Now there is no record that the early Christians ever expected their earthly lives to pass directly into heavenly lives at death in exactly the same way as their Lord's had done. What they did believe, however, was that by faith in Christ and by means of baptism, which was the necessary concomitant of that faith, they were so intimately united with him that they could never finally die. They had received eternal life. The 'many infallible proofs' were necessary to convince the original inner circle, the literal witnesses. That done, they had served their purpose. From then on it was possible to proclaim, not merely that Christ had risen from the dead, but that he *is* the Resurrection and the Life; and that he who believes in Christ, though he were dead, yet shall live (John 11 : 25). To believe in him, to be baptized, is to be in him, a member of his body. The Christian is already 'risen with Christ' and earthly death is undergone (in the words of the Burial Service) in sure and certain hope of the resurrection to eternal life.

But, it must finally be said, Christians are not primarily concerned with individual 'survival' or even with individual salvation, despite a popular opinion to the contrary. From within Christianity, so essentially the life of the Body, these seem almost to be by-products of Christian belief and practice.

If God was made Man in the Incarnation of Jesus Christ, then that birth and the life, death and resurrection, together with all that follows from them, are events of cosmic significance. And if we may isolate one event from the series, it is the Resurrection which most vividly conveys this significance. For it is, in a sense, the Great Reversal, wherein the universal human principle of decay and death is swung back upon its axis and made to serve the cause of life: more abundant life: an altogether new quality of life. 'The Resurrection,' wrote Bishop Westcott, 'is the central point of history, primarily of religious history, and then of civil history, of which that is the soul.'

The dreams of man have customarily looked both back and forward: nostalgically to a Golden Age, irretrievably lost in the past, or hopefully to a bright Utopian future. Both dreams may be found in the poetic literature of Israel. The experience of exile found natural expression in poignant longing for home and the Prophets sometimes recalled the racial memory of the forefathers of the race and their nomadic life in the wilderness, conceiving it as a period of relative innocence (the romanticizing of Eden is a later development). But on the whole, the fiercely realistic Hebrew mind was little given to nostalgia. Its typical dream, which would be better dignified with the name of 'vision,' was of a glorious future. But this vision must be sharply distinguished from any notion of inevitable progress to a man-made Utopia. The future Golden Age was, for the Hebrews, an article of faith —faith in God who had done so many 'marvellous acts' and who could be relied upon, in his own time, to bring in the New Age, the Day of the Lord. The language is not that of longing or of human aspiration: it speaks always of Return and Restoration.

The writer of the Epistle to the Hebrews, looking back on the history of his race from the hither side of the Resurrection, most movingly depicts the Father of that race, looking 'for the city which hath the foundations, whose builder and maker is God' (11 : 10) and of succeeding generations who 'died in faith, not having received the promises, but having seen them and greeted them from afar.' 'They desire,' he says, 'a better country, that is, a heavenly—for God hath prepared for them a city' (Hebrews 11 : 13f.).

Of that city the Risen Christ is the chief cornerstone. The Resurrection is a new and authentic 'marvellous act' of God: Easter Day is the long looked-for Day of the Lord. In him the work of Restoration is begun. The time for dreams and visions is at an end and this is the summons on the lips of the Risen Lord: 'Awake, thou that sleepest, and arise from the dead, and Christ shall shine upon thee' (Eph. 5 : 14).

F

PART II

INTRODUCTION TO PART II

BOOKS on Christian Doctrine traditionally begin with an essay on the existence of God, then go on to speak of his nature, his authority, his revelation of himself, and so proceed to Jesus Christ, the Holy Spirit, the Church, the behaviour of a Christian man, etc.

This book however starts from Christian experience—the experience of Christ and his Resurrection and thus too of all that prepared the way for that. Part I might indeed be entitled 'The Facts.'

Only now do we go back and reflect upon these Facts. We try to make a rational assessment of what has been taken for granted in Part I: God's existence, how we should think of him; the cosmos which he created; and the flaws in that cosmos, especially in man its most significant inhabitant. This Part II might be entitled 'The Reason for the Facts.' It is assumed that Christians will be prepared to use their reasons (since reason too is created by God) to inspect and weigh their experience: piety is no valid excuse for mental laziness.

CHAPTER I

FR. MARTIN JARRETT-KERR, C.R.

DIALOGUE ON THE EXISTENCE OF GOD

ALL the essays so far in this book have made one simple but enormous assumption: that there is a God. If that assumption were untrue, everything that has so far been written would have no more value (though perhaps no less) than runic charms or bedtime stories told to pre-sputnik children. Can such an assumption, then, be justified?

Let a believer argue with an ordinary agnostic on the subject. We shall call the believer a Religionist, and the agnostic an Empiricist. For most of this essay the Religionist will not need to be a Christian: a Jew, a Moslem, some kind of Hindu, or a Unitarian would be able to subscribe to his beliefs. The Empiricist will show his hand as he proceeds: all he needs to start with is a scepticism of any statement for which the evidence of experience ('empiria') cannot be produced.

For this is how the Empiricist will undoubtedly throw down his challenge. He will say, as the Mosotho said in the 1830s to the early French missionary in Basutoland, 'I will go up to the sky first and see if there really is a God, and when I have seen him, I'll believe in him.'[1]

In other words, he will say:

Empiricist. 'I am used to doubting everything until it has been proved from experience. I know from experience that whenever I mix *sodium carbonate* with *sulphuric acid* the result will invariably be *sodium sulphate*. That's what I mean by proof from experience. So unless you can give me evidence for God's existence, based on experience, I shall conclude that the three letters of the alphabet in the combination G.O.D. have as little meaning as three other letters in the combination (say) F.Q.X.'

Religionist. 'But you must understand that God is unique:

he is far above human experience. If we could "see" him, in the way I can see your tie, he would not be God. Indeed, it is the strength of our position, we Religionists, that no man has seen God at any time.'

Empiricist. 'Strength? Ha! I am reminded of Malinowsky's Trobriand Islanders. They believed in a mythical island called KAYTALUGI, inhabited only by fierce and nymphomaniac amazons, who enticed men to the island in order to assault them sexually and then kill them. When Malinowsky expressed his doubt as to the reality of this island they said that it was all very well to be sceptical, but he had better not try to go there for he would never escape. They added that all white men would like to go to KAYTALUGI, but were afraid to do so. "Look, not one white man has been to KAYTALUGI!"—an irrefutable proof of its existence.' [2]

Religionist. 'I don't mean that God's invisibility proves his existence. I mean that if he exists, he exists invisibly: so that if we thought we saw him we should be mistaken—it wouldn't be he at all.'

Empiricist. 'So you can't prove that he does exist?'

Religionist. 'Wait a moment. Let me first find out what you mean by "prove." When you demand evidence based on "experience" how much does that word include? The five senses?'

Empiricist. 'Well, yes—to begin with.'

Religionist. 'So unless I can persuade you either to see, feel, hear, taste, or smell God, you won't believe in him?'

Empiricist. 'More or less, yes . . .'

Religionist. 'More or less? You mean—?'

Empiricist. 'I mean, of course, that there are some things which I believe in and yet which I can't either see, feel, etc. But they must be inferred, directly or indirectly, from what I can see, feel, etc. Such as . . .? Such as, up to a little time ago (he was talking before the Russian Moon Rocket) our old friend the Back of the Moon. No one had ever seen it directly; but when the first Lunik returned, this told us that our inference that the moon has got a back was justified.'

Religionist. 'Suppose the Lunik had found nothing at the back. Suppose it had found that the moon is like a tennis ball sliced through—just a hollow behind?'

Empiricist. 'Even if they had that wouldn't show the moon hadn't got a back: it would show it had a hollow back. After all, a sliced tennis ball was once an unsliced one.'

Religionist. 'All right. In other words you infer that certain things which you can't see conform to the rules you deduce from the things you can see (or hear, or smell, etc.). You assume that if you could see them you would find them so conforming. And if you didn't, you would merely say, "Ah, I see. I supposed these were going to come under Rule A. My mistake. I ought to have said, under either Rule A or Rule B. This time it's Rule B. Silly of me. I'll widen the possibilities next time." In any case, it's bound to be under some Rule or other? Right?'

Empiricist. 'Right.'

Religionist. 'But why? Why *any* Rule?'

Empiricist. 'Because it always works that way.'

Religionist. 'You mean it always has worked that way? How do you know it always will?'

Empiricist. 'Because explaining or understanding a thing means seeing what Rule it comes under.'

Religionist. 'And if you found something which you could not fit under any Rule?'

Empiricist. 'I should either say I couldn't (as yet) explain it; or I'd make it the basis of a new Rule; or (which comes to the same thing) I'd wait till the Rule that could explain it turned up.'

Religionist. 'I see. In other words, you'd make an act of faith that there would be a Rule somewhere—where, exactly, you don't at the moment know—which would explain it?'

Empiricist. 'Of course. I've just said that that's what we *mean by* explaining. And that's how, e.g., scientific discovery works.'

Religionist. 'You realize that this act of faith is not itself empirical? I mean, it is based on several assumptions: That "things" are understandable and explainable; that the future will be like the past; that the evidence of "experience" is reliable— or where it isn't, that we can distinguish between sight and hallucination?'

Empiricist. 'These assumptions have never let any one down before. The conclusions invariably justify them. The invariableness is so highly "statistically relevant," as the sociologists and others say, that it would be insanity not to rely on it.'

Religionist. 'That means that you make another act of faith in man's ability to distinguish sanity from insanity?'

Empiricist. 'Yes. Anyway, we should be in a poor way if we couldn't.'

Religionist. 'I agree. But I must insist that this is an act of faith, which is not itself based on what you call evidence based on experience.'

Empiricist. 'Yes it is. It's based on our experience of what sane and insane people do.'

Religionist. 'Sorry. You haven't got me. Why do you think that our experience of what sane and insane people do enables you to be confident that everything comes under a Rule?'

Empiricist. 'Because that experience enables us to explain things—which in a wholly insane world we'd never be able to do.'

Religionist. 'Quite. In other words, you first make an act of faith that things can be explained, and then go on to find the Rules under which you can place them. But the act of faith—whether you realize it or not—has to be made first.'

Empiricist. 'You make it sound very complicated. Call it an "act of faith" if you like. That sounds a bit abstract for me. Surely, it's simply that I know I'm a man; I know how man's reason works; so I know roughly how to identify insanity; and so I go ahead, in the only way man's reason can go, and explain things by bringing them under the Rules experience has taught us to apply.'

Religionist. 'And as you talk you assume I understand you. Suppose there's no me here to do the understanding?'

Empiricist. 'Well, you answer my questions all right.'

Religionist. 'It seems so. But you might be dreaming my existence, and my answers too.'

Empiricist. 'Ah, I know: "solipsism." "How can I prove that there is anybody in the world but me?"'

Religionist. 'Well, it is difficult to disprove solipsism. It's like what one of the leading Empiricist philosophers of the day said about...'

Empiricist. 'Yes, what Mr. Bertrand Russell said about ultimate scepticism. You can't catch me out on the sacred texts. He said "No arguments are logically possible either for or against complete scepticism, which must be admitted to be one among possible philosophies. It is, however, too short and simple to be interesting." ³ I agree with that.'

Religionist. 'In other words, what matters is not that a belief should be true, but that it should be interesting.'

Empiricist. 'Oh, I think Russell had his tongue in his cheek you know. What matters is that empiricism works. Anyway I don't see what all this has got to do with proving the existence of God.

Religionist. 'Wait a minute. You say that what matters is that empiricism works. That means that you've got a religion of your own. It's called Pragmatism; and it is based on several acts of faith. I've told you what they are: faith that things can be explained; that there is order in the world; that the future will be like the past; that reason is trustworthy; and that there are rational beings like yourself with whom you can communicate. You can't prove any of these five dogmas, because you have to assume them in any proofs you use. But let me go on to the next stage. Some of your assumptions are more basic than others. For instance: you inferred what shape the back of the moon is.⁴ But it doesn't much matter what shape it is, so long as it has a back. In other words, the similarity of one sphere to another sphere is more basic than their accidental differences of detail (whether one is more corrugated or less hilly than the other). Or take a village: having houses in it is a more basic property of a village than having particular kinds of houses—a village of mud huts is as much a village as a village of modern bungalows. But again, you can have many kinds of bungalows—some tin-roofed, some thatched, etc.; so being one-storied is a more basic property of a bungalow than being thatched, or being made of concrete rather than bricks, etc. But now go upwards from villages: you can have human communities without having villages. So the property of "dwelling together in community" is more basic than the particular way of dwelling together—it can be done in blocks of flats, in megalopolis, in groups of caves like the Desert Fathers, just as well as in villages. Here is an ascending series: the type of bungalow is accidental to the basic structure of being a bungalow; the type of dwelling (bungalow or mud hut) is accidental to the basic nature of a village; the type of community-grouping (village or urban conglomeration) is accidental to the basic principle of "dwelling-together in community"—and so on. This ascending series is true of everything in the world: you could have trees without having gum-trees; you could have vegetation without having trees; you could have mountains without vegetation; you could have earth without mountains; you could have (I suppose) eroded planets without any earth: you could have a universe without planets. . . . In each case the lesser term is accidental to, or contingent upon, the more inclusive; or the more inclusive is basic to the less. But what happens when you get to the most inclusive, or the most basic, of all? Everything else must be accidental to *it*. In this sense we say that God is the only ultimate, "necessary" being. All else is accidental to him: all else could have been this way or not, could be dispensed with; God alone exists "necessarily." '

Empiricist. 'I knew you'd try to drive me into an Infinite Regress. "How could you have cows unless they grew from calves; but how could you have calves without cows to bear them?" I challenge the whole argument. For instance: there are telephone directories for large towns; so you might say "But now we need a directory of all town directories." Someone else might go further and say, "Different countries will then have national directories of all town directories: but we need a world directory of all national directories of all town directories." I suppose you could go on to other planets—but what would be the point? One lot of telephone directories is enough, without any Infinite Regress of Directories. And anyway, what do you mean by "God exists necessarily?" You can talk about "a necessary proposition" (i.e. what philosophers call "analytic") Or you can talk about this being necessary to that. God isn't a proposition. So you must mean that he is necessary to the universe? In that case, if there were no universe, there would be no necessity for God—and bang goes your "ascending series." '

Religionist. 'Yes, and bang would go God: for we certainly can't agree that God is necessary to any one. And I'm afraid you're right. The "Cosmological Proof" (which is what I've been giving you, in picturesque form) is out of favour now. Let me offer you something less ambitious, less grandiose, instead: the "Cosmological awareness," or as a young philosopher has called it, "Cosmological intuition." [5] "Intuition" is rather a non-U word these days; but we do get this kind of awareness from time to time. Don't you, for instance, sometimes get a feeling that life is empty, meaningless, not worth the effort? And when you do, can you dismiss it by saying it's due to indigestion, or a secondary neurosis? What poets call "The Tragic Sense of Life" is an example of such an intuition. Or the sense that everything we know—not only my existence and yours, but this whole world, every existence we can imagine—might not have been. People do have that sense sometimes—often it comes suddenly, with a shock, unexpectedly. Don't you ever get it?'

Empiricist. 'Never. And even if I did it would be a silly thing to have. I couldn't do anything about it; nor can I imagine what an absolute "might-have-been" is. After all, it would cancel itself out, wouldn't it? If there had been nothing from the start, then there wouldn't have been any one like you or me to appreciate that it was nothing, or to argue that the nothing might have been something!'

Religionist. 'And what a relief that might have been. These arguments are tiresome anyway. Still, here we are—arguing. As an empiricist you'll admit that?'

Empiricist. 'Yes. So what?'

Religionist. 'So you can't deny that lots of people (like me) get sometimes to wondering "why anything rather than nothing?" Put it this way: a trusted friend lets me down—and at once I have that awful sinking feeling: "Golly, is there anything, anybody I can rely on now?" You know—the earth disappears under my feet; I fall into space; I have the terrible sense of the relativity of all human values . . . etc. Now universalize that: all existence, every galactic system, everything is secondary, not ultimate.'

Empiricist. 'I can see some people in poetic moments might have that sort of feeling, but I don't see that it proves anything. Except that there are too many manic-depressives around.'

Religionist. 'Thank you. What I wanted. Because not all poets are manic-depressives; even some who are write great poetry; and anyway, it is possible to distinguish a healthy from a pathological feeling of this kind. For you will agree: it is good for our characters to realize that we aren't indispensable, isn't it?'

Empiricist. 'Yes . . . ?'

Religionist. 'I can even remember reading a psychologist who said, of the Teleological Argument for the existence of God, "Although the argument from design does not convince us of the objective existence of God, it does induce in us a more becoming intellectual humility" (*sc.* than was common in the "first flush of pride" of the rationalist era).[6] All right: it is good, ethically good, for me to learn I'm not indispensable. Universalize this, man! Universalize it! It is good for men to learn that their world is not indispensable, the universe is not indispensable . . . What does that mean? Why, that God could have done without it all.'

Empiricist. 'I see. You're using "feelings" as a proof. I "feel" I'm not indispensable so the world might feel it was not indispensable, so—there's a god who *is* indispensable. Is that it?'

Religionist. 'Not quite. You're being a bit hard on "feelings" aren't you? Surely we can distinguish reliable ones from unreliable. "I know there's a god because I get a nice feeling in church." That's no use, I agree. Actually it's no use in religion either, so we join hands here. But you yourself "feel" there must be a meaning in the world, because otherwise there would be no point in doing scientific experiments, seeking scientific explanations, etc. Is that a respectable kind of "feeling"?'

Empiricist. 'Of course—if you must call it a "feeling." Because it works.'

Religionist. 'Good. I'm glad to find your religious devotion to pragmatism withstands all assaults. But I think we're getting nearer the heart of the matter. For in a way I think Pragmatism is a sensible kind of belief. But then, I think it's sensible because I believe in an ultimate reason which makes our own acts of reasoning, and our acts of faith behind them, justifiable. I supplement your religion by a superior and a more inclusive religion. That's all.'

Empiricist. 'That's all! You've "sure spilled a bibful" as the Americans say. I suppose your "ultimate reason" is what you call God? A very abstract kind of god.'

Religionist. 'Yes, if that's all you can say about him.'

Empiricist. 'But he, or it, is rather a gratuitous assumption.'

Religionist. 'Well; but can you really defend Pragmatism without him? Will naked Pragmatism do? To put it crudely: Is a theory true because it works, or does it work because it's true?

Naked Pragmatism says the first (and you seem to be saying it often enough). Theistic realism says the second. If I'm not mistaken, it's not altogether your fault, for philosophy to-day (I speak of Anglo-Saxon philosophy, not of the murky adventures on the continent) is the child of three hundred years of Pragmatism. The young Oxford thinkers are all talking about language to-day. They don't say "Here is reality," as their grandfathers did; they don't say, "Reality is metaphysics, and metaphysics is nonsense," as their fathers did; they say "Tell me what you think, and I'll tell you which language-system you're using." In other words, the modern philosopher is content to be a caddie: he says, "Tell me what stroke you want to play, and I'll choose the right club for you." He's like the economist, who says "Don't ask me what a society should do. Tell me what your society wants, and I'll tell you the advantages of Method A, or the snags of Method B, to achieve it." So if I say to the young philosopher, "What are the true values? What is the meaning of life?" he will reply, "Men dictate their own values, according to what works best. And life has only the meanings men put upon it." And if you're not satisfied with that answer, he says "Sorry: I can't offer you any more. Of course, if you're threatening to commit suicide because you can't find this meaning, then go away and consult a psychiatrist." One of your own philosophers has said, in language that (strangely enough) is very close to that of a continental "existentialist" like J. P. Sartre, "Life has for each of us whatever meaning we severally choose to give it. . . . To live without values of any kind is practically impossible, but there is no well of truth, whether natural or supernatural, from which they can be drawn. . . . In the last resort, therefore, each individual has the responsibility of choice; and it is a responsibility that is not to be escaped. . . . The questions how men ought to live is one to which there is no authoritative answer. It has to be decided by each man for himself." ' [7]

Empiricist. 'We don't always agree with Prof. Ayer, you know.'

Religionist. 'No? But most of you tend to talk like him. Anyway, to get back to our history lesson. I said "three hundred years of Pragmatism": for behind your "feeling" that there must be meaning in the world, lies David Hume's "strong and lively impressions" or "feelings" that are the only evidence for a universal cause-effect link. And behind that again lies Descartes who demanded "clear and distinct ideas" as the only guarantee of truths. Small wonder that we cave in so easily when the discoveries of modern physics persuade us that we live altogether in a subjective world. But perhaps the most awful warning, in connection with naked Pragmatism, is what Kant's followers made of Kant. There was a man called Vaihinger who developed "The Philosophy of *Als Ob*." He accepted Kant's distinction between the "phenomenal world" (which we can know) and the "noumenal world" (which we can't); and concluded that we have to act "as if" (*als ob*) things were true which we can't know about—to live "as if" we were free (though we only feel free and can't prove it); "as if" God and immortality existed (though we only posit them and can't prove them). This is what I mean by naked Pragmatism. And it sounds a bit like naked deceit. "We know that the emperor has got no clothes on—this child has just pointed out the fact. But we shall continue to act *als ob* he had, because the venerable institution of monarchy might otherwise be threatened." I suppose you wouldn't be prepared . . .'

Empiricist. 'Of course I wouldn't be prepared to defend that. But the child has let the cat out of the bag—the deceit is that they are pretending what they know is not true. Our Pragmatism isn't like that: because we *don't* know that the world hasn't got a meaning, and we do know that giving it a meaning helps us to live in it.'

Religionist. 'Agreed. I was being unfair, dragging in the emperor (who must be very chilly by now, poor man, from all the arguments he's had to figure in). But even the more modest formulation you've just given me is objectionable. "Giving the world a meaning helps us to live in it," you say. No, it doesn't. No, no. *Finding* a meaning that's there: that helps us to live in it. But "giving"? Do you really want to reduce life to a child's make-believe?—"Let's pretend the carpet is a sea, the sofa a battleship." . . . You can have a good romp like that, but even the child knows it's only a game.'

Empiricist. 'I don't accept your analogy, of course. But even if it were a valid one, what else can we do? If there's no means of knowing the truth, isn't a therapeutic game better than either ethical anarchy on the one hand, or arbitrarily-imposed dogmatism on the other?'

Religionist. 'It's my turn to reject the description. I'm not, I hope, offering you an arbitrarily imposed dogmatism. What I'm trying to do is this: We see, even from what you call the "therapeutic" point of view, that life must have a meaning to those who live it, just as a road must have a direction to those who walk along it. (Imagine the universe as one vast Hampton Court Maze: the inhabitants would surely all be dotty in a couple of days?) We see that it isn't enough (at least, this is what I am insisting on) to "impose" a meaning on life: for surely that would be like asking the artist to kneel and worship his own self-portrait, or the nun to worship the mitre she's just embroidered for the bishop. In fact, naked Pragmatism is a sort of bogus Ritualism, the sort of superstitious or even blasphemous game which some Protestants accuse some Catholics of playing. On the other hand, we do see that some people have *found* a meaning in life, a meaning which, they are convinced, was there already before they found it—just as the three angles of a triangle equalled 180 degrees even before Euclid lived. And these people have, by doing so, coped satisfactorily with life. And . . .'

Empiricist. 'Aha. Aren't *you* being a Pragmatist now?'

Religionist. 'Wait. I hadn't finished. I was just going to say that we do *not* conclude from this fact "Therefore there is a meaning in life. Q.E.D." I agree, that would be the same naked Pragmatism as yours. We say "Therefore we have to ask where man got this idea of 'meaning' from in the first place." My thirst in the desert doesn't (alas) prove that there's a nice oasis round the next sand-dune. But it does prove that water was made for throats, so to speak. And it proves something more: that if three different *marabouts* appear before you on the horizon, each promising to lead you to a well if you will trust him, you've got to choose between one of them or die of thirst where you are.'

Empiricist. 'You're making it sound all very dramatic. How does one choose, anyway?'

Religionist. 'Ah. Now you're asking. But I'm afraid the answer belongs to the chaps next door, and I mustn't pinch their trade. Let me give you an introduction to my friends, the historical theologians. What—not now? Later, then? All right. But before you get embroiled with them, just two more things that I can't really keep out, though you may not think they belong to this argument at all. You see, we've really (I don't know whether you noticed it) been talking all the time about the nature of man. You've said that you know you're a man, and you know how man's reason works, and so you derive a common-sense, empirical, pragmatic philosophy from it. I say that man's reason is how you describe it—but that that's not all: that man needs to find things, not just to make them up: and from that need I argue to the kind of universe in which such a need could make sense. But there are two more things about man that are important here. *First,* it is a matter of empirical fact that the Hebrew-Christian tradition is a kind of oddity among world-religious-systems, in that it thinks of history as having a beginning and an end, as going somewhere. All, repeat, all, the others have a picture of history going round and round in circles. If you want to read about that, look at one of the most learned experts in comparative mythology to-day, Professor Mircea Eliade.[8] This Hebrew-Christian tradition has influenced all Western thought, and you and I can't get away from it; indeed, it may be partly responsible for us both looking for a "meaning" in life.

'And, *second,* there is this odd fact, also empirical, that anything that is really going to be of any use to us always has to be more than just "of any use." The meaning has got to be "over-determined," I think the psychologists would call it. A calculated friendship, for instance, isn't a friendship at all. Leaning over the water and making the right arm- and leg-movements isn't swimming: you've got to be right in. Or, as Pascal says, "Passion can not be beautiful without excess. When one does not love too much, one does not love enough." '

Empiricist. 'I agree with that. But what does it prove?'

Religionist. 'I'm not using it to prove anything. But I am going to ask why these things are so. And my answer is simply the traditional one; that "Man is a fallen creature." Whatever he knows he too easily twists to his own selfish ends. Whenever he is given something nice he tends to use it, or rather misuse it, to minister to his own pride. Give him a leek, stuffed with vitamins, and instead of feeding it to his stomach he puts it on his cap to show off—or even to start a tribal war with. That's why "Reason is not enough." By which I don't mean to commend irrationalism: it is perfectly reasonable, given man's condition, to conclude that reason cannot solve all his problems. A distinguished palaeontologist has said, "In one thing man, as we know him to-day, is over-specialized. His brain power is very over-specialized compared with the rest of his physical make-up, and it may well be that this over-specialization will lead, just as surely to his extinction as other forms of over-specialization have done, in the past, for other groups."[9] This is saying the same thing, from a different point of view, as the psychologists say when they suggest that modern man needs to "reintegrate his unconscious" into his psychic life; or as the theologian, Paul Tillich, said when he averred that "Protestantism . . . has emphasized the conscious religious personality, his intellectual understanding, and his moral decisions. It has become a 'theology of consciousness.' . . . (As a result) The personality was cut off from the vital basis of its existence. . . . The subconscious levels remained untouched, empty, or suppressed, while the conscious side was overburdened with the continuous ultimate decisions it had to make. It is not by chance that in Protestant countries the breakdown of the conscious personality has occurred on such a large scale that the psychoanalytic return to the unconscious became a social necessity."[10] The real basis for the "Cosmological Proof for the Existence of God" is the sense of man's non-indispensability. The real basis for the Teleological Proof (or Proof from Design) is his sense of need for a "meaning" in life. And so the real basis for the Moral Argument is his sense of being a "fallen creature." It isn't that "*I ought* implies *I can*": it is rather that "*I wish I hadn't* implies *I ought*." You can put it that man needs more than his principal to pay his debts. And that is why his God must be more than a demonstrated God. Suppose I had convinced you with all my arguments . . .'

Empiricist. 'You haven't.'

Religionist. 'I thought not. I didn't really expect to. But suppose I had: what good would it have done? Not much. For you'd be suspicious if I brought you God on a plate and presented him to you. You'd think: This can't be God surely? And you'd be right. For you'd be understanding God as we do. Who, or what, is God? One of your kind of philosophers has said, " 'There used to be a god, but isn't any more,' seems to conflict with the concept 'God.' "[11] In other words: if God exists, he must exist "necessarily." (Oh yes, I don't forget your difficulty about "necessary existence"; but in this context you'll see what it means.) Of course this doesn't prove he exists—we all know the defects of the Ontological Proof. It isn't a proof at all: it's a reminder of what kind of a god there is if there is a god. And unfortunately it lands both of us in an impasse: because whatever you may say to me, I've always got a "knock-you-down" reply. Even if you proved I was wrong, I should merely come back with the words our Lord used to Pilate: "Thou wouldest have no power against me, except it were given thee from above" (John 19 : 11). In other words: even your arguments to disprove God's existence would be excogitated by the reason he gave you in the first place. And you will naturally reply that that means my argument is "Heads I win, tails you lose." So it would be if it were just an argument. But what we ask you to do is not merely to listen to an argument but to choose. The argument is only there to cheer you up. I mean, it is there to persuade you that we're not executioners saying, "Look: here's where you put your neck" . . .'

Empiricist. 'You'd have some neck to do that!'

Religionist. 'Yes. Anyway, we're saying: The choice you are offered both is and is not in line with man's universal history. So it's both a difficult choice and an easy one. It isn't in line with universal history, because it's a choice of something from outside, something that comes at us at a tangent, that goes against the grain; something that even at moments seems irrational and arbitrary. So it's a difficult choice. But it is also easy because it is in line after all: at least, that's what we find when we've made it. We find, unexpectedly, that it turns out to be fulfilment rather than denial. Our greatest philosopher (St. Thomas Aquinas) has put it thus: that grace does not destroy nature, it perfects it. And a higher authority than that has said the same thing in a different way: "I came not to destroy, but to fulfil" ' (Matt. 5 : 17).

Some suggestions for reading:

ALASDAIR C. MACINTYRE : *Difficulties in Christian Belief* (SCM Press, 8s. 6d.)
CHARLES GORE : *Belief in God* (Penguin, 3s. 6d.)
ST. AUGUSTINE : *Confessions* (Fontana, 2s. 6d.)
BASIL MITCHELL (ed.) : *Faith and Logic* (Allen and Unwin, 18s.)
A. G. N. FLEW & A. MACINTYRE : *New Essays in Philosophical Theology* (SCM Press, 21s.)
M. B. FOSTER : *Mystery and Philosophy* (SCM Press, 12s. 6d.)
FREDERICK FERRÉ : *Language, Logic and God* (Eyre & Spottiswoode, 15s.)

And standard works:

A. E. TAYLOR : *Faith of a Moralist* (2 vols.)
L. S. THORNTON : *The Incarnate Lord*
AUSTIN FARRER : *Finite and Infinite*

CHAPTER II

FR. WILLIAM WHEELDON, C.R.

THE LIVING GOD

WHEN I began to think about religion I imagined that Christians regarded God as an old man with a beard ruling the world from a heavenly throne. And though I often slipped petitions in his direction, I was not prepared to take such a being very seriously.

Not that I was ready to take the world at its face value. I felt that it had another dimension or a directing force somewhere in its depths. A vague belief in some sort of life-force, or an unfolding purpose seemed not only more intellectually respectable than belief in a heavenly monarch, but it was exciting and satisfying. Yet perhaps I had here a true, though muddled, insight into the Christian belief about God, for God is indeed at the heart of things, guiding and sustaining them. So in rejecting what I thought was Christian belief about God, I was only rejecting beards and thrones, though properly understood, they too might have corrected my ideas about life-forces and emergent purposes.

It is failure to grasp what Christians mean by the word 'God' and perversion by Christians of the idea of God that, for many, stands in the way of seriously listening to the Christian gospel.

What then do we mean by 'God'?

'Maker of heaven and earth and of all things visible and invisible,' says the Creed. And before this is dismissed as a variant of the old man and the beard let it be made clear that the Christian doctrine of creation is not simply an attempt to prove that the universe came into existence at some dateable time in the far distant past, but rather it says something about the world as we experience it here and now. Christians are not committed to any particular account of the beginning of the world, and it is a pity that some have acclaimed the theory that the universe began with a big bang at a date in the past which may soon be scientifically ascertained, as if it proved that the universe is the work of a creator. On the other hand the present rival cosmological theory of the continuous 'creation' of new matter is not what we mean by the doctrine of new creation. Either theory could fit in with creation as Christianity understands it, but neither is a full account of it.

In saying that the world is created we mean that it is fundamentally dependent; that at no time does it stand by itself, but is at all times and at all points dependent upon, held in being by, something other than itself which underlies all change and all existence. So creation is not simply a beginning of existence, but also a sustaining and conserving of it. The universe has a total dependence on God, and without him would not just disintegrate but vanish.

Now, for the Christian, God is in no sense part of the world. And so if he is to be known it can only be through his actions, through the effects which he produces as the source of all our experience. So if the world is seen as at all points radically dependent we shall know God as that which is the source of all creative and sustaining power, and the richer the universe is seen to be, the richer must the source be.

Now this view of the world as through and through dependent may come home to us through different angles as one aspect or another of it holds our attention. So the bare fact of existence and change as we experience them in the world about us or as we know them in the mysteries of personal life within us may lead us to see it all as upheld by or grounded in a mysterious background of power and permanence. How the movement of thought which leads us to think in this way should be described; whether it is inference or insight, is not part of our subject here. But by whatever means it takes place, we are led to affirm, however vaguely, that in contrast with the world of direct experience there is beyond it a depth of self-sufficient being whose nature we cannot express except in contrast with and yet as source of our experience.

God is this depth [1] and ground of all existence. Yet it is not simply that the world has unknown dimensions of its own beneath its surface, as an iceberg has hidden depths. We point rather to a depth *in* which all experience is set and *from* which it springs. 'In him we live, and move, and have our being' (Acts

17 : 28). But what is at the heart of things is yet other than those things. It draws us and yet it causes us to tremble.

Formal Christian theology expresses this depth, which is the source of and yet other than the world of our experience, in a variety of ways. God is the fullness of life and existence. God is infinite; not that we can conceive him as extending for ever and ever, but simply that we deny of him the limitations of the world we know. God is absolute, not dependent for his fullness upon his relation with this world or any other, and man is created by him not so that he might have the pleasure of our company, but so that we might have the joy of loving and praising him. God is omnipresent, for his power is applied intimately and directly to all created things. God is omniscient and nothing is hid from his eyes for all things are his, not only the physical world but also the minds which know it. God is almighty for he is the fullness and perfection of existence. But the principles on which he exercises that power are never fully known to us, so that his government of the world often seems to belie his omnipotence. Yet it is truer to say that some things cannot be done, rather than that He cannot do them.

All this, which formal theology sets out in its detail and logical connections, is a drawing out of the implications of that depth in which our existence is set.

It is, of course, possible to live on the surface of life; to be entirely taken up by the struggle for survival, or to move from one diversion to another. But to most of us come times of reflection upon the world about us, or more likely in an age that is taken up with its ability to conquer and manipulate nature, times of reflection upon the inner self. It is then that, beneath the insubstantial shiftings of experience, the soul reaches out to affirm and acknowledge, however vaguely, a depth beneath and about all things. In some degree we share the experience of St. Augustine, 'With the flash of one trembling glance I arrived at that which is.'[2]

This is God, the self-sufficient source that underlies and penetrates all things at all points and yet is not part of them. Nothing less is God. He is not just the mirror of all that we admire in man, for we instinctively fear him who knows us through and through and whose hand we cannot escape; the attributes which formal theology ascribes to him do not give us a neat picture of him. They point rather to the mystery of his being and guard us from the constant tendency to think too meanly or too cosily of him.

The Bible speaks of this depth and mystery of his being as his holiness. The word means 'that which is set apart' and as applied to God it points to his separation from all else, his transcendent otherness, his immensity and majesty. When its presence is felt man is crushed and overwhelmed and knows himself in contrast as radically different, as a creature. This sense of God may fill him with trembling and awe as he encounters that which is wholly other than himself and which shows him the 'precarious and threatened nature of his existence.' [3] It brings home with crushing reality the great gulf between Creator and creature.

But the holiness of God involves not only his majesty which fills man with awe and fear. It expresses not only man's encounter with the source on which he is utterly dependent, but also the richness and excellence of that source which draws him to the religious attitude of reverence and adoring worship. The mystery of God is both awe-full and fascinating. So man is drawn to God as the inexhaustible source of all perfection, that which is utterly desirable and which alone can satisfy the inarticulate longing of his soul. And in the face of that adorable perfection he is crushingly aware of his own impurity.

This religious awareness of God's majesty and perfection is expressed most profoundly in the great vision of God in the sixth chapter of Isaiah: 'I saw the Lord sitting upon a throne, high and lifted up, and his train filled the temple. Above him stood the seraphim: each one had six wings; . . . and one cried unto another, and said, Holy, holy, holy is the Lord of hosts: the whole earth is full of his glory. And the foundations of the thresholds were moved at the voice of him that cried, and the house was filled with smoke. Then said I, Woe is me! for I am undone; because I am a man of unclean lips, and I dwell in the midst of a people of unclean lips: for mine eyes have seen the King, the Lord of hosts' (verses 1–5).

Here the depth which is the being of God is experienced with inescapable and bewildering force, beside which the arguments and formulae of formal theology seem fumbling or futile. This is echoed in the overwhelming experience which Pascal recorded as having taken place on Monday, November 23rd, 1654, the day of St. Clement. This experience was so momentous that he wrote it on a piece of parchment and sewed it into the lining of his doublet where it was found at his death.

'Fire. God of Abraham, God of Isaac, God of Jacob, not of the philosophers and the learned. Certitude. Joy. Certitude. Emotion. Sight. Joy. Forgetfulness of the world and of all outside of God.'

Not the God of the philosophers and the learned. Certainly the idea of God set out by formal theology—the eternal, the immutable, the infinite, the altogether simple God may seem by comparison to be a bundle of bloodless categories. But this account of his nature is not meant to reduce the God of revelation and experience to order or to strain out the richness and incalculable mystery of his being. Properly understood, it should guard the holiness and glory of God against our attempts to put them on a level with our own standards and experience.

It is not only as we turn from the movement of life and fix a steady contemplative gaze upon the world and ourselves that we meet this depth which is God. It meets us within the movement of life too. The creative power of God sustains and directs not only the very existence of all things but also their change and movement.

But man's life is in some degree personal. Much of it may flow along, directed by sheer necessity, by appetite or social pressure, but from time to time, at least, a man is faced with the burden of free decision. If God is to direct him even at this point it must be by some way other than physical law or implanted instinct.

As we weigh alternate courses of action we may become aware that the right course is one for which we have no natural inclination. Perhaps it is one that seems to threaten our security and prosperity, but none-the-less it may press on us with what can only be called a steady and inescapable demand. We may hold that an action, an intention or a state of affairs which may be brought about has value in itself without reference to the will of God, so that in themselves honesty and self-sacrifice are better than cheating and cowardice and would still keep this value in a God-less world. That may be so. Yet the demand, the obligation that we feel ourselves to be under, cannot be fully described except as the demand of a personal will. Perhaps only as we resist the claim of a certain course of action does the personal demand come to the fore, but as we meet it in the stress of temptation and decision we find that the call of duty or obligation does involve something more than an ideal which we may reject or accept as we judge expedient.

Yet this demand brings with it a sense of ultimate security. Though the way ahead threatens us with complete personal loss, there is with the demand an assurance that it is not futile, that in some way all will be well. We may be called to sacrifice our own well-being so far as we can see, and yet we know that it will be in the hands of an order of existence that is in final control. To use Professor Farmer's terms,[4] absolute demand is accompanied by an assurance of final succour. And this can only be the case if that demand springs from that same depth which upholds and penetrates all things. This is not based on experience that honesty is the best policy. In knowing the good we know it, however vaguely, as the eternal and secure, in which we can trust.

So in the movement of life, in the crises of moral decision we find ourselves both challenged and upheld by a depth of being which directs and sustains our personal and social life. We are not faced with an ideal of life which we may admire and then reluctantly pass by as too high for attainment. The particular force of its insistent demand is that of a personal will, and we are called to obey and worship, not simply to contemplate and admire.

This depth which underlies and surrounds all existence is not just an underlying refined and passive spirit, but a directing personal will. And not only does it direct, but it must also control. For together with the demand comes an assurance of our deepest well-being.

The personal will of God seeks us out so that the whole creation, including that part of it which is able to choose its own line of action, may be directed towards his own purposes. Just as his presence and sustaining power are inescapable, so is his will. And so God's omnipresence becomes no longer a dry deduction about the nature of a hidden God, but an urgent and oppressive reality. God is inescapable. His knowledge and his will penetrate every secret corner of our lives, though we ignore or deny him. We want to have a corner of our life which is not subject to his will or his knowledge, to be left alone, to forget that we are nothing apart from the sustaining action of his will. But all our powers and gifts are dependent from moment to moment on him, and the very power by which we turn away from him is his. Yet we imagine that we are independent centres of power and we try to flee from the inescapable presence and will of God with its absolute demands. We all echo the voice of the Psalmist (Ps. 139): 'O Lord, thou has searched me, and known me. Thou knowest my downsitting and mine uprising, Thou understandest my thought afar off. . . . Whither shall I go from thy Spirit? Or whither shall I flee from thy presence? If I ascend up into heaven, thou art there: If I make my bed in Sheol, behold, thou art there' (verses 1–2, 7–8).

Neither in self-satisfaction nor in atheism is there any escape from his insistent will. We cannot deny our awareness of responsibility.

Now it is sometimes said that to think of God as personal is to create a father-figure to comfort us in the bewildering spaces of the universe.

But when we speak like this of God we mean first of all that he directs all things by his intelligent will. The universe is not just an inevitable emanation from an austere general principle but it depends solely on the free decision of God. That is the distinctive character of real creation. It involves the free production of something new. And that involves the free decision of a personal will. And so God must be personal, at least to this extent. Furthermore to say that the depth from which we spring and in which we live and move and have our being is personal intelligent will that has produced beings really distinct from itself confirms our conviction that we ourselves are distinct and responsible persons.

We have seen that the awareness of God's personal will challenging our own in moral crises brings with it the sense that this will springs from the power which is in final control of all things and so will ensure our ultimate security if we obey. No power, no condition in which we may find ourselves can keep us from our ultimate good; 'neither death, nor life, nor angels, nor principalities, nor things present, nor things to come, nor powers, nor height, nor depth, nor any other creature, shall be able to separate us from the love of God' (Rom. 8 : 38f.). This is primarily what we mean by the providence of God. Not that he should make things go smoothly and painlessly, but that he should be bringing about his ultimate designs and make all things contributory to this. Belief in this providence can never be adequately based on our observation of historical events. We cannot see how all things that happen are for the best. And so we can never point to proofs that things do not happen haphazardly or according to impersonal law. For providence does not mean the elimination of pain and difficulty. These seem inseparable from all the production of the highest personal values in life as we know it. We come to belief in providence, not through undeniable instances of it, but through the conviction that God is deeply concerned with man, and that nothing lies outside the power of his will.

How providence works is another matter and our conviction that it does operate is not dependent on our having a convincing theory of how it does or could work. But certainly it need not involve constant breaking of 'laws of nature.' Our own free initiation of events in the world does not involve that, and God who has a far closer relationship to the rest of the world than we have must have far more subtle ways of determining its course. And furthermore, regularity and predictability in our environment is indispensable to our growth as persons with creative designs of our own. Unless the world about us behaved with some degree of regularity, we should be incapable of intelligent action and simply resign ourselves to be jostled about by unpredictable forces. Only when we can be sure that the world is steady enough for us to rely on most things happening in the same way from day to day are we able to make plans and to form intentions and so exercise that freedom which is the essence of personality. It is not fanciful to see man's growing ability to control the world through the development of scientific knowledge as the fulfilment of the purpose of God hinted at in Genesis that man is to be lord of creation. And this can only be possible if regularity, with which we have to come to terms and which may involve pain and hardship, is part of the world order. So the pain of the world may fall in this way under the providence of God and serve the wider purpose of personal development in the world as a whole. That it does fall under the providence of God we believe in any case. Just how it does so is a matter for speculation. We must beware of assuming that all things are meant for our convenience, and that we have to put up with small inconveniences so that we may gain wider ones. The providence of God is his over-ruling action, however it may take place, which makes the free actions of men and the order of nature serve the purpose of God himself. And though submission to his demands carries with it the security which lies in his will, resistance to his demands carries with it the futility and ruin that lies in resistance to the foundations of all life. So, then, judgment upon resistance to God's will lies within that providence which brings about his ultimate designs. The all-ruling power of God brings both salvation and judgment into the confusion of human history.

Yet this underlying pattern is by no means obvious and we do not arrive at belief in it by a simple deduction from the facts of history. Indeed the course of history brings us up against the agonizing problems of the triumphs of evil and the sufferings of the weak and poor. The vision of the majesty of God may quieten our perplexity, but it brings us little nearer to seeing just how history serves his purposes. We cannot deduce from the tide of events that someone cares. That can only come from our knowledge of the personal will which lies behind the events and in whose hands we know ourselves to be.

Yet if the course of historic happenings which remains so inscrutable to us is the field in which God is working out his purposes, it would most surely give us some insight into the character of God, so far as it concerns us, if only we could read those events aright. But if God is to be known here, there must be a God-given understanding of the significance of those happenings. Christians believe that this understanding has been given, that God has revealed himself here.

Revelation takes place when there is a coincidence of divinely controlled events and minds, divinely illumined to read it aright [5] as Archbishop Temple put it. And the Bible is the record of this self-disclosing activity of God in the history of a small and insignificant people. This revelation is not given just to satisfy the curiosity of man. If that were the case it would seem incredible that such a revelation should be given. Revelation is given so that man may recognize what God is doing and what God wills to do, and to show man that God desires him to be in a particular relationship to himself. For God does not move men as counters on a chess board. He calls them into a free acceptance of his will. He reveals that will so that men may follow, and he reveals his concern for man so that we may respond to him in love.

God then works in and directs history through his revelation. It is because the prophet cries, 'Thus said the Lord,' that the history of a nation takes on a particular direction. It is because he shows himself as lord of history that a people is led to put its trust in him alone.

If God were concerned with individuals alone he might move them to do his will simply by the inner promptings of conscience. But he shows himself concerned with the social and corporate life of man. He calls a people into special relationship with himself and purifies them in adversity, and he does this not for their sake alone but so that from them his law should go out to all nations.

God reveals himself in his actions, and that revelation becomes fruitful in further action as men are moved by his word to take up a new relationship with him, as men are moved from enmity with God to reconciliation with him. The whole of God's action is concerned with this new life, that is to say, with salvation. And this action reaches its consummation at the point where he himself takes flesh, a complete human nature, into union with himself under all the conditions of pain and shame which belong to man's state of estrangement from God. And so, accepting those conditions to the point of death as the judgment of God on sin, and yet remaining a faithful mirror of God's will, he becomes the mediating link through which all men may be reconciled to God and with each other.

So God acts and reveals himself in a human life. Jesus Christ shows us God, not simply by what he says, but by what he is. He is a mirror of the mind of God. So the word which was heard imperfectly through the prophets is embodied in a life. 'The Word became flesh and dwelt amongst us and we beheld his glory, glory as of the only begotten from the Father.'

It is here in this history as he chooses and purifies, judges and saves a nation and speaks to it through its prophets and chroniclers, and above all as he shows his mind and will when he takes flesh and dwells amongst us, that we can know what God is like.

First, God reveals himself as the sole ruling lord of all things, and so commands the entire obedience of all men. 'I am God, and there is none else' (Isa. 45 : 22).

But this is not a bare statement that there is one unchangeable reality behind all things, nor simply an assurance that the world has been created by him. God reveals himself as actively ruling the affairs of men, as being deeply concerned not only with bringing individuals into line with his fixed will, but with man as the member of society. And he shows that men are not simply at the mercy of blind fate, utterly indifferent to their well-being, for even the terrifying military powers of the heathen nations are subject to his over-ruling will. Even Cyrus and Nebuchadnezzar are his servants. It is because men know God as the unrivalled sovereign that they come to know him as the only God. 'To whom then will ye liken me, that I should be equal, saith the Holy One. Lift up your eyes on high, and see who hath created these, that bringeth out their host by number' (Isa. 40 : 25f.).

Only one who has no rivals can rightly be called God. And he who has absolute control has it because he has made all things and is the source of what power they have.

This basic faith in the sovereignty, the unity, the almighty creative power of God is not reached by reflection on the heavens above us or the life within, but it springs from the actual historical experience of a God who delivers his people from their enemies and judges their unfaithfulness.

No doubt these events which are said to reveal the power of God are capable of other explanations. They might be the result of purely natural and human forces, of natural selection at work in history. Because a strong east wind made a passage through the Red Sea God is said to have delivered his people. But if the sea had not opened and Israel had been led back to bondage no doubt God would have been said to have punished a people who were already murmuring against Moses their captain. God himself must enlighten men to know what is going on in history.

But that there is such a pattern of the judgment and deliverance of God in history is confirmed by the event to which they lead and foreshadow, the resurrection of Jesus Christ from the dead.

The Resurrection and the whole life of the Church which springs from it is known by the believer who is living in the new life, to be the act of the living God. And looking back, the same pattern of divine action is seen in the history which leads to Jesus Christ. The Resurrection and the life in the Spirit confirm and clarify the prophetic interpretation of history. They assure us that the unrivalled power of God is ruling in the affairs of men, and that all things are subject to him, for they are his.

Again the Resurrection confirms our glimpses of a depth in which all things are set and from which they spring. The lord of life and death is he on whom all things are utterly dependent.

'It is he that hath made us, and we are his; we are his people, and the sheep of his pasture' (Psalm 100 : 3).

God shows himself as the lord and giver of life. But his rule over men is not like that of a chess player. He has made man with freedom to accept or reject his commands because he desires from us a free response. Deep as the gulf is between the being of God and that of man, yet God's will is that we should walk in obedience and fellowship, in friendship with God. This is not a natural right of ours. We cannot claim the friendship with God which is heaven as a natural reward for good conduct, though many people seem to assume this to be so. It is only by the grace, by the good pleasure of our maker that this can be brought about. We have no natural kinship with him as the heathen imagine themselves to have with the nature-gods. This is simply God's will, his promise. And for this we have been given the gift of free will by which we can make the response of love.

But man's moral state is a bar to such friendship. God is he who is 'of purer eyes than to behold evil, and that canst not look on perverseness' (Hab. 1 : 13).

God is deeply concerned with the moral order, which is an expression of his own nature, and will not overlook the transgression of it. So man's sin stands in the way of that end for which he was made, fellowship with God. This is not because God is a fussy rigorist who insists on keeping to the rules, but because the stain of sin mars the perfection of friendship with

God who is perfection, or rather makes such friendship impossible.

It is the passion of Christ which reveals the depth of God's concern for sin, the greatest evil which afflicts man and which bars him from his only final happiness. The destruction of sin and guilt is the only way by which we can be delivered from our predicament.

So God shows himself as the holy one who cannot compromise with evil. The apparent ease and hypocrisy with which Christians have condoned injustice and cruelty, and by which they have compromised with evil to extend the power of the Church, is a condemnation of their idea of God. So through a right and holy zeal for justice some men have been driven to deny this false god which Christians have set up and, not knowing any other God, have become atheists for the Kingdom of God's sake.

Belief in the God who is a consuming fire against evil should be an awful and terrifying thing. But we have tamed him, and our reaction to the fact of his existence is, to quote something which T. E. Hulme wrote in another connection, 'as if you pointed out to an old lady at a garden party that there was an escaped lion twenty yards off, and she were to reply, "Oh yes" and then quietly take another cucumber sandwich.' [6]

But above all God reveals himself as the God of love, and first of all in calling men into fellowship with himself. This is not, as we have said, a natural right of man or a due reward of his labours. He gives man the capacity for knowing him and for friendship with him, and so sharing the beatitude which belongs to his infinite perfection. Man is not entitled to this, but neither does God need our company, though we tend to assume that he does.

That friendship springs only from loving obedience, but our pride finds the cost too high, for it reminds us that we are nothing apart from God, and we prefer the sense of our own importance and self-sufficiency. Because we have some degree of freedom we can refuse the surrender which is the way to the joy for which we were made. And yet in spite of man's unfaithfulness God remains faithful to his purpose for us. He remains steadfast in his love. The awful truth is that God our maker, from whom we turn away and try to forget, pursues us with his unspeakable gift, determined that in spite of our insulting rejections he will thrust it into our hands. This revelation of the heart of God shines out as he, our rejected Lord, meets the sinner on the Damascus road, 'whilst we were yet sinners, Christ died for us.' That is what struck St. Paul with trembling wonder. And here, in the life and death and resurrection of Jesus, the love of God is made known. This is how God loves us, for this is what He does to make possible that fellowship with the infinite and eternal God for which we were created.

In Christ, God comes out to meet us, and being joined to Christ, we have fellowship with God. We are called into the union which exists between Jesus Christ and his Father. But that perfect union, which held unbroken through suffering and shame and darkness is itself the reflection of an eternal unity, 'the glory which I had with thee before the world was' (John 17 : 5). The love of Jesus Christ for his Father, and the love of the Father for the Son, show us an abiding love which we are called to share.

We know God because he has revealed himself in his condescension towards us. That action continues in the life of the Church, and he is known there too. That is why the Acts of the Apostles is not just an apologia for Christianity directed towards a suspicious Roman governing class but part of the gospel itself. The starting point of early Christian preaching was that a mighty force was at work in the world, and so the Apostles began by pointing to the extraordinary power which had gripped them, 'This is that which hath been spoken by the prophet Joel; and it shall be in the last days, saith God, I will pour forth of my Spirit upon all flesh' (Acts 2 : 16f.). And in the New Testament epistles Peter and Paul encourage and comfort the young Church by pointing to the new and divine basis of their existence, the Spirit who reproduces the life of Christ in them. 'The Spirit of God dwelleth in you. But if any man hath not the Spirit of Christ, he is none of his' (Rom. 8 : 9).

Christian life means the extension of that pattern of life which we see in the Gospels, its reproduction in the disciples.

Jesus is he to whom the Father 'giveth not the Spirit by measure' (John 3 : 34). He begins his ministry as he is visibly anointed by the Spirit and 'through the eternal Spirit' (Heb. 9 : 14) he offered himself unto God. But before he dies he tells the disciples that it is expedient for them that he should go away so that the Comforter, the Spirit of truth, should come to guide *them* and be the principle of *their* life. And this is what Christians claim does happen. To be a Christian is not simply to follow the example of Christ, but to be made like him by the same Spirit which rested upon him. We are 'in Christ' and so are possessed by that Spirit which was with him. But also Christ is in us, reproducing his life in us. Yet that life is the fruit of the Spirit, 'love, joy, peace, long-suffering, kindness, goodness' (Gal. 5 : 22).

Now Christians believe that Christ is divine, not only because of the evidence of the Gospels, but because he does a divine work in them. Only God can reconcile us to God. And similarly we believe the Spirit to be divine, for he produces a new life in us. As Professor Hodgson puts it, the doctrine of the Trinity, that is the Christian doctrine of God, is that which is 'implied by the earthly life of Christ when that life was reflected upon by Christians in the light of their experience of being adopted to share his sonship.' [7]

In Jesus Christ we meet the paradox of God who is wholly receptive, 'the Son can do nothing of himself, but what he seeth the Father doing' (John 5 : 19). It is the very substance of his life to receive all and to obey, 'My meat is to do the will of him that sent me, and to accomplish his work' (John 4 : 34). Here, Christian tradition uncompromisingly asserts, we see God indeed, but the majesty of God is shown as not only irresistible power but also as astounding humility. It is our poverty, not our greatness, that stands in the way of humility. We are unsure of ourselves, and so we either clutch at all we can lay our hands on, or else, like men with an inferiority complex, we assert ourselves and delight in humiliating our neighbours. But in Christ we may learn that God is still God in receiving all, and so to rejoice in the fact that all we have is given to us and that to offer it back in obedience is indeed divine.

So God is known to us as the Father and the Son; as giving and receiving.

The reproduction of the pattern of the Son's life in ourselves is the work of the Spirit, God's gift by which we are liberated from the small circle of our own concerns. But this is not through the infusion of an irresistible force. It is the work of a personal presence directing in us that response to the Father which is eternal life. He is the agent of a rebirth in us which is a putting on of Christ. He is not the Son, yet he is never found apart from him, for we can never have him on any terms except willingness to be conformed to the likeness of the Son. As the Son is God who receives all, so the Spirit is God who is given, the divine life and love being bestowed.

Christians believe in a living personal God whose life is revealed to us through Jesus Christ and in the present experience of the Church.

'The Father is God, the Son is God : and the Holy Ghost is God. And yet they are not three Gods : but one God' (Ath. Creed).

The Church was bound to assert this if it saw in Christ and in the Holy Spirit something other than parts of the created world, for she could not accept a hierarchy of subordinate Gods. There are only two orders of existence; the created order including men and angels as well as the rest of nature, and the divine and uncreated order which is the creator alone. What is less than the infinite source of all is not God. And yet if Son and Spirit are not God the Christian message is a fraud.

At the same time God is one and indivisible, one Lord ordering all things and so giving unity to all things, one Lord of one world. We have sinned against this one God, and this one God has brought us back to himself. And this same God now works in us and gives us a sort of likeness to himself which makes friendship possible.

Christian experience and Christian tradition hold fast to both the unity of God and the real distinction of Father, Son and Spirit, and theology safeguards this in the formula : 'three persons in one substance.'

It is doubtful if this 'explains' anything. Its main function is to prevent us from explaining things away. But it is important to know just what is being said.

'Person' here does not mean an independent individual, but neither does it point to a mode of being which the Godhead can assume, a phase of existence. The use of the word is to mark a real and permanent distinction between the three. Dr. Prestige tells us that in the Greek version it indicates 'that which stands up to pressure, that which possesses a firm crust, and so an object in the concrete, something which is not a mere attribute or abstraction.' [8]

But yet there is one substance; not just that the three are made out of the same divine 'stuff,' but that there is one unique being embodied in three distinct though inseparable ways. So the whole riches of the Godhead is expressed as a whole in each person, in the relationship of Father, Son and Spirit; a threefold movement of personal life of which the sending of the Son and the gift of the Spirit are the outward revelation. These appearances in history are a mirror of eternal relationships in the being of God.

We cannot form a picture of this reality. It has no parallels in our experience. But there are two types of analogy which illustrate in some measure the eternal relations of the Godhead.

First there are the psychological analogies which take as their starting point God considered as mind and its inward acts. St. Augustine traces the three-fold unity of memory, or the stored experience of mind, understanding or the act of self-awareness, and will, by which we love or are concerned with the self of which we are aware. The three movements are distinct and yet not separable. It is one self, acting in three interdependent and simultaneous ways. The memory, as source of knowledge, is thus an image of the Father; the understanding, as the expression of this, is an image of the Son; and the will or love and the bond between memory and the understanding, is an image of the Spirit.

This is not to suggest that the Father is in fact memory in the Godhead or that the Son is understanding, for all knowledge and love and all things are common to the three persons. But it does go some way as an illustration of the one nature expressed entirely in each of the three distinct though not independent ways, whose actions take place always together. Yet it seems to fall short of doing justice to the fullness of the mutual relations between the three.

This is better brought out by analogies which take as their basis the nature of God as love. The Trinity helps us to see how love can exist in God apart from any created object, for he is never, like Keat's bright star, in lone splendour hung aloft the night of the void before creation. God is personal love, and love, presupposes one who loves and another who is loved. And again, love finds its fulfilment in a mutual gift.

This analogy emphasizes the distinction of persons, but in itself it tends to give us a picture of three gods, or of one substance which is passed from one point to another.

In fact trinitarian thought tends to suggest either that the threeness is a parcelling-out or that it is an outward aspect, and that the central core (so to speak) of God's being is exempt from the threeness.

But we have to assert that, however much we are incapable of imagining it, God's being is essentially and eternally three-fold in its very nature. 'God-stuff' is threefold stuff, one undivided threefold nature which has no parallels in experience.

'The paradox is that the Three is as primitive as the One. It participates in the structure of absolute Being . . . love is therefore as primary as existence.' [9]

But we try to make the doctrine of God something more basic than the doctrine of the Trinity, like the streamer at the Irish Corpus Christi procession emblazoned with the motto 'God bless the Holy Trinity.'

The doctrine of the Trinity is not just an abstract theory of higher mathematics but the pattern of Christian life. Through the work of the Spirit we are conformed to the likeness of the incarnate Son and so abide with him in that love of the Father from which we proceed. 'Through him we both have our access in one Spirit unto the Father' (Eph. 2 : 18). The basic truth about created beings like ourselves is that we have nothing that we do not receive from God. We find it hurts our pride to accept this to the uttermost. But in the incarnate Son we see one who rejoices in his dependence and who trustfully accepts all that happens as from the hand of the Father. This is the pattern of life, the only terms on which we can know the friendship and intimacy with God which is the heaven to which we are called. And yet this pattern can only be worked in us by God's own action, the life-giving Spirit through whom we become sons in the Son.

This life in union with the Blessed Trinity is the Christian answer, as Professor Hodgson suggests,[10] to those ways of thought which see in man a spark of divinity which, in a dedicated life, may grow so that it becomes the guiding force of our being. Some would see in Jesus the supreme example of such a life, showing possibilities which are open to all of us. But the main tradition of Christendom holds that there is an absolute distinction of nature between the Creator and the creature, and that though man lives and moves and has his being in God, not even his 'real self' is divine.

Yet such speculations about a divine spark in man, as a natural endowment, are perhaps echoes of a real sense that man is made for intimacy with God. And the life as adopted sons in union with the life of the Blessed Trinity answers that longing, so that it has been daringly spoken of by a persistent Christian tradition as 'divinization.' This not attained by any technique of prayer or knowledge of inner mysteries, but only as we submit to the providence of the living God in the affairs of daily life, and so share the pattern of crucified Christ-life through the power of the Holy Spirit.

CHAPTER III

BR. DUNSTAN JONES, C.R.

CREATION AND THE FALL

I

IT is the contention of this essay that, in the Bible, the doctrine of Creation cannot be separated from the doctrines of the Fall and of Redemption, but is intimately related to them.

Very often, the Creation and the Fall are considered together under one heading for no other reason than that they are understood to be the first and second principal events in the spiritual history of the world—there is not supposed to be any intrinsic connection between them. The doctrine of Redemption is thought to be related to the doctrine of Creation only in the uninteresting sense that, if there had been no world, there could have been no Fall, no Incarnation, no Crucifixion and no Resurrection. And no necessary connection is thought to exist between the work of Christ and the actual *manner* of the Fall.

There are two reasons why such a view is inadequate—one arising out of modern scientific knowledge, and the other out of the study of the Bible itself. As commonly understood, the Bible represents the Fall of man as resulting from an act of self-will on the part of the first man, and the corruption which has entered into the non-human creation is held to have resulted from this. It is not thought surprising that man himself could be the object of temptation by spiritual forces. Nor is the Fall of the angels thought to need explanation, or even any consideration at all. Now the study of fossils over the past century and a half has shown that there were living creatures on the earth for hundreds of millions of years before man appeared, and has suggested that the relations between these creatures were often such as we feel constrained to look upon as evil—in particular, the preying of one creature upon another. It thus becomes difficult to maintain the view that all the evils in the world result from an act of rebellion of man. This gives us an incentive to look at the revelation in the Bible again.

Secondly, when we consider the Bible itself, we find that there is not one simple account of Creation and the Fall, nor even only two accounts of the Creation in Genesis, but other forms of Creation myth stated or referred to in other parts of the Bible, and two accounts of the Fall. To complicate the picture further, in large parts of the Old Testament, there is no interest in the Fall (as such) at all. It is left to St. Paul, in the New Testament, to draw out the doctrine of the Fall as significant and to fix upon one version of it.

II

There are many ways of dealing with the text of Scripture. It may be treated textually for its own sake. It may be treated, where appropriate, as a statement of historical fact. It may be treated as teaching the moral demands of God upon men. It may be treated as an allegory of the spiritual life. But it may be treated in a more complex fashion, according to which the meaning of each part of Scripture can only be appreciated in relation to some or all other parts of it. In particular, the Old Testament can only be properly understood as used in the New Testament. This is an important manner of treatment; since modern criticism and historical knowledge have made it difficult to accept the historicity of many supposedly historical reports, and difficult to overlook the fact of the development of moral teaching in the later, as compared with the earlier written, parts of the Bible.

The Bible sets itself forth, as a whole, as at once the Revelation of God and the report of the Revelation of God. That is, there are certain divine acts which are reported in the Scriptures and which are themselves the self-manifestation of God; but the Scriptures are not only the *report* of God's self-manifestation, but also in a sense *part of it*. Where, therefore, higher criticism makes any part of the Bible to be other than it appears to set itself forth to be; or independent historical knowledge makes supposedly historical reports in the Bible to seem to be false; or the consideration of the ethics of the New Testament makes the ethical teaching of portions of the Old Testament to appear to be morally defective; there, if these passages are still part of the Revelation, they must be interpreted in a different way from that which we had thought to be the obvious way.

CREATION AND THE FALL

The original meaning of the text (i.e. as intended by the writer) is important, but the relation of one text to another, as seen under the inspiration of the Holy Spirit, is even more important. The factual content of any text is important, if it can be established, but its relation to other texts is also an important part of Revelation. If its factual content cannot be established, the text is *still* important in relation to other texts, and this relation now gives it its only importance. This point of view has obviously to be taken into account when we are considering stories of the Creation and the Fall whose historicity has been made extremely doubtful. And, further, it may help people who are anxious as to the spiritual significance of passages whose superficial meaning can no longer be accepted as true.

One assumption (among others) which we are no longer obliged to make is that all texts must follow the historical order of the events to which they refer—Creation at the beginning, Redemption somewhere in the middle, the Consummation of all things at the end. Admittedly, a superficial study of the Bible may suggest that it follows this order, but we are no longer obliged to assume that it does so in detail. We are thus freed to look *throughout* the Bible for revelation relative to any given process, and not to look only in one particular place.

III

This granted, one particular *motif* which we can recognize running through the Bible is that of *creation through conflict*. This was a common feature of the myths of the peoples surrounding the Chosen People, but it is sometimes said that this *motif* has been removed from the principal creation-myths in Genesis, and that occasional references to it in other books of the Old Testament have as it were slipped in by accident. If we take the whole Bible as the self-declaration of God, we are no longer able to pass over these texts as accidental intrusions, but must take them as part of the Revelation—though, of course, they may still need interpreting.

In the cosmogony of the Babylonians, the gods are first born of Apsu and Tiamat (the fresh water of the rain and the salt water of the sea), but then Apsu and Tiamat plot against the gods to destroy them. No record has come down of the defeat of Apsu; but the gods elect Marduk as their champion, who fights against Tiamat, splitting her in two, one part being made heaven and the other part earth. In fact, in the myths as they have come down, Tiamat is the power of chaos and Apsu is insignificant.[1]

In biblical accounts of, and references to, the Creation, this idea of conflict is present, but the polytheistic setting has been stripped away. Yahweh (Jehovah) is the sole divine agent, though the origin of the hostile power is not made clear. In the so-called 'Priestly Narrative' (the last to be written of the four documents which scholars consider to have been combined together to form the first five books of the Old Testament), which was written during the exile of the Jews in Babylon, even the *motif* of conflict is at a minimum. We are only told that: 'In the beginning of God's creation of the heaven and the earth—the earth being chaos and darkness over the deep, and a wind of God hovering over the waters—then God said, "Let there be light."'[2] The Hebrew *tehom* (chaos) corresponds to the Babylonian *tiamat*.

In other parts of the Bible, however, though still strictly monotheistic and giving the whole initiative to Yahweh, there are clearer references to a battle between Yahweh and a great sea-monster.

Awake, awake, put on strength, O arm of the Lord; awake as in the days of old, the generations of ancient times. Art thou not it that cut Rahab in pieces, that pierced the dragon?
(Isa. 51 : 9)

Thou hast broken Rahab in pieces, as one that is slain;
Thou hast scattered thine enemies with the arm of thy strength.
The heavens are thine, the earth also is thine:
The world and the fulness thereof, thou hast founded them
(Ps. 89 : 10f.)

He stirreth up the sea with his power,
And by his understanding he smiteth through Rahab.
By his spirit the heavens are garnished;
His hand hath pierced the swift serpent (Job 26 : 12f.)

CREATION AND THE FALL

> *Thou didst divide the sea by thy strength:*
> *Thou brakest the heads of the sea-monsters in the waters.*
> *Thou brakest the heads of leviathan in pieces,*
> *Thou gavest him to be meat to the people inhabiting the wilderness* (Ps. 74: 13f.)

And we can compare with these another passage from the Book of Job:

> *Am I a sea, or a sea-monster,*
> *That thou settest a watch over me?* (Job 7: 12)

In the Bible, however, this primeval battle is treated as an antetype of the deliverance of the Israelites from Egypt:

> *Art thou not it that cut Rahab in pieces, that pierced the dragon? Art thou not it which dried up the sea, the waters of the great deep; that made the depths of the sea a way for the redeemed to pass over?* (Isa. 51: 9b, 10)

For this reason, perhaps, Egypt also was called Rahab (Isa. 30: 7).

In apocalyptic in the Book of Isaiah, too, this story is treated as a type (in prophecy) of the final redemption:

> *In that day the Lord with his sore and great and strong sword shall punish leviathan the swift serpent, and leviathan the crooked serpent; and he shall slay the dragon that is in the sea* (Isa. 27: 1)

It is not to be overlooked that, in Christian theology, the Exodus from Egypt has been thought of, in turn, as the type of Christ's Resurrection, delivering man from bondage to sin and the devil, that 'spiritual' serpent.

In Hebrew, 'victory' is always 'salvation'; and creation and deliverance are both forms of salvation. We are beginning to get a hint, therefore, that Creation and the Resurrection are not far apart in the thought of the Bible.

IV

The doctrine that the world was created out of *nothing*, might, however, seem to contradict this, for there cannot be battle with nothing. Let us consider how this contradiction arises. Hebrew beliefs begin, not from speculations about the origin of the world, but from the almost unbelievable deliverance of the Israelites from Egypt. All Hebrew prophecy refers back to this. Reflection on this always reacts upon earlier beliefs about the constitution of the world; but the sense of deliverance is always more important than the beliefs which it may serve to modify. The conviction to which it gives rise is of the supremacy of Yahweh over all other forces, whether celestial or terrestrial. This did not at once become a full belief in omnipotence. It was believed that there were other gods in the world, though none so powerful as Yahweh. Through the revelation by the prophets, Yahweh was represented as greater and greater, and other powers as less and less, until there was a change of category of thought, and Yahweh came to be looked upon as the *unlimited*. He was no longer looked upon merely as stronger than any and all other powers, but his operation was now thought of as entirely *effortless*—this is probably the implication of the word translated 'created' in Genesis 1 : 1.[3] But even at the time of the composition of the 'Priestly Narrative' (during the Exile, i.e. sometime between 597 and 520 B.C.), the unlimitedness of Yahweh and his effortless operation were not thought to be inconsistent with a pre-existent 'somewhat' upon which he operated. Provided this 'somewhat' could offer no resistance to the divine operation, the absolute divine initiative was not felt to be contradicted.

This pre-existent was held to be formless, but, unlike the undetermined, static space of Greek thought (called *chaos*), the conception seems to have been of formlessness in the sense of milling confusion—chaos, in fact, in precisely the modern English sense of the word, rather than according to the original Greek usage. It should probably be interpreted in the light of 'Jeremiah's vision of Chaos-come-again'[4]:

I beheld the earth, and, lo, it was waste and void;
and the heavens, and they had no light. I beheld the
mountains, and, lo, they, trembled, and all the hills moved to
and fro. I beheld, and, lo, there was no man, and all the

birds of the heavens were fled. I beheld, and, lo, the fruitful field was a wilderness, and all the cities were broken down at the presence of the Lord, and before his fierce anger
(Jer. 4 : 23–6)

and of a passage from Deutero-Isaiah:

*The creator of the heavens, he is God,
The former of the earth and its maker, he established it.
Not Chaos* (tohu) *did he create it, for dwelling did he form it* [5]
(Isa. 45 : 18)

The concept of creation out of nothing is a logical development, but one late in appearing. If Yahweh has the absolute initiative in all things, then not even a formless stuff can exist without his will, nor can there even be the *possibility* of existence apart from him. But if this be admitted, it is not necessary to hold that the creature is formless before receiving its form. If all depends on Yahweh, Yahweh can as easily create determinate things as create an indeterminate stuff or a bare possibility and then impress determinations upon it. To speak in terms of later theological concepts, prior to the creation of things there was not just ME ON—nothing in particular—but OUK ON—nothing at all. As we have said, however, this conception was late in appearing. There is no certain reference to it before 2 Maccabees (written in the late second century or the first century B.C.): 'I beseech thee, my child, to lift thine eyes unto the heaven and the earth, and to see all things that are therein, and thus to recognize that God made them not of things that were, and that the race of men in this wise cometh into being' (2 Macc. 7 : 28).

Thus the belief that God is all-powerful in conflict has led to the conviction that nothing can exist that does not depend on him—the supposition of creation out of a pre-existent is contradicted, and creation through conflict seems to become an impossibility. This is one of those matters in which, if the Bible be taken at its face value, one part of it contradicts another. We must look for another interpretation. But first the doctrine of *creatio ex nihilo* must be further considered in itself.

Strictly speaking, it is not, as so often supposed, a philosophical notion at all. In Hebrew-Jewish religion, it is not the conclusion of speculation about the origin of the world, but an inference from (or, indeed, a part of) the Revelation of God as other than the world but having the absolute initiative in it. When one speculates, independently of this Revelation, as to the origin of the world, several conceptions are possible. The world may be unoriginate, and either with, or without, a beginning or ending of time. It may have evolved out of a pre-existent entity. It may depend for its existence upon the will of a creator, and this either with, or without, a beginning or ending of time. Further, if the world depends for its existence on a creator, the creator may be either subject, or not subject, to time; and, if subject to time, either with, or without, a beginning in time and with, or without, an end in time.

Since all these possibilities are conceivable, there is no *logical* necessity that one should be true rather than the others. These considerations and the so-called proofs of the existence of God form the obverse and reverse of one another. There is no *logical* contradiction in supposing that the world came into existence without anything to give rise to it, or that it has a certain form without anything to give form to it. That is, from a consideration of the world itself, we can prove neither that there must be a creator nor that the world must have been created.

This may be seen for another reason also. If God creates and sustains the world, he must sustain all things continually. There is, therefore, no conceivable possibility that we should be able to compare the effect of his presence with the effect of his absence. There is no *observable* difference between a world that is created and one that is unoriginate. The knowledge of God, if we have it, must therefore be obtained in another way—that is, by divine self-revelation.

v

It may, however, be asked how there can be self-revelation of God if the world gives no indication whether it does, or does not, depend upon a creator. This question shows a failure to understand the nature of Revelation as conceived in the Scriptures. Revelation consists partly of *special* interventions by God in the course of history; i.e. of interventions other than God's general dispensation of Providence. It is because these events are special—out of the normal run—that they are recognized as significant. Revelation also consists partly of meaningful communications to the prophets, interpreting these special events and indicating the purposes of God. Revelation, further, is not something undeniable like mathematical truth. The acceptance of the communications and the recognition of certain events as special divine interventions depend on faith, and faith can be given or withheld as an act of will on the part of the person to whom the revelation is given.

If one came into a room every morning and found it rearranged according to what seemed to be a new plan, one would suppose that someone entered the room every night and rearranged it, even though one never saw him. This conviction would become even stronger if one found new written messages there every morning. But there is no *logical* necessity to accept this explanation, even though there appears to be no other that makes sense. It *might* 'just happen,' though we do not believe this to be the case. The self-revelation of God in the Bible is very similar to this, for God's existence is never proved, but meaningful communications are given to men. The conviction *that* God is, and the conviction as to *what* he is, both therefore rest on the messages transmitted by the prophets.

Lest it be said that the prophets form only part of the Bible, distinct from the narrative, it must be remembered that all the narratives of the Old Testament were transmitted by the prophetic schools, and cannot be separated from the prophetic interpretation of the history of Israel. Similarly the narratives of the New Testament (i.e. the Gospels and the Acts of the Apostles) are transmitted by apostles, or by writers under the influence of the apostles or of the general mind of the early Church. They cannot, therefore, be separated from the early Church's understanding of the life and work of Christ. Conviction *that* God is and of *what* God is arises out of the discovery of a coherent communication in the Bible and the recognization that this communication makes sense only if God, whose communication it represents itself to be, really exists.

Such a view would seem to be more acceptable to the empiricist temper of thought, common nowadays, than is a rationalist theology. It would seem that, in a created universe, the Creator can only make himself known in precisely the way that Judea-Christian belief holds that he *has* made himself known. As we have seen, the assertions of rationalist theology (proofs of the existence of God, for instance) are invalid, while a self-declaratory communication must always require a responsive act of faith in its acceptance.

If this be granted, then, as we have seen, the doctrine of creation out of nothing is a necessary deduction from God's self-manifestation as he who has the absolute primacy of initiative in all that takes place in the world.

According to the prophets' interpretations of history, it is not merely the interpretation of events which is Revelation (as so often thought), but the events themselves are part of the self-revelation of God. Indeed, we may suggest that the great divine acts may be called 'the primary revelation,' while the interpretation given through the prophets may be called 'the secondary revelation.' If this be so, then the greatest of all the divine acts, Creation itself, must itself be looked upon as part of the primary self-revelation of God. So Revelation consists at least of Creation, history and prophecy (i.e. scripture). But since God is revealed as having the absolute initiative in all things, his self-revelation must be free and not in any way subject to necessity. In particular, there is no necessity that creation should be as in fact it is. We ought not, therefore, to look upon the creation as the realization of eternal patterns, forms or exemplars in the being of God, but should rather recognize God's absolute freedom to make the creation whatsoever he would. In the tradition of the Western Church, found in St. Augustine and supremely in St. Thomas Aquinas, the pattern of the creation is contained in the very being of God! God's freedom to create whatsoever he wishes is better recognized in Eastern Orthodox theology.[6]

VI

The Bible sets forth certain great images [7] under which God chooses to make himself and his purposes known. The word 'chooses' is used deliberately in view of the discussion in the last paragraph. But the greatest of the images under which God represents himself is that of Man. It is common to pay attention only to Genesis 1 and to say that God made man his own image. But the converse may profitably be considered: that God is like man. This is stated in Ezekiel: 'And above the firmament that was over their heads was the likeness of a throne, as the appearance of a sapphire stone: and upon the likeness of the throne was a likeness as the appearance of a man upon it above' (1 : 26). It is not improbable that this was written before the 'Priestly Narrative' of which Genesis 1 forms a part.

The one text tells us that, in his creative activity, God has made man in his own image: the other text tells us that the figure of a man is a suitable image for God. It may be asked, however, in what sense the figure of a man is the image of God. In Genesis God said: 'Let us make man in our image, after our likeness' (1 : 26).

All the great images under which God represents himself or his activities and purposes are in some sense metaphorical. Further, they are not applied to God by men as men gain insight, and search for suitable words in order to express their insight, but *God* chooses these images as the images under which he will represent himself and his activities and purposes, and *the images are under the control of God*. This is as true of the figure of a man as of any other image. Nevertheless, the figure of a man is represented as *more* appropriate to the self-manifestation of God than any other image and, while no image is either inevitable or exhaustive, we must conclude that, of all created beings, man is closer to the divine nature than any other.

This must be so because God does not merely *represent* himself under the human image, but actually unites himself to it. Indeed, recognizing that the images are under God's control, and that there is no necessity in his use of any image, we must say, not that God *can* unite himself to human nature *because* man is in the image of God, but that God in the Old Testament manifested himself under the human image *with a view to the Incarnation which was yet to take place*. This makes attractive the view that God intended the Incarnation of God the Son whether there had been a Fall or not. This has been suggested from time to time in the history of Christian theology. The name of Duns Scotus is that most commonly associated with this view, but there have been others—our own Bishop Westcott evidently favoured this

I

view of the matter in the last century. Perhaps this view can never finally be established from the Scriptures, but it is worthy to be taken seriously.

For another reason God's choice of the figure of a man to be an image of himself cannot be entirely arbitrary. St. Paul writes of putting off the old man and putting on the new man which is being renewed after the image of him that created him (Col. 3 : 9f.), implying that the image of God has been lost in man by sin and needs to be (is being) restored. Yet, if we ask, Where can we see the true human image? the answer is, Only in God Incarnate. So when the figure of man is taken as the most suitable image of God, it is only the figure of the God-Man, Jesus Christ, God incarnate upon earth, that is meant. It is a relief to discover this, for palaeontology (the study of fossils) has made it almost insuperably difficult to believe in the existence of a perfect man on earth at the beginning of the human race.

VII

It is in this context that we may most profitably consider the Creation of man. St. Irenaeus and the Eastern Orthodox theologians understand 'made in the image and likeness of God' to mean, not '(already) conformed to the pattern of God,' but 'made within the Second Person of the Trinity who is not only himself the image and likeness of the Father, but also the *locus* of Creation, and to whom man is *yet to be* conformed.' We have seen the difficulty in believing in the existence of a perfect man in the distant past. But we now see that such a belief is not a theological necessity. Irenaeus insists that man was not created complete but had still to grow to maturity. Further, man was suborned by Satan, and the process of growth interfered with. This is a quite different conception from that of the gratuitous rebellion of a perfect man.

Notwithstanding this, God has made man but little lower than God (Ps. 8 : 5) (i.e. in ultimate intention and by participation in Christ), and made him to have dominion over the works of God's hands (Ps. 8 : 6), while according to St. Paul the redeemed will judge angels (1 Cor. 6 : 3). It was the view of Jewish writers prior to the time of our Lord that man is both the vice-gerent of God in the creation and the high priest of creation before God. This,

CREATION AND THE FALL 131

of course, was to be summed up in, and expressed through, the Messiah. Christians identified the Messiah with Jesus, but also recognized him to be God the Son. Yet he exercises his vicegerency and high priesthood as Man and through men. Further, Irenaeus and other early writers assert that the Son took a share-in human nature in order that men may share in the divine nature.

So far we have considered the story of the creation of man as given in Genesis 1, and this represents man as created in the image and likeness of God. We have also to consider the story of his creation in Genesis 2. Here the breathing into man's nostrils of the breath of life may be understood to represent the inbreathing of the *Holy Spirit*. This is incomplete (since man is immature) and, in any case, interfered with, since man is in bondage to Satan. Yet it points to a time when man will be completely possessed by the Holy Spirit. Thus the human being conformed to the divine pattern will be both united to God the Son, by the effects of his Incarnation, so as to be a sharer in his divine sonship, and also possessed by the Holy Spirit. Some early writers, and more recent Eastern Orthodox writers, do not hesitate to use the word 'deification,' but this is only a following of the Second Epistle of St. Peter: 'That . . . ye may become partakers of the divine nature' (2 Peter 1 : 4). It is clearly understood that the participation in divine sonship and the possession by the Holy Spirit are both brought about in such a way that there will be no confusion of human persons with divine Persons.

VIII

Now that the aim of God in the creation of man has been recognized we may begin to discuss the loss of the divine image which is, or is part of, the Fall. There are two things in the world which the religious man has to explain: suffering, with its intrinsic character of contradiction; and sin, the rebellion of free beings against their creator. The idea of a Fall lies dormant in Scripture and does not become 'active' till we come to St. Paul. The Jewish theologians held the peculiar doctrine of 'the two wills'—the good and evil will—both implanted by God. The logical necessity of free will to the idea of man's responsibility to God had not yet dawned on them, and they felt no sense of contradiction in supposing that God should implant in man a will to disobey God and then punish man for so disobeying. Even Paul himself hardly sees the contradiction: 'So then he hath mercy on whom he will, and whom he will he hardeneth. Thou wilt say then unto me, Why doth he still find fault? For who withstandeth his will? Nay but, O man, who art thou that repliest against God?' (Rom. 9 : 18–20)—which is no answer at all. But Christians began to realize that an antinomy must be accepted—the antinomy of the Creator (without whom nothing can be done) limiting himself to bring about the actions willed by men in actual disobedience to his own will!—*not* the antinomy of a creator who *makes* men disobey himself and then punishes them for doing so.

As we have said, the two oddities of the world which the religious man must explain are the fact of contradiction in a created universe, and the fact that men find it easier to disobey their creator than to obey him. The fact of contradiction inspires myths giving pictures of its origin. This is the original purpose of the Fall story in Genesis 3. The sense of sin leads to the development of these pictures into the concept of original sin—that men have inherited tendencies which make it easier to be disobedient than obedient.

The coming of Christ serves only to make the sense of sin and failure more intense. Before that, men felt that they were sinners because they could not keep the law. Now they know that they are to be 'partakers of the divine nature' (2 Peter 1 : 4), they disobey and rebel against the call of God at the same instant as they rejoice at it. Israel in bondage to Egypt, the Jews captive in Babylon, Jonah in the belly of the great fish, are all images which may serve to represent the intolerable bondage that a man finds himself in when he is confronted with Christ. 'For I delight in the law of God after the inward man: but I see a different law in my members, warring against the law of my mind, and bringing me into captivity under the law of sin which is in my members. O wretched man that I am! who shall deliver me out of the body of this death?' (Rom. 7 : 22–4).

If the divine image never yet was attained in man, yet it is ever present as a pattern to which man is to be conformed; and God *will* conform man to it, even if man does not wish to be so conformed. Man must either be conformed to the divine image or be cast into outer darkness. And there can be no rest for man unless and until the former is brought about.

IX

The Fall, then, whatever it may consist in, is not the inexplicable, gratuitous and profitless rebellion of a perfect man, but some event, process or state in virtue of which man's conformation to the divine image has become a painful process, enforced upon man by God against man's repeated desire to withdraw. But it is not only man who is involved. St. Paul says that 'the earnest expectation of the creation waiteth for the revealing of the sons of God. For the creation was subjected to vanity, not of its own will, but by reason of him who subjected it, in hope that the creation itself also shall be delivered from the bondage of corruption into the liberty of the glory of the children of God. For we know that the whole creation groaneth and travaileth in pain together [*or* with us] until now' (Rom. 8 : 19–22). 'He who subjected it' is plainly God, not man or the devil; but St. Paul does not in this passage say *why* God subjected the creation to vanity (i.e. failure to attain its proper end) though it seems clear, from the next verse, that the suffering of men and the suffering of sub-human creation are linked together, for 'we ourselves also, which have the firstfruits of the Spirit, even we ourselves groan within ourselves, waiting for our adoption, to wit, the redemption of our body' (Rom. 8 : 23) and the sub-human creation expects its redemption in the 'revealing of the sons of God.' This is in tune with St. Paul's teaching in other epistles. In the Epistle to the Colossians he tells us that 'it was the good pleasure of the Father that in him should all the fulness dwell; and through him to reconcile all things unto himself, having made peace through the blood of his cross; through him, I say, whether things upon the earth, or things in the heavens' (Col. 1 : 19f.). A similar passage is to be found in Ephesians: 'to sum up all things in Christ, the things in the heavens, and the things upon earth' (Eph. 1 : 10). So the 'blood of his cross' which avails for the reconciliation of men to God, avails for the reconciliation of *all things*. And whereas in Romans we are probably right in understanding 'the creation' to mean the sub-human creation, in Colossians and Ephesians it must include the angelic creation also. The Fall of man therefore is linked to the Fall both of the angelic creation and of the sub-human creation, and the means of redemption for the one is the means of redemption for the others also.

The myth of Genesis 3 was composed in order to account for the sufferings of men. St. Paul takes it and turns it into an explanation of the universal tendency of men to rebel against the deifying work of God: in doing so, he changes the relative importance of different parts of the story. The work of the serpent becomes less important than the consent of the man. The part of the woman is treated as not in itself greatly blameworthy, the whole blame falling on the man for not keeping her in order. At the same time, St. Paul considers the whole human race to have been implicated in the effects of the man's wrong choice. The whole race, summed up in the first man, is placed in a separation from God in which, not only cannot any man by his own efforts be pleasing to God, but even correspondence to God's sanctifying grace (i.e. living the life which God's grace makes possible) must be painful.

The original writer of the story evidently intended one purpose in writing it, while St. Paul has used it to a quite different purpose. We may still ask whether St. Paul has really attached to it the true, or the necessary, meaning. And we may further ask whether any conclusion is to be drawn from the fact that *two* stories of the Creation are given in Genesis 1-3, and that the Fall of Adam forms part of only one of them. It is pleasing to find an interpretation of the early chapters of Genesis in which Adam is seen as the type of Christ and Eve as the type, sometimes of the Church, sometimes of the whole Creation.[8] Genesis 2 : 4ff. is understood to represent the creation of the world within the Second Person of the Trinity as its *locus,* and as posterior to his own eternal begetting from the Father. Genesis 1 : 1–2 : 4, on the other hand, is seen to represent the constitution of the Church, the *totus Christus,* and indeed the *whole creation* recapitulated in Christ, as the crown of the work of creation. In this poem (Gen. 1 : 1–2 : 4) it is the perfected work of God which is referred to—the story anticipates the Consummation of all things —and the Fall is therefore not mentioned. In Genesis 3, however, the corruption of creation (Eve) brings down the true Adam,

Christ, not indeed into actual sin, but into the suffering which sin brings in its entail,[9] and 'him who knew no sin he made to be sin on our behalf' (2 Cor. 5 : 21). (That Eve tempted Adam has commonly been used in making strictures upon women (1 Tim. 2 : 14), but it has been more rarely used *theologically* in the attempt to understand the purpose of this scripture. This treatment seems to do precisely that.)

x

If this view be legitimate, then we are free to look back to a Fall of all creation prior to, and not in consequence of, human sin. The nature of this Fall is less certain. Here only speculation is possible, and no one is bound to accept any such speculations. We are at least free to suppose that spiritual agencies (i.e. what we call the powers of evil) have been operative on the material creation, and that, they themselves having rebelled against God, they have corrupted it. In consequence, it might be supposed, man, when he was created out of 'the dust of the ground,' inherited this corruption. N. P. Williams tentatively suggested the existence of a World Soul which rebelled against God.[10] Dr. Mascall considers, no doubt rightly, that this involves too drastic a departure from the main body of Christian tradition.[11]

Ignoring N. P. Williams' suggestion, it may still be felt that the idea that spiritual powers corrupted the material universe and the material out of which man was made runs counter to the teaching of the Bible that 'God saw everything that he had made and, behold, it was very good' (Gen. 1 : 31). It may indeed seem that our speculation belongs to Manichaeism or some form of Gnosticism rather than to the religion of the Bible. Manichaeism is dualistic, holding that the world is the battle-ground of uncreated good and evil powers, and that matter is the creation of the evil power. But we are not suggesting this at all. The spiritual beings who rebel against God are themselves created by God, and matter also is created by God. Matter must be good, i.e. pleasing to God, in its beginning, for it owes its origin to no one but him. Similarly, the spiritual powers themselves were pleasing to God as he created them; but he delegated to them a certain measure of his own initiative, and this (as they were free to do) they have used against the Creator who gave it to them.

Further, it is not inconsistent with Genesis 1 : 1–2 : 4, as we have interpreted it, to suggest that God allowed these spiritual creatures to corrupt the material creation. As we have said, in this first poem of Creation, 'it is the perfected work of God which is referred to—the story anticipates the Consummation of all things—and the Fall is therefore not mentioned.' It would seem that a further implication of this manner of interpretation of Genesis 1 : 1–2 : 4 is that, in a temporal sense, the sabbath rest of God still awaits the Consummation of all things in Christ.

XI

If this be so, we may ask, precisely what is involved in this work of the completion of Creation? It is plain that the Incarnation of God the Son is involved and, central to it, his Passion, Crucifixion and Resurrection. That is, the conflict-and-victory *motif* is central to the picture of the creative activity of God. Not only may the poem of Genesis 1 : 1–2 : 4 be interpreted as referring to the *completed* work of God, but the creation-through-conflict passages mentioned at the beginning of this essay may be referred to the restoration and consummation of creation brought about by the Crucifixion and·Resurrection of Christ, rather than to some supposed spiritual battle in the dim past of the universe.

Nor can it be some pre-existent 'somewhat' which resists the moulding will of God, for that, as we have seen, would be to detract from the absolute primacy of God's initiative. We must say, therefore, that the creation, or some part of it, resists its own creation in the very act of being created.

If God has the absolute primacy of initiative, he is no more limited by time than in power. Creation, therefore, is not a process in time. Time is a characteristic of the created world, not of the act of Creation. The world is not only created in all its parts; it is also created in all its instants. God creates things as doing what they are doing at all instants. If then the world or some of its parts resist their creation, they resist their creation in the timeless act of their being created.

This resistance to being created can only be the desire to un-be. This aim cannot be attained, since it is not in the power of the creature to decide whether it shall be created or not. Hence this determination to un-be must be manifested as a refusal to be what God would have the creature to be. This plainly is only possible to creatures of self-knowledge and free-will; and it is the mystery and antinomy of free-will that God concedes a certain limited modicum of his own initiative to certain creatures, and limits himself according to the exercise which they make of this delegated creativity. Sin then is basically the determination to resist creation, and since this aim is in fact unattainable, it appears as a determination to be other than what God wills— a determination which, within limits, and for a limited time, God permits. This rebellion in its fullness we attribute to spiritual creatures. Judging from God's Revelation, these are not in his sight so important as man. Their fate is described as to be cast into the pit and the fire that burns for ever and ever. We must recognize this as figurative language for something that cannot be expressed in words. It is also part of God's Revelation that he will go to the uttermost to save man from a like fate, and that the sub-human creation is to be delivered from woe through the salvation of man. God works in his creation, supremely in the work of the Cross and Resurrection, to bring his creation to final perfection, united to the Second Person of the Trinity through the Body of his Incarnation.

Though the total work of Creation is timeless, it can only be known by men in time; and, as known in time, can be completed only in the final Consummation, which itself is only possible through the victory of the Resurrection following the battle of the Cross. This whole picture is shown in Ephesians 1 : 3–14. The final Consummation is planned in the eternal will of God, but attained only 'through his blood,' 'unto a dispensation of the fullness of the times,' 'to sum up all things in Christ,' 'unto the praise of his glory.'

XII

It is not, therefore, artificial to relate Creation and the Fall to the Resurrection of Christ. The effect of the Fall is overcome by Christ's Resurrection, and the purpose of God in creating the world attained only through the effects of his Resurrection. The creation-through-conflict passages in the Old Testament are not mere vestigial remains of primitive cosmogony, but, under the Holy Spirit, they indicate an essential action in the work of

Creation. God's perfect intention for the creation is not attained except by overcoming the resistance of some creatures to their own creation and their corrupting of the rest of creation through this resistance. These creatures, if they do not repent, will be 'cast into the fire'; but men who accept the redeeming work of God will be brought into communion with the Father through the Son by the Holy Spirit, and all the rest of creation will be brought to perfection. God in his eternity is in perfect rest, but the Sabbath rest of creation, as of the people of God, awaits the fruition of the work of Christ which he will bring about in the Consummation of all things.

CHAPTER IV

FR. NICOLAS GRAHAM, C.R.

THE HOLY SPIRIT

THE words spirit and 'spiritual' are so loosely and variously used that there is no wonder that the Christian doctrine of the Holy Spirit is little understood. Nor does the term 'Holy Ghost' (a survival from sixteenth century usage, when the word 'ghost' was interchangeable with 'spirit') do much to dispel the general vagueness which commonly surrounds this whole subject. Moreover the title 'comforter' which appears in our English Bible suggests something cosy and woolly : whereas the word *parakletos,* which it translates and which sometimes appears in Christian writings in its English form Paraclete, is a strong and bracing word. Its exact connotation is not easy to determine but it can mean advocate or exhorter, as well as consoler. When Comforter was chosen to translate it, no doubt that word carried more of its Latin sense of co-strengthener. Meanwhile since 'Paraclete' carries no particular meaning to the English ear, it is no wonder that the third Person of the Holy Trinity is actually thought, by some people, to be a bird. This wild speculation is, in turn, given some colour by a passage in the New Testament where, at our Lord's Baptism, the Holy Spirit is said to have appeared in the form of a dove.

There is, then, a good deal of haze and some positive misconception to be cleared away before we can even begin to get a true outline of what Christians mean by Holy Spirit.

Perhaps we can best begin by looking to see under what symbols the Holy Spirit appears in the New Testament. First of all, the word Spirit itself is symbolic or figurative. Its Hebrew and Greek equivalents both mean 'breath' or 'wind' (the Greek word is *pneuma,* familiar to us in the derivatives pneumatic and pneumonia). The cognate English words which still retain the connection between spirit and breath are e.g. inspiration, respiration and expire. So we arrive at the metaphorical (but useful) picture of the Holy Spirit as holy breath, the Breath of God. Thus we may say, as long as we remember that we are using imagery, that the second person of the Holy Trinity is the Word uttered by the Father and that the third person (the Holy Spirit) is the Breath with which the Word is uttered.

Further, the coming of the Holy Spirit on the Day of Pentecost is described as being accompanied by a sound 'as of the rushing of a mighty wind,' and also by the appearance of tongues 'distributing themselves, like as of fire' (Acts 2 : 1–4). The important word in this rather obscure expression is 'tongues,' since it points to one of the Holy Spirit's activities, that of giving the power of inspired speech. And this seems close to the image of 'breath.' The Holy Spirit not only enables God to utter his Word, but enables men to speak in an inspired (or inbreathed) way.

Now for the image of Wind, to which the sound as of a rushing mighty wind at Pentecost adds colour, if not definition. There is a passage in St. John's Gospel where our Lord himself compares the motion of the Holy Spirit to that of the wind : 'The wind bloweth where it listeth, and thou hearest the voice thereof, but knowest not whence it cometh, and whither it goeth : so is everyone that is born of the Spirit' (John 3 : 8). Here the same word 'pneuma' is used for both wind and spirit and indeed the first phrase could be translated 'the Spirit breathes where he will,' but this would destroy the force of the illustration. It is typical of our Lord to teach by simile or parable. The Spirit, he says, behaves, in certain respects, like the wind : you know of his presence by his effects.

Lastly we should consider the image of the Dove. This has become a favourite way for painters or sculptors to depict the Holy Spirit, no doubt because it provides a concrete image ; while hymn writers have made something of 'hovering' and 'brooding' (do doves, in fact, hover or brood?). The appearance of the Holy Spirit in the form of a dove is confined, in the New Testament, to accounts of our Lord's baptism and it is doubtful whether, for the understanding of the doctrine of the Holy Spirit, the image of the dove is widely useful. Yet a glance at its Old Testament ancestry may be illuminating. In the prelude to Creation, in the first chapter of Genesis, where primeval chaos is thought of as a dark or formless waste of waters, we read that 'the spirit of God moved upon the face of the waters. And God said . . .' (Gen. 1 : 2–3) and there follows a series of creative utterances. A few chapters later, when earth has once again been reduced to a formless waste by the Flood, it is a dove which Noah sends out of the ark. On its second flight it comes to the ark with an olive leaf in its beak, thus bringing the news that the flood is abating and that the world is (as it were) being recreated. Taking these two passages in connection we have first the Spirit of God and then a dove moving upon the face of the waters, heralding in the first instance an act of creation and in the second, an act of restoration. It is possible, then, to see in the dove descending on the waters of our Lord's baptism, the Holy Spirit heralding the far greater recreation and restoration—the 'making of all things new' which began with that declaration of our Lord's divine sonship and which may be called the coming of the Kingdom of Heaven on earth : to which, moreover, the entrance for us is through the waters of Baptism.

The image of Breath seems the most helpful, since breath, unlike wind (save in a limited medical application), is intensely personal. Breath is often equated with life itself. The separate life of the infant begins when it draws its first breath; that life ends when a man exhales his last breath—when, in biblical language, he 'gives up the ghost (or spirit).' The breath of God, then, is the Spirit of God, the life of God. And this idea paves the way for the fully developed doctrine that the Spirit is God himself.

There is one other scriptural image of Holy Spirit, namely water. This may have some relevance to the Rite of Baptism, but in general it would seem to represent the function of the Spirit in fructifying what is barren and in cleansing what is impure.

To return once more to the passage in which our Lord compares the action of the Spirit to that of the wind : it will be well to deal here with a very common misconception which perhaps has its origin in a misunderstanding of this passage. This misconception is common among Christians, and perhaps especially among those who might be described as being on the fringes of orthodoxy. It runs something like this : 'The church (or churches, according to the point of view) is institutional, over-organized. Orthodoxy is stuffy, restrictive and dull. Surely all this dogma, this emphasis on going to church, on the sacraments, on a validly ordained ministry, all tends to quench the Spirit?' The Spirit, in this context, is identified with all that is spontaneous, sincere and free, and set over against the historic church, which is seen as formal, insincere (not to say hypocritical) and shackled by tradition and convention. Only recently a church dignitary, writing in the church press of one of his predecessors, said in effect (the exact quotation is not to hand), 'He was no pillar of orthodoxy, but he was a fearless apostle of the religion of the Spirit,' and this was said in a clearly complimentary sense, as if 'the religion of the Spirit' were somehow purer, nobler, more real than the religion of the Church.

Now, it cannot be denied that this misconception has arisen from the often lamentably 'spiritless' appearance of institutional religion. It is largely the Church's fault if she has given the impression that orthodoxy is dull, that she is chiefly concerned with liturgical niceties and fine-drawn legalities, while ignoring the things of the Spirit. But conceding all that and more, it is still both theological and logical nonsense to set a 'religion of the Spirit' over against the religion of the Church. However much the Church may have marred the beauty of her heritage, however often she may have deserved her Lord's denunciations 'Ye hypocrites,' she *is* still the divinely founded household of God, the mystical Body of Christ and the living temple of the Spirit. The Holy Spirit is God, the third person of the Holy Trinity, and it is not merely blasphemous, but meaningless, to accuse him of (or congratulate him upon) being unorthodox. He is the fount of orthodoxy—that is of right worship and right belief. He is even demonstrably liturgical, in that he chose, for his first full descent upon the Apostles, the Jewish Feast of Pentecost, just as the second Person, Jesus Christ, chose to identify his sacrifice with the Feast of the Passover. Moreover it was upon the assembled Church that the Spirit descended and not upon a few scattered free-lance preachers.

The text comparing the action of the Spirit to that of the wind cannot be pressed to mean that the Spirit is capricious. 'He breathes where he wills' sounds perhaps to us like 'where whim or fancy takes him,' but the will of the Spirit is the will of God, supremely purposive and directed. You hear the sound, you see the trees bending—that is how you know the wind is blowing. The presence of the Spirit is known by his effects. These are not necessarily dramatic, as on the day of Pentecost. There is no sign that St. James was in an ecstasy when he gave his summing up from the chair at the Council of Jerusalem, using the words: 'It seemed good to the Holy Ghost, and to us . . .' (Acts 15 : 28). Or again St. Paul, giving plain paternal advice to the Corinthians, ends a passage as sober as any Vicar's letter in a parish magazine, with the words: 'I think that I also have the Spirit of God' (1 Cor. 7 : 40). Indeed one could multiply instances from the New Testament of this calm familiarity with the will and work of the Spirit, which suggests that it was the everyday experience of the early Church; nor need this surprise those who, living within the Church, act daily in the belief that they have the Spirit of God and that he will, as promised, lead them into all truth. The late Archbishop Temple well remarked: 'That a respectable citizen should love his neighbour as himself is less likely to be announced in double-column headlines than his utterance of ecstatic gibberish in a public place; but it would be quite as unusual, and a far surer sign of the divine presence and activity in him.'[1]

Having tried, then, to clarify the use of certain images and to clear away some popular misconceptions, in the hope that by these means the outline of the Christian doctrine of the Holy Spirit may begin to appear, it is time to try to complete that outline and attempt a positive portrait.

A moment's thought, however, assures the Christian writer that this is strictly impossible. Nobody but a Christian is likely to want to describe the Holy Spirit and when he tries to do so, he immediately becomes aware that he cannot (so to speak) look squarely at the Holy Spirit because the Holy Spirit is the Power by which he does the looking.

His picture is bound to be as incomplete as would be a description by a man of his own eyes as seen in a mirror. He cannot see his own eyes in motion (and mobility is one of the most characteristic features of eyes), nor can he see them looking at anything except the mirror.

Bearing this difficulty in mind, however, it is still possible to say some useful things about him. It will be noticed that in that sentence and throughout this essay the Holy Spirit has always been referred to as 'he' or 'him,' not as 'it.' He is a Person, not a thing. Christianity has no dealings with an impersonal Life Force or with vaguely benevolent influences. Our limited everyday use of the word 'person' and our impersonal use of the word 'spirit' (e.g. 'a spirit of friendliness pervaded the meeting') both tend to make it difficult for us to accept the statement that the Holy Spirit is a Person. He behaves in a manner very unlike that of the persons (i.e. individual human beings) we know and talk about. He is evidently able, according to the New Testament, to be equally and fully present to, or even in, any number of different people simultaneously: he is invisible and intangible and so forth. In fact, of course, this difficulty of conceiving him as a person applies equally to our attempts to conceive the person of the Father, but we unconsciously are more ready to accept the personality of the Father, just because we call him Father and father, unlike spirit, is a concrete image. The word person, as used in speaking of the Persons of the Godhead, is perhaps unfortunate, but human language is likely to prove inadequate to the strain of describing Godhead and at least the retention of the word 'person' safeguards the essential personality of God in all three persons, and rules out such impersonal concepts as 'force' or 'influence.'

Dogma is always the outcome of experience; religious dogma of devotional experience. Statements of dogma may sound cold and obscure, but they are only the best attempts to crystallize religious experience. In fact the dogma of the Holy Spirit took longer to crystallize out than any other of the basic dogmas of Christianity. In the New Testament we see some of the living experience which went to formulate the dogma. And that experience at all times confirms both the divinity and the personality of the Holy Spirit.

We have already quoted the phrase 'It seemed good to the Holy Ghost, and to us.' St. James was not just 'taking the feeling (spirit) of the meeting' he was clearly aware that their decision was in accordance with the will of God and this is his way of saying it. In the Gospels our Lord speaks of a sin against the Holy Ghost, and he calls him 'another Comforter' whom the Father will send in his (Christ's) name. St. Peter, in the Acts, accuses Ananias of lying to the Holy Ghost, St. Paul speaks of grieving him. He is said to teach, to bear witness and to make intercession for men. These and other similar references when considered cumulatively leave no doubt that to the writers of the New Testament and to those they wrote about and wrote to, the Holy Spirit was a person. He *has* a force and an influence, but that is not to say that he *is* a force or an influence. Contact with the Spirit of God is comparable to contact with any strong personality—one feels and is influenced, perhaps guided, by the strength of his character and personality.

Now the question arises: 'Was this a new experience, something not felt before the Christian era?' The answer is both Yes and No. The actual term Holy Spirit is rare in the Old Testament (Ps. 51 : 11 and Isa. 63 : 10, 11), but the Spirit of the Lord is frequently mentioned. (It should be remembered here that 'the Lord' in our Bibles most often stands for the personal name YAHWEH and is therefore a name not a title.) This Spirit of Yahweh descends on individuals and fills them so that they are enabled to prophesy (that is to speak authentically in the Name of God) or to perform specially wonderful acts. A recent writer on this subject says: 'We cannot think of the Spirit of Yahweh as in any sense something separate from God himself. It is more true to say that the Spirit is a fluid extension of God, coming upon or into people with greater or less power, according to their capacity of soul.'[2] Here again the image of Breath and perhaps also that of Water, is operative. That of Breath has already been sufficiently discussed: water can be seen to fill dry pools, to freshen springs or torrents, to make dry ground fruitful and also to cleanse, and hence, in a figure, to sanctify.

In some instances of Hebrew prophecy we have something similar to that 'possession by the God' which we meet in descriptions of divinely inspired prophets in classical literature. This, however, is not to suggest that the greatest Hebrew prophets, far less the Christians of the New Testament, are at all comparable to mediums; it is only intended to emphasize the personal and divine character of the Spirit.

As for those who hold that all inspired or ecstatic utterance is attributable to hysteria or self-hypnosis or to some artificially induced state of emotional excitement, one can only say that it is difficult to believe this of the prophet Isaiah, of the thirteenth

Chapter of St. Paul's first Letter to the Corinthians—or, for that matter, of Homer, Dante or Shakespeare.

Ideas about the Spirit of God underwent certain developments during the period covered by the Old Testament and further during the four centuries or so which lie between our two Testaments. These need not be pursued in detail. It is perhaps enough to say that to the question: 'Was the Christian experience of the Holy Spirit an entirely new thing?' part of the answer is 'No.' Had it been entirely new it would hardly have been possible for his hearers to attach any meaning to the statement of St. John the Baptist that there was one coming after him (that is, the Christ) who would baptize with the Holy Spirit.

But part of the answer is also 'Yes,' and that, just *because* 'he who should come' had meanwhile come. God had appeared in the flesh in the person of Jesus Christ.

The Incarnation, that is the coming of God in human flesh, is of course, central to Christianity and it has its proper place elsewhere in this book. For our present purpose it is enough to say that it was, at once, both the continuation, the development or (to use the scriptural word) the fulfilment of the Old Testament, *and* an entirely New Thing, a New Creation, the inauguration of a New Era or Dispensation. By the same token, it was at once an end and a beginning. It was an end, in that it was that to which the Old Testament had looked forward in faith and prophecy, although, 'seen from afar,' the full design of God had never been guessed in all its startling simplicity; nor indeed was the full truth of the Incarnation grasped until after the Resurrection. It was a beginning, in that it made possible the foundation of the Church, the outpouring of the Holy Spirit and the fullest revelation of the nature of God possible to man, the doctrine of the Trinity. The Incarnation, while it was a 'liberating' of God into the world and into the understanding and experience of men, was also a 'limitation' of God in the Incarnate Lord himself. 'How am I straitened!' (Luke 12:50) he himself exclaims and he promises that after his departure from the world, his followers shall do greater things than he himself has done. The Incarnate God is necessarily limited to the actual time and space which he occupies in human history: his return to the Father will bring about the 'Coming of the Holy Spirit' who will know no such limitations.

One may perhaps usefully regard the dealings of God with the world under the analogy of a drama with three acts of (temporally) very unequal length. Act I was from the Creation to the Annunciation. Its chief event is the catastrophe of men's fall and thereafter its principal theme is the preparation of man by God for his recovery and redemption. Act II, which is the shortest in time, is none the less the most crucial in the development of the drama. It runs from the acceptance by Mary of the divine desire to become Incarnate in her womb to the Ascension or return of the Son to the Father. In this Act the catastrophe of man is recovered and reversed in the person of a Man who is also God himself. The saving act of redemption is performed by the voluntary and sinless sacrifice of Jesus Christ, Son of Man and Son of God, and is seen to be vindicated by his triumphant Resurrection. Act III opens ten days after the Ascension and it is still going on. The document which tells us of the opening scenes in Act III, the Acts of the Apostles (St. Luke Volume II), gives us, in a striking sentence, the clue to what may be expected to be the course of the drama. Referring back to his Gospel, St. Luke says that this, his first volume, told 'concerning all that Jesus *began* both to do and to teach, until the day in which he was received up' (Acts 1 : 1f.). The implication is that Volume II (The Acts) will tell of what Jesus will *continue* to do in the world now that he has been taken up from the world. How can Jesus continue to work in the world when he is no longer in it? The answer, which would be perfectly plain to his readers, is 'by the Holy Spirit.' This is just what Jesus had promised : 'When the Comforter is come, whom I will send unto you from the Father, even the Spirit of truth, which proceedeth from the Father, he shall bear witness of me' (John 15 : 26). Again, 'If I go not away the Comforter will not come unto you; but if I go, I will send him unto you' (John 16 : 7) and again : 'When he, the Spirit of truth, is come, he shall guide you into all truth' (John 16 : 13).

Here clearly is something more than an exhortation, as it might be from the deathbed of a beloved Master to his followers to 'go on living in my spirit.' We should indeed have been left comfortless at his departure if all that was left was to go on trying to live 'in a Christian spirit.' Such a description of the Holy Spirit is far behind even the crudest descriptions of the

Spirit of Yahweh in the Old Testament. What makes the experience of the Holy Spirit in the New Testament something new is that the Spirit, whom Jesus promises and who fulfilled that promise on the Feast of Pentecost in Jerusalem, is none other than the Spirit of Jesus (as the New Testament sometimes calls him) now fully liberated to work in a world where the primary initial acts of redemption have been once for all performed by the Son.

The Incarnation and consequent Passion had truly humiliated the Son; but the Spirit 'shall glorify me' says Jesus, 'for he shall take of mine, and shall declare it unto you. All things whatsoever the Father hath are mine: therefore said I, that he taketh of mine, and shall declare it unto you' (John 16: 14f.).

Here is as full and clear an expression as we are entitled to look for in Scripture of the intimate union and co-operation of the three persons of the Godhead.

Provided we hold fast to the conception of the eternal co-inherence of the three persons, we can rightly say that Act I was the dispensation of the Father, Act II of the Son and Act III of the Holy Spirit. The work of each person is the work of all three. Creation, redemption and sanctification are the continuous work of the Three-in-One. To him there is no slowly unfolding drama; to him Acts I, II and III are seen simultaneously.

For us, however, it is safe to call the present time the Age of the Spirit, since to our necessarily time-bound minds it is just a matter of historical fact that there was a time before God came into the world and there is a time since he left it. And in this connection it is worth remembering that God has actually experienced our condition of time-space limitation.

So we return to the essential difficulty of writing about the Holy Spirit mentioned earlier in this essay. In attempting to describe the truth of the Spirit, one is aware that it is only by the very Spirit of Truth himself that one is enabled to say anything even nearly true about him or anything else.

Yet, as we have seen, the presence of the Spirit, like the blowing of the wind, is to be known by his effects. Further we have also considered that these effects are not necessarily to be expected outwardly dramatic, striking and strange. Indeed it would seem to be the normal principle of God's working that he brings about his will in and through what we call the ordinary processes of Nature. After all he created Nature and might be expected to know the nature of Nature and to have created the instrument best suited to his hand.

This is not the place for a discussion or defence of miracles. The existence of the miraculous in the Christian documents has given offence to many an honest mind and, at first sight, might seem to give the lie to what has been said above about God's normal working. So here let just two things be said. First, that abnormal conditions might be expected to require abnormal actions. No one can say that it was exactly *normal* for the Son of God to be at large in the world. At such a time, if at any, miracles might be expected to be *seen* to be miracles (and hushed up). Meanwhile who shall say that the growth of the flower from the seed, the plucking of sound and pictures from the air, the assimilation of food in the animal body are really *normal*, except in so far that they happen all the time? Nature herself is miraculous, in the simple sense of 'wonderful.' Secondly, a very large number (though admittedly not all) of the miracles of the New Testament are what might be called 'natural.' God does quicken the life in every egg and womb (why not once, for a special purpose, directly in the womb of a virgin?); he does multiply food and heal sickness and turn water into wine all day and every day. Moreover the greatest miracle of all—the Incarnation itself—was never *seen* to be a miracle at all. What was there to wonder at in the birth of a baby in a cave in Bethlehem, save perhaps the inhumanity of those who let it happen there? No miracle recorded in the New Testament is grotesque; conjuring tricks and wizard's magic are sternly refused—stones are *not* turned into bread. As it is with God the Father and with God the Son—so is it with God the Spirit.

That brief digression was thought necessary in order to emphasize the 'ordinariness' of the Spirit's work in the world to-day. After all you don't have to wait for the roof to blow off or for trees to fall before you become aware that there is a wind blowing.

Everything, then, which is specifically and perceptibly Christian in the world to-day (for that matter throughout the period known as A.D.) is the work of the Holy Spirit. At once let it be said that men, even good men, retain the power to hinder or obscure the Spirit's work. This is the risk God took when he created men in his own image—that is with wills of their own.

All that is specifically Christian in the world to-day throughout the history of Christendom—that is a sweeping phrase. Nowhere is the frustration of the Spirit's work by the sins of men more plainly visible than in the Spirit's greatest masterpiece—the Church. None-the-less it is to the Church that we must look for the typical activity of the Holy Spirit. A great cathedral does not cease to be an architect's masterpiece because hooligans throw stones at the windows and smash up the carvings. And the architect of the Church has the means of continual repair and restoration and the ultimate certainty of bringing his work to perfection.

A spirit cried out for a body. Disembodied spirits simply do not enter into our experience, nor even into our imagination. If any one doubts that, let him try to visualize a disembodied spirit. Instinctively, indeed necessarily, he clothes it with a body —maybe a very refined and gaseous body, but still some sort of material envelope. True, the experience of Eliphaz the Temanite is one which many people have shared: 'A spirit passed before my face; the hair of my flesh stood up' (Job 4: 15). But even he goes on to say: 'an image was before mine eyes.' None of this proves that there are not such things as pure spirits—spirits without bodies—but the human spirit is not one of them.

Neither, in a sense, is the Holy Spirit. I hasten to say that I do not mean that the Holy Spirit 'has a body,' but that he desires always to be embodied (as far as this world is concerned). He acts—perhaps *can* only act—in and through matter, in his mission to men, and that is what we are concerned with.

Christianity, it can never be said too often, is not a 'purely spiritual religion.' If indeed such a thing exists, it could only be practised by pure spirits. The devil's religion, if he has one, must be purely spiritual, for we are taught that all angels, fallen and unfallen, are pure spirits (that is 'pure' in the sense of 'unmixed,' not in the sense of 'sinless'). The word 'spiritual' is not a synonym for 'holy,' 'high-minded' or 'vague.' Christianity is the religion of the Whole Man for the Whole Man—indeed for all creation. God has chosen for his full and final revelation of himself to men, to become incarnate in Jesus Christ who is called both Son and Word of God, and the principle of incarnation runs right through the Christian religion. One of the great Biblical titles for the Church is The Body of Christ and this is more than a metaphor. There is a striking parallel between the conception of Jesus Christ and what may be called the conception or birth of the Church.

The Holy Spirit 'fell upon' the Apostles and their companions at Pentecost and they became the Body of Christ, the Church.

And anyway what use is a body without a spirit to animate it?

So it is primarily in and through men and women—their souls and bodies—that the Holy Spirit acts in the world: but not just any man and woman anywhere anyhow. It does not follow that because God chooses certain people for his purposes, he necessarily excludes others.

There is an interesting passage in the Old Testament: it seems to be a kind of primitive ordination. Moses, at God's bidding, and for the practical purpose of lightening his own work, gathers seventy elders from among the people and the Lord 'took of the spirit that was upon him (Moses) and put it upon the seventy elders,' with the result that 'they prophesied.' Two men, however, who did not go to the meeting of the elders (though probably they were meant to) also received the spirit, in the camp and also 'prophesied.' On hearing this, Moses' young aide-de-camp, Joshua, indignantly asks Moses to forbid them, but Moses answers, 'Art thou jealous for my sake? would God that all the Lord's people were prophets, that the Lord would put his spirit upon them!' (Num. 11 : 24–9).

God chooses, then, whom he will: 'The wind bloweth where it listeth . . . so is every one that is born of the Spirit' (John 3 : 8).

There is nothing either capricious or 'favouritizing' about God's choice of persons who are to receive the Spirit. Still less is the Spirit to be thought of as having a kind of roving commission, or working as a divine free-lance.

At Pentecost the Spirit comes in his fullness on a small group of men who had been most carefully prepared and trained by Jesus himself. They, in their turn, were empowered to become the vehicles of the Spirit to others. It is clear that the Apostles themselves received very definite commission to perform certain specific functions, namely, to 'preach the Word with power,' to commission others to be officers in the Church, to forgive or retain sins, to 'break bread,' to baptize and to confirm: in short to preach and celebrate the sacrament. Ultimately all these functions they were enabled to pass on to others, in a way similar to that in which Moses had done under the Old Dispensation, though with far fuller powers than he.

Most important of all, the Apostles became not merely the organizers of the Church, but an essential and (in some respects) unique part of the organism, the Body of Christ, which is the Church. Their teaching, their sacramental functions, their ordering of the Church's worship made the essential nucleus around which and in definite relations with which, the Church was formed. It is recorded of the first Christians that 'they continued stedfastly in the apostles' teaching and fellowship, in breaking of bread and the prayers' (Acts 2 : 42).

Here, then, in the foundation of the Church, is the supreme and essential work of the Holy Spirit. God is a god of order, the Spirit is a spirit of order. And order means more than efficient organization; it means the growth of an organism in accordance with the laws inherent in the germ or seed. Nobody speaks of an acorn being organized—still less of its organizing itself—into becoming an oak tree. So the Church, the mystical Body of Christ, grows according to its pre-ordained pattern, as surely as the divinely fertilized cell in the womb of Mary grew to be the natural body of Christ. It could be argued that the goal of all God's purposes from the fall of Man onwards was to produce Mary of Nazareth; one who was able to be both his Spouse and the mother of his Son. So now, we may say that the goal of the Holy Spirit's purpose is to perfect the Church, which is sometimes called the Bride of Christ, until she can be presented before God, a chaste virgin, 'not having spot or wrinkle or any such thing' (Eph. 5 : 27) to be the mystical wife of the Lamb (who is the Christ).

It seems that the Church is as yet far from achieving her destiny. Yet it must be remembered, in this context, that by far the greater part of the Church (numerically) is no longer on earth and it may well be that she is nearer perfection than can appear on earth.

THE HOLY SPIRIT 153

Meanwhile it is with the work of the Holy Spirit on earth that this essay is principally concerned, and it is contended that if we would see and understand the typical nature of his work we must look, ideally at any rate, to the Church to see it. Nor is it proposed here to make a very close or exclusive definition of the Church. All the baptized are members of the Body of Christ and those who adhere with loyalty or conviction to a particular part of divided Christendom must be, without abating one jot of their conscientious convictions, warned by the rebuke which Joshua received from Moses. Writing as a convinced Catholic with loyalty to the Anglican communion, I must be able to say with my hand on my heart, 'Would God that all the Lord's people were Catholics' while most carefully and joyfully respecting those outside the visible 'tabernacle' in whom the work of the Holy Spirit is clearly discernible. For if one thing is certain it is that the Holy Spirit is working always towards understanding and unity.

We are told that no one can call Jesus Lord except by the Holy Spirit. If it is true that the principle of Incarnation runs right through Christianity—the principle which I have described as 'The Spirit crying out for a body'; if it is true that an essential part of the experience of Christianity is that of being a member of a Body a partaker in common worship and works; it is also inescapably true that no individual can truly call himself a Christian unless he can say from his heart, 'Jesus is Lord' and all that that implies for personal faith and trust in and love for a personal Saviour in Jesus Christ. This also is the work of the Holy Spirit.

The Holy Spirit, it was promised by Jesus, would lead us into all truth. His work is the work of sanctification—of making holy the chosen people of God. All the means of becoming holy are really the means by which the Spirit makes us holy, taking of 'the things of Christ' and showing them to us. Of these, personal faith and practising membership in the common life of the church are the two principal means. Common worship, especially eucharistic worship (because that was divinely instituted) corresponds to and promotes the corporate Christian life—the steady adherence to the Apostles' teaching and fellowship. Personal prayer corresponds to and feeds the life of personal Christian faith.

The Spirit's work in our prayers is vividly portrayed in a passage of St. Paul's letter to the Romans: 'We know not,' says St. Paul, 'how to pray as we ought' (and how heartily every practising Christian can echo that satement), 'but,' he goes on, 'the Spirit himself maketh intercession for us with groanings which cannot be uttered' (8 : 26). The deepest prayer of Christians is the prayer of the indwelling Spirit—crying out for the true end of all Christian life—to be united in the fellowship of the Holy Trinity.

And here this attempt to write of the Holy Spirit must be brought to an end, with the writer more conscious even than when he began, that the truth can only be told by the Spirit himself in words which cannot be uttered; yet in the knowledge that he cries out for a body and will not altogether disdain the pen and paper of a Christian whose heart is inditing of a great matter, however unready the writer.

PART III

INTRODUCTION TO PART III

IF Part I of this book could be entitled 'The Facts,' and Part II 'The Reason for the Facts,' Part III might be called 'Christian Response to the Facts.' Here we consider the foundation, and nature, of the Church; the Church as a worshipping body; the essential unity of the Church, expressed in 'one Baptism'; the privilege of the presence of God in the Church —i.e., the call to prayer; and finally the power of Christ as shown in one particular situation, which is but one among many—the Christian's confrontation with and use of suffering. Here we leave the somewhat intellectualist level of Part II, and speak of problems and encouragements which meet the ordinary Christian every day of his or her life.

CHAPTER I

FR. ANDREW BLAIR, C.R.

THE APOSTOLIC CHURCH

THE British visitor to the city of Boston is soon made aware that he is on holy ground. As he goes through the streets he will observe here and there sign-posts bearing the inscription 'Freedom Trail' : these, he will discover on inquiry, mark the route of Paul Revere's famous ride in April 1775 to rouse the Patriot Militia of Lexington and Concord with the news of the British advance. Revere, so we are told, hid in the marshes on the Cambridge bank of the Charles River until he saw the prearranged signal—two lamps burning in the tower of the Old North Church—which told him that the British troops were on the move. Mounting his horse, he rode through the night rousing the farmers as he went: by dawn the Minute Men, as the Militia were popularly known, were drawn up on the green at Lexington to await the British, and at Concord Bridge 'the shot was fired that echoed round the world.' It was a small affair indeed compared with the battles the twentieth century has known : and many years were to roll by before the United States became the nation we know to-day: a whole continent still stretched to the west to be conquered and tamed. None-the-less, it was a turning point: had the Patriot Militia not stood their ground that day on Lexington Green the whole of later history might well have been very different indeed. On that day a colony ended and a nation began to be forged : and, little though the participants probably realized the historic event in which they were taking part—still less the immense future which began to unfold that day—the conscience of America has rightly regarded this episode as determinative in the nation's history and has enshrined the battlefields of Lexington and Concord as 'The Cradle of Liberty.'

It is from a similar angle, *mutatis mutandis,* that we may contemplate the first Christians in the period immediately following our Lord's Ascension. They were not a large body of people nor, from the point of view of contemporary society, were they at all important. The events of our Lord's life and Passion, taken in the context of the immense canvas of contemporary history, seemed hardly to have ruffled the surface of human affairs. We can hardly imagine that, any more than it was given to the peasant soldiers at Lexington and Concord to see the great future to which their bravery had opened the gates, they were able to see with a prophetic eye their little group becoming a vast body extending beyond the bounds of the known world and still growing. But just as the Minute Men had certain knowledge of one fact, that they had faced a professional army and held their own, and took heart therefrom for the next step, so the first Christians had one fact, and one only, to hold on to—the fact that 'Christ is Risen.' More than that they did not know. The implications of it all had yet to be thought out. The New Testament was as yet unwritten and it would be many years before the Creeds would be formulated. The theology of our Lord's Person had not been seriously considered nor had the exact nature of what had been accomplished by his life, death and resurrection been worked out. All that they knew was this one fact—that Jesus whom they had known, whom they had seen die and whom some of them had helped to bury, had risen to a new life, no longer bound by the limitations of space and time. It was a fact about which it would be no easier to convince their contemporary auditors than it would be to-day. Indeed in many ways it would be a good deal more difficult. Many of those to whom they preached had seen Jesus die and would be hard to convince. Contrary to what many sceptics seem to assume, the Jews of the first century were a hard-headed race, not easy to convince: and risings from the dead were no more commonplace events two thousand years ago than they are to-day.

One thing was clear to them: just as the American patriots in 1775 believed that a new age had dawned for which all their previous history had been preparing them, so the first Christians were convinced that what they had witnessed—the life, Passion and Resurrection of Jesus—was the centre of all history. A new age had dawned for which all past history was the preparation. The Day of the Lord, to which the Old Testament prophets had looked forward, had truly broken. 'This is that which hath been spoken by the prophet' (Acts 2 : 16). 'The things which God foreshewed by the mouth of all the prophets . . . he thus fulfilled' (Acts 3 : 18). 'All the prophets from Samuel and them that followed after . . . they also told of these days' (Acts 3 : 24). 'The promise made unto the fathers . . . God hath fulfilled the same unto our children in that he raised up Jesus' (Acts 13 : 32–3). In St. Mark's Gospel, which is generally thought to be the earliest in time of the four, the first word in the mouth of our Lord is 'The time is fulfilled, and the kingdom of God is at hand: repent ye, and believe in the Gospel' (1 : 15). As the 'manifest destiny' of 1775 proclaimed that the American patriots were the true heirs of the old colonial system, so the witness of the Scriptures at the beginning of the Christian era proclaimed that Christ had fulfilled the teaching of the Old Testament writers and prophets and that in his followers the promises made to the ancient people of God would be fulfilled. 'In thee shall all the families of the earth be blessed (Gen. 12 : 3) was the oath which God had sworn to Abraham and in Christ it had its fulfilment (Luke 1 : 73–4).

The first Christians as we find them described in the early chapters of the Acts of the Apostles seem to have been little distinguished outwardly from their Jewish neighbours. They were all Jews by race and continued in their outward practice to adhere to Jewish religious ways: the practice of circumcision was continued, the Sabbath was observed, the services in temple and synagogue were attended regularly and the Jewish law on such matters as clean and unclean food was kept. To this practice they added the observance of Sunday as the Lord's Day, a weekly commemoration of the Resurrection: and this was marked by common participation in the Eucharist—'the breaking of bread'—in obedience to the Lord's command. (It is possible to interpret some passages in the sense that the Eucharist was celebrated daily, but scholars are not all agreed upon this point.) In theory what marked them off from their Jewish brethren was the belief that it was no longer a question of looking forward to the fulfilment of the promises of Scripture because these promises had already been fulfilled. All that remained to look for was the Second Coming of the Lord in glory to judge the living and the dead, to wind up the earthly economy of things and to establish his eternal kingdom openly with glory. This event the first Christians expected to take place comparatively soon, within the lifetime of most of those who had been the witnesses of Christ's Passion and Resurrection. In the later documents of the New Testament we notice how the Christians had to readjust their outlook on this point as it became clear that their expectation of Christ's early return had been based on a misunderstanding of some of his sayings. They were a compact little body, outwardly not unlike other contemporary Jewish sects—Pharisees, Sadducees and Essenes—and in the expectation of the early return of Christ and the winding up of the earthly order of things they practised a common ownership of property (Acts 2 : 44–5 ; 4 : 32).

This little body was bound together by a common Rule of Faith : we are told (Acts 2 : 42) that 'they continued steadfastly in the apostles' teaching and fellowship, in the breaking of bread and the prayers.' They were an apostolic fellowship because the Apostles were the link which bound them together. The original Twelve, it is not difficult to see, fulfilled in the new Israel the part played by the Twelve Patriarchs in the older dispensation. After the defection of Judas care was taken to complete the Apostolic College by the choice of another witness to take his place (Acts 1 : 15–26). To the twelve had been given Christ's commission to teach all nations, baptizing them in the Name of the Father, Son and Holy Ghost (Matt. 28 : 19): to them Christ had said after his resurrection 'As the Father hath sent me, even so send I you' : to them he had said, 'Receive ye the Holy Ghost: whose soever sins ye forgive, they are forgiven unto them; whose soever sins ye retain, they are retained' (John 20 : 22–4). As the Church grew beyond the possibility of the immediate care and supervision of the Twelve it was they who commissioned others—Timothy, Titus and such-like—to take the oversight of the various local churches. As it became clear in the process of time that the Second Coming of our Lord was less likely to take place within the lifetime of the first generation of Christians than had at one time been expected, Apostolic authority for the care of the Church was conferred by the Twelve upon approved successors : and as the Church spread from its original homeland to Europe and the farther parts of the Roman Empire the Apostles and their successors in their various seats of authority were the links in the chain which bound the whole scattered Church together.

The Christians continued in the Apostles' doctrine. The fundamental article of their belief was, as we have seen, the fact that Christ was risen: and the chief function of the Apostles was to bear witness to this fact. It will be noted that when the question arose of filling the gap left by Judas the chief qualification required of candidates for the vacancy was that the chosen man must be one of them 'which have companied with us all the time that the Lord Jesus went in and went out among us, beginning from the baptism of John, unto the day that he was received up from us; of these must one become a witness with us of his resurrection' (Acts 1 : 21-2). As we have seen, the full implications of this great fact had yet to be thought out: the only Scriptures possessed by the infant Church were the Old Testament writings, and it was only in the long future that the Canon of the New Testament and the formalized Creeds as we know them to-day were settled. Conformity with the Apostolic *paradosis* or tradition was the hall-mark of Christian belief and practice: and important matters on which there was disagreement or misunderstanding were referred to the Apostolic College for their decision (Acts 15).

They continued in the breaking of bread and the prayers. In addition to the usual Liturgical practices of the Jews, the Christians were united by Apostolic worship. In obedience to Christ's command, as we have seen, the Holy Eucharist was observed as the Christians' characteristic act of worship—certainly on the Lord's Day in commemoration of the Resurrection, and probably at other times as well. So far as we are able to gather, this act of worship was normally presided over by an Apostle or by someone appointed by apostolic authority.

The Church soon had to face the usual problems of a growing body. From a small, rather intimate group, comparatively easy to manage, it began to develop. Even while its membership was largely confined to Jerusalem it became necessary for the Apostles to delegate some of their functions to specially appointed officers. These seven, St. Stephen and his companions, are traditionally

L

thought of as the first deacons—the ancestors of the third Order of the Ministry of our day (Acts 6). If this is so, it illustrates how the Church developed its various functions as need appeared. The actual occasion of the institution of the diaconate was the sort of situation which is familiar enough to any one with experience of the problems of parochial administration : a section of godly people begins to feel (and apparently in this instance not without a certain measure of justification) that with the growing claims upon the time of the clergy not enough attention is being paid to its particular interests, and begins to make difficulties. Something had to be done to meet the situation : and the Church was flexible enough (as it has not always been everywhere in its history) to rise to the occasion. It would appear from the Scripture narrative that the original function of the Seven was to look after what might be called pastoral administration, distribution of alms, care of the sick and so on, leaving the Apostles free to concentrate on their own more specialized work (Acts 6: 4). But it also seems (and this again is not a unique experience in Church history) that the Seven developed considerable gifts as teachers and evangelists out and beyond their primary duties. St. Stephen, in particular, was noted for this. Mainly as a result of his activities along this line the persecution to which the Church had hitherto been exposed only sporadically, was considerably stepped up in vigour and persistence. St. Stephen himself was the first of a long line of Christians to lay down his life for the faith : and the Church itself, from being a compact body in and around Jerusalem, became scattered about Judea and Samaria for security reasons, at the same time forming a kind of Christian underground movement wherever it went (Acts 8 : 1).

Two consequences followed from this event which were to be of great import for the future of the Church. In the first place the removal of its main sphere of activity from the closely Jewish environment of Jerusalem brought the Christians for the first time into direct contact with the Gentile world. In Acts 10 and 11 we read of the conversion of the centurion Cornelius and of the problems which this raised. It has to be remembered that the Church was born into what was spiritually rather a *fin-de-siècle* age. The traditional religions of Greece and Rome (as the late

G. K. Chesterton showed in his fine book *The Everlasting Man*), though officially recognized as the Imperial Cultus, had ceased to be taken seriously by thinking people. The rigid legal separation of Judaism had preserved it from the synthetic process which had whittled away the particular characteristics of most of the ancient cults: and with its lofty morality and austere monotheism it was proving an attractive force to many earnest people who were dissatisfied with things as they were. In most of the larger cities of the Mediterranean seaboard there were synagogues to which local 'seekers' looked for some spiritual hope. In its own limited way Jewry had become a light to lighten the Gentiles. But over against this Judaism was a largely ossified system: at its heart and centre the leaders were concerned more with the political hope of the revival of the Davidic monarchy with Jewry triumphant over a prostrate Gentile world than with anything which could be called evangelism: and its principal teachers were mainly devoted to the giving of detailed commentaries on the *minutiae* of the Mosaic law. A limited number of Gentiles, after a period of instruction, accepted the rite of circumcision and became known as 'Israelites in all things,' but they were always a small minority and contemporary Judaism could not by any means be called a missionary faith. A strong prejudice against Gentiles—not unlike the colour-prejudice to be found among some Europeans in South Africa and the Southern States of America in our own day—was characteristic of the ordinary Jewish people, and it seems clear that the first Christians shared this to the full. St. Peter, in dealing with Cornelius, seems to have treated the case on its own merits and, after a certain preliminary hesitation, baptized him without going further into the principle involved. In any event Cornelius is described (Acts 10 : 2) as 'one that feared God': and the phrase 'God-fearer' had a technical application to those Gentiles who had embraced a considerable amount of Jewish belief and practice without having attained the status of 'Israelites in all things.' St. Peter was able to persuade the Apostolic College to ratify his action in this case, though their assent, too, appears to have been given without any great consideration of principle as far as we can judge from the scriptural record.

The second consequence of the martyrdom of St. Stephen—

and one which, though it manifested itself later in time, was of equal if not of more importance for the Church—was the conversion of Saul, later to be known as St. Paul. It would be hard to over-estimate the importance of this event for the developing life and work of the Church. St. Paul, a Pharisee and a university graduate, with the prestige and cosmopolitan outlook belonging to his status as a Roman citizen, brought a new element of life to the Church. The original apostolic band had been a group of country folk and small traders, of little education beyond that of the ordinary Palestinian Jews, and with a full share of the prejudices which attached to this class of person. St. Paul had, so far as we can learn, never known Christ in the flesh: and for a period which is not easy to define he had devoted most of his considerable energy and influence to the rooting out of this new sect by every means at his command. We first hear of him (Acts 7 : 58) as looking after the outer garments of those who had laid them aside while occupied in stoning St. Stephen to death. Though he continued for a period not clearly specified after this event to persecute the Church, it is difficult not to believe that the martyrdom of St. Stephen was the first real jolt which started him rethinking his position. A vision of the Risen Christ on the Damascus Road (Acts 9) was the turning point for him: he accepted baptism and placed himself at the disposal of the Apostolic College. From this time onward the mental and physical vigour which he had hitherto devoted to the persecution of the Church was dedicated to the service of Christ. It was no easy decision for him to make : it meant the renunciation of a brilliant career in the service of his church and nation and uniting himself with those who were regarded as heretics by that church and as traitors by that nation.

St. Paul, as a non-Palestinian Jew from Tarsus, quickly saw that in the question of the status of the Gentile converts a matter of deep principle was involved. After his introduction to the Apostolic College he had been sent by them, not unnaturally, to proclaim the faith to his own folk in his native city. In that cosmopolitan environment, far away from Jerusalem and the temple and the hierarchy, the question of the Gentiles rapidly became acute. Were they, as a preliminary condition to Baptism, to undertake the whole responsibility of observing the Jewish law? To answer no was to face a head-on collision with the whole inherited prejudice of the Jewish Christians: but to answer yes, as St. Paul saw, was to make the Christian Church nothing more than another Jewish sect like the Pharisees or the Sadducees or the Essenes. Looking back after the event it is impossible not to conclude that had it not been, under God, for the brave stand made by St. Paul, the Christian Church must have gone down with the fall of the Jewish Church-State in A.D. 70 and would not have been heard of again.

The controversy grew hot, but at last a decision was made by the Apostolic College at Jerusalem which in effect bound the Gentile converts to the moral law of Jewry, but left them free in regard to the ceremonial and ritual law (Acts 15).

It was long, however, before this decision was accepted by the Church as a whole. It seemed to contravene the whole traditional belief in God's promises to his children : a great part of St. Paul's writings—notably the Epistles to the Romans and the Galatians —is devoted to trying to impress upon his readers the vital importance of the principle at stake. The observance of the Jewish law, with the glosses and comments of the doctors, had long been an almost intolerable burden, as no one knew better than St. Paul himself : and to impose this upon the Gentile converts seemed to him not only likely to hamper and cripple the developing life of the Church, but, more important than that, to deny the very gift of freedom which Christ had come to bring. The Gentiles had had their sacrifices, their priests, their prophets and philosophers, their virtuous men and women, and all these were for them what the law had been for the Jews—a preparing for the coming of the Lord (Rom. 2 : 14–15 and cp. Heb. 1 : 1). What Christ had accomplished was the last of the many siftings to which the ancient people of God had been subject since Abraham was separated from Lot, Isaac from Ishmael and Jacob from Esau. The Jews who had rejected Christ had rejected the promises of God and with that had rejected their status as the People of God : the true Israel consists of those—Jews and Gentiles alike—who have accepted Christ in baptism (Rom. 9 : 6–12). As the law had been for the Jews a tutor to lead them to Christ (Gal. 3 : 24) so in dim types and shadows had the priests and teachers and philosophers of the Gentiles been to them. Christ had healed the division between Jew and Gentile (Eph. 2 : 14) and made of both one people of God in whom the promises made to Abraham had their fulfilment. This is the charter of freedom of the Catholic Church in which fellowship in Christ is the decisive factor and in which distinctions of colour and nationality have no place. Justification by faith in Christ, sealed by baptism, was the underlying principle upon which the People of God was to be built up. It is in the teaching of St. Paul that this doctrine is first clearly discerned. The history of revelation, as it has been succinctly put, is 'one continuous process from the Call of Abraham down to the last Lambeth Conference.'

But this is not the only theological debt which the Church owes to St. Paul. For many generations Jewish teachers had felt dissatisfied with a conception of salvation which was mainly concerned with obedience to an external law with its accompanying sanctions. As a permanent picture of man's relations with God it seemed somehow lacking in completeness. 'Behold, thou desirest truth in the inward parts' the Psalmist (51 : 6) had written wistfully. Jeremiah (31 : 33–4) had looked forward to a time when God would write his law in the heart and conscience of his people—when their response to God would be a co-operating obedience freely given and not exacted by external sanctions : Ezekiel (11 : 19–20; 36 : 26–7) looks forward to a similar state of affairs. St. Paul links the event of Pentecost, when the Holy Spirit, which is the very Life of God, came to indwell the infant Church, with the fulfilment of these prophecies. He was, we may confidently assume, not unmindful of the fact that the first word spoken to him by the Risen Lord was 'Why persecutest thou me?'—not, as we might naturally have expected, 'Why persecutest thou my people?' His acute mind drew all these various pointers together and he presents us with a picture of the Church as the outward manifestation of the Life of God Himself —the very Body of Christ. The faithful are by baptism infused with the Risen Life of Christ and ever nourished through the sacramental system of the Church with fresh inpourings of this grace (1 Cor. 6 : 19). Hence schism becomes a very serious sin (1 Cor. 1 : 13) for it is a rending of the Body of which Christ is the Head (Col. 1 : 18) and of which we are the limbs or members (1 Cor. 12 : 12–27). The Church according to St. Paul is not a group of like-minded people associating themselves together voluntarily in order to propagate certain principle and opinions like a political club or a Trade Union, but something which springs alive from the very heart of God himself, instinct with his Risen and Victorious Life. To be a Christian and to be a member of the Church are, according to the New Testament, synonymous things. A Christian who is not a member of the Church is a phenomenon not to be found in its pages.

Two observations may perhaps be made in closing this discussion. The first is that the New Testament knows nothing of the word 'Churches' as it is often used to-day. When e.g. St. Paul is spoken of as 'Strengthening the Churches' the word refers to the groups of members of the one Church scattered about in different parts of the world, such as the Church of Jerusalem, the Church of Rome, the Church of Corinth, the Church of Antioch etc. The use of the word to describe separate groups of Christians in mutual disagreement on many of their fundamental teachings and often working in competition with or opposition to each other is a concept unknown to Scripture and is indeed alien to the whole doctrine of the Body of Christ as revealed therein.

Secondly, in the early years of the present century there was an influential school of theologians, mainly deriving their inspiration from Professor Harnack and other German teachers, who held that St. Paul had revolutionized—even perverted—Christian teaching by imposing upon an original simple Gospel of ethical perfection taught by Jesus in Galilee a whole apparatus of sacramental practice which he had borrowed (apparently without acknowledgment) from the Mystery Religions current in the Roman Empire. These cults were generally centred round some semi-mythical figure such as Osiris, Mithras or Attys and were characterized by initiatory and sacramental rites which had certain external points of affinity to Christian sacramental practice: they claimed to offer to their initiates the gift of eternal life (*Renatus in aeternum* is the phrase used in some of their inscriptions to describe their initiates) and enjoyed a certain ephemeral popularity in pious circles in the generally rather decadent religious atmosphere of the Augustan Empire when, as we have seen, the old religions of Greece and Rome had ceased to offer any spiritual appeal. It was contended by the teachers of this school that St. Paul, with a view to extending the popularity of the Christian Faith in Gentile circles and at the same time to strengthen his own theological and ecclesiastical authority in the face of the traditionalist Jewish Christians in Palestine (who, as we have already observed, were for long greatly scandalized by St. Paul's liberal attitude to the Gentile converts), had adapted these sacramental practices with the doctrine of a supernatural Church and imposed them upon the original simple ethical gospel of Jesus. This view, though it has left its mark in some circles, has largely been discarded by scholars in recent years. There is no substantial evidence in the Bible for any great controversy such as so revolutionary a proceeding must inevitably have aroused. That St. Paul had to fight for the Catholic nature of the Church against those who wished to maintain it as little more than a Jewish sect and that he did not have an easy victory—of this, as we have seen, there is plenty of evidence. And it is not to be considered that such a much more radical alteration of the Christian system could have been carried through without leaving its mark on the Scripture record. Moreover, despite certain superficial resemblances between the practice of some of the Mystery Cults and the Christian Sacramental system, there is one fundamental difference: the Mystery Religions traced their origins to semi-mythical heroes who lived, if they lived at all, in the dim mists of pre-history. Christianity is based on certain quite definite events concerning a definitely historical person which took place in a perfectly definite place at a perfectly definite time—in the fifteenth year of Tiberius Caesar, Pontius Pilate being Governor of Judea (Luke 3 : 1). Of those with whom St. Paul had to deal many had known Christ intimately in the days of his flesh and were well acquainted with his teaching and were in a position to react strongly against any such perversion of the primitive Christian doctrine as is here suggested. *Crucifixus etiam pro nobis sub Pontio Pilato* is, in this connection, a key phrase of the Creed.

So we leave the Apostolic Church: like the American volunteers on Lexington Green they are still a small body, and doubtless their eyes were no more open to the illimitable future of the People of God than were the eyes of the 'embattled farmers' to the great destiny of the American nation of which their action had been the necessary prelude. But, like them, it is a body conscious that it is a new nation, brought to birth through the tremendous fact of the Incarnation, Passion and Resurrection of our Lord; and certain that nothing can ever be quite the same again because in these same stupendous events questing humanity has been brought to the city which has foundations, whose builder and maker is God. They were opposed by the fanatical hatred of the church and nation from which they were derived and by the executive and political power of the greatest Empire which the world up to that time had ever known. The august history of the Church of God in face of these facts, despite the frequent failure and worse of many of its members, is the sufficient testimony of how well their hope was founded.

CHAPTER II

FR. MARK TWEEDY, C.R.

THE WORSHIP OF THE BODY

Looking hither and thither, huddled into the shadow of the wall, he moved briskly and stealthily along, every moment narrowing the fear-filled gap between his home and that of Publius. Would he make it to-day? he wondered; and would he ever return home? One could never be sure. . . . Since last Sunday Flavia had disappeared: they must have taken her up soon after she had left the house of Publius, red-handed, actually carrying her little box enclosing the *Dominicum*. . . .

To contemporary Christian minds' eyes the story of which this is an imaginary type is almost too familiar—the reconstruction of the atmosphere of the Church's worship in the days of persecution. We sometimes forget that our grandparents, and even many of our parents, never spent a moment in such visions. In so far as they were not completely content with 'our incomparable liturgy,' as they loved to call the Book of Common Prayer, they tended to hark back in imagination to a considerably idealized picture of an English yokel fingering his beads (agreed, he should rather have been attending to the service, but they could not get round that on the evidence) in a riotously coloured, dimly lit medieval gothic building wreathed in clouds of incense.

No two pictures could be more different. An outside observer would hardly recognize any similarities at all between the two celebrations of the one service.

To begin with, the very idea of incense in the days of the Roman persecution would have been unthinkable. Was it not a fearful symbol of that Power which sat in Satan's seat demanding its quota of nominal worship in front of Caesar's image? The offering of a few grains of incense in itself meant nothing, and by most citizens was intended to mean nothing: the Romans of the Empire were far too cynical and blasé to worship anything. Yet for the followers of Christ it was the very razor-edge. Loyal to the state they would be if they could, following the great apostle's instructions; but even the most conventional worship must be reserved for God alone. Better risk the torments of the Colosseum than the torment of the loss of life eternal.

So their worship was characterized by a sense of *urgency* and a sense of *immediacy*.

To begin with, no one knew for certain whether he would get home again after the service. But there was more to it than that. The worshippers might indeed be interrupted by the arrival of the police, and therefore no one in his senses would be likely to attend unless he believed that the practice of Christ's religion was a matter of the most urgent importance: but in the view of the earliest Christians something more immediate even than the arrival of the police might happen. At any moment, so they were taught, the trumpet might sound, and suddenly in the twinkling of an eye they would all be changed (cf. 1 Cor. 15 : 52). As this would most probably happen in the middle of the night—and what night more likely than that leading to a Lord's Day?—these first Christians from time to time kept most of Saturday night in vigil. If it did not this time culminate in the manifested second coming of their Lord, then with breaking of day they would once more renew his first coming and his making himself known to them in the breaking of bread.

It is hardly an exaggeration to say that the whole pattern of primitive Christian worship was governed by an imminent expectation of either of two interruptions: the arrival of the police or the arrival of the Lord Jesus. There was no dallying. What had to be done was done without unnecessary fuss or ceremony. Bread and wine were brought up by the worshippers, the ordained leader (normally the Bishop) exchanged greetings with them and then broke into his great thanksgiving prayer, the bread was broken, and then bread and wine alike—now lifegiving 'Spirit'—were taken and received by every one present. That was all. They had no time for any lofty devotions as they were hustled out of the back door, carrying their little supply of the holy Bread to sustain them each day through the week till they met again in the Body.

This sense of immediate urgency was very soon lost. It became apparent that the first Christians had misunderstood the Lord's words about his coming again, which was not necessarily to be looked for in the immediate future. And some 250 years later they knew the police would not be coming either. For great Caesar himself had bowed the knee, the empire was supposedly converted, and the phenomenon of the Christian state was born into uneasy existence. It was very natural that the Church's worship, which before had been predominantly concerned with the breaking into time of eternity (in the Person of the Eternal), now becomes far more engrossed with time itself. Christianity henceforth will be above all an historical rather than an eschatological religion. So the Kalendar is born. Instead of every Eucharist being a celebration of the entire mystery of redemption, the events of the Lord's earthly life are commemorated one by one. With personal danger removed, the ceremonial becomes more leisurely, more elaborate. No longer is it necessary to worship furtively in someone's private house. Church buildings make their appearance, and in doing so start that misapprehension of the primary meaning of the word *Church* which has continued ever since.

With the eclipse of the western imperial power it is henceforth in the spiritual sphere that Rome exercises her authority and leadership. East and West fall gradually apart, but not before the Church in the east has contributed a certain amount of enrichment together with a good deal of ceremonial dross to the western Eucharist. Next comes the golden age of Rome, in the years immediately following the great Pope Gregory, the same who dispatched his fellow-monk Augustine on the mission to England. Though by now the bare simplicity of the primitive order of service was in places overlaid by frills from the Orient, the structure of the rite was still clearly discernible. In obedience to the Lord's command, 'Do this,' something was clearly and evidently done by all his faithful people met together. But soon the vision fades; Rome is swallowed up in the age of darkness. Now, however, a new beacon shines forth in the north, with the coming of Charlemagne (800). But the semi-barbarians under Frankish rule would not be content with the sobriety of the Roman service books which their Christian monarchs had had copied for them; they demanded more colour, excitement, elaboration. As none was forthcoming from Rome, they set to work and made their own additions. A few more centuries, and these elaborate gallicanized forms of worship had found their way back across the Alps, and the whole of western Christendom (by now completely separated from the east) was worshipping with rites so splendid that our early Christians would have been hard put to it to recognize in them the simple actions they themselves had performed each Lord's Day. Soon came decay and decadence. The formal beauty and outward magnificence of the Mass if anything increased: but it was now only a spectacle for all except the clergy. No longer did the layfolk either give or receive, bring or take away bread and wine. True, the mystery still took place. Bread became the Body of the Lord, wine his Blood; but only for people to gaze at. The active participation of the members of the Body had been suppressed. Long centuries before, the old idea of urgent expectation, of every Eucharist as something outside time, an actual foretaste of the second coming of the Saviour had been irretrievably lost. Now not even the Church's march through time, through the seasons, meant much to the laity. So far as they followed it, it would be more by means of pageantry outside the Mass than by the words and ceremonies of the Mass itself, of which they could understand hardly anything.

So came the inevitable upheaval of the sixteenth century, which we call the Reformation. The Church in the West—for the East was unaffected, being still in complete separation—was rent asunder by schism and by heresy. These sad pages of history need not concern us now: enough to believe that our mother church, battered as she was from all sides, still managed to remain herself, the catholic Church in this land. Archbishop Cranmer of Canterbury did far better for her than he intended. Himself deeply under the influence of heretical beliefs from the continent about the nature of the Eucharist, he was cut off from this life before he had worked them out in full fruition. On balance we owe him thanks for bequeathing us English rites in matchless language, which served us well enough for nearly four hundred years. After all the jewel was found to be still there; it was only the setting which had suffered much damage. But the jewel, though unharmed, was so encrusted with extraneous matter that now a trained eye was needed to discern through the mass of protestant exhortation the essential elements of the Lord's own service. The backbone of the structure had been broken, deliberately.

A determined attempt had been made to replace the age-long Sacrifice of the Lord's Body and Blood by what someone unambiguously called 'the new service of bread and wine.' But the pendulum swung and swung again. Thanks humanly speaking to the Englishman's dislike of any extremes, orthodoxy was barely preserved; a thin golden line of high church divines handed down the torch. Practice was as it were put into cold storage for a century or two, while any sort of enthusiasm or even interest in worship was considered out of place. But the age of enlightenment was succeeded in Queen Victoria's reign by the age of romance. While the theologians of the Oxford Movement, partly inspired by the evangelical revival of a previous generation, reached back in history to translate the Fathers of the undivided Church into contemporary English idiom, so as to show the world that England's faith had never really changed, their successors the ritualists set their sights a little closer. Their right-minded aim was to clothe the bare bones of the reformed English Eucharist with enough of the traditional colour and symbolism to make really clear what it meant. The words they left alone: but now the worshippers would see a meaning of them portrayed which, they were instructed, was that of the 'ages of faith.'

But when were the ages of faith? Information about the conduct of the Eucharist in the age of the Fathers was generally lacking a century ago. What was by no means lacking were detailed descriptions of the ceremonial of the middle ages. Many copies were made and adapted. Strange things were seen in church at the turn of the century. But the ritualists were not all of one hue. As time went on, more and more of them revolted against what they dubbed the antiquarian outlook of the medievalists. Why seek the living among the dead? was their cry; and forthwith a large number of those who could afford it took ship for France, Italy, and Spain. They did not realize that the ceremonial of the Latin rite which they so eagerly imported to this country was living indeed but hardly lively. Ever since the tragedies of the sixteenth century Rome had continued rigid, embattled, reactionary. To the worshippers kneeling or standing packed in the nave, what went on at a continental altar was no more meaningful than a piece of English medieval magnificence witnessed from a comfortable box pew. To change from one to the other—even to remove the pew—did not greatly help. Since then most of us were born. In the course of this half-century there have been a good many things to engage our attention besides the niceties of religious ceremonial. Above all, for churchpeople, there has been the experience of returning to the primitive age not in luxurious thought but in agonizing fact. For the first time for sixteen hundred years it is not generally popular to go to church. It may cause derision. Only in the matter of active persecution is there a difference; in this country it has not so far been employed. But the folk of England as a whole, when it comes to counting heads at Christian worship, are just about as pagan as the folk of ancient Rome.

In these circumstances it need not be surprising that churchmen everywhere are tending more and more to revise their eucharistic ritual forms by reference to the considerable knowledge we now assume that we possess of the Church's worship in the earlier age of paganism. Can we do anything to revive that sense of immediate urgency which so characterized the early Eucharist? Before answering that question it may be well to make sure that we understand, so far as is humanly possible, what the Eucharist is, this great treasure bequeathed and entrusted by our Risen Lord to us his members.

What is it that we do when—as priests or laymen—we come to the altar of God? All Christian worship is summed up in this service, this meeting of the Church in the sense of the assembled people of God gathered under Christ their Head as members of his Body. What happens at it? Exactly what is going on? What do we mean by 'the Worship of the Body'?

At once we are brought up against the mysterious idea of *sacrifice*, which for weal or for woe has pervaded all Christian thinking about the Eucharist from the earliest days. The New Testament seems to make it clear that our Lord intended his followers to think of his death in sacrificial terms and that in fact they did so. (See Mark 10 : 45; 1 Cor. 5 : 7b; Heb. 9 : 26; 10 : 12.) Where churchmen have often differed is in the question how far and in what manner the Saviour intended to link his special actions at the Last Supper on Thursday with his sacrificial death on the Cross on Friday. Here we may at once claim official sanction for a positive view in the *Reply* sent by the English archbishops to Pope Leo XIII's condemnatory Bull on Anglican Orders in 1897. They stated unequivocally: 'We truly teach the doctrine of the Eucharistic Sacrifice . . .'

In what then does the sacrifice of the Eucharist consist?

It is by Christians universally believed, and in our service of Holy Communion is made abundantly clear, that our Lord Jesus Christ in dying on the Cross made of himself the one and only all-sufficient Sacrifice in expiation for the sin of the whole creation. In him God was reconciling the world to himself (cf. 2 Cor. 5 : 19). Here at last was the offering of a perfect human life to the glory of God. Once for all it was offered, once for all it was accepted. Christ the God-Man in taking our nature upon him became in a real sense the Head of the human race, and henceforth all who believe in him are incorporated into him, in other words become members (or limbs) of his Body, which we call the Church. It is by the sacrament or sign of Baptism that this incorporation takes place. From that moment the Christian man or woman is made a partaker, in a true and literal sense, in the perfect offering of Christ on earth; not as something in the past, for the sequel to the death on the cross was the empty tomb on Easter morning. The Resurrection and Ascension have made of Christ's offering an eternal fact, independent of the passage of time; being very God, it was not possible that he should be 'holden' of death (cf. Acts 2 : 24). This then is our faith: Christ 'when he had offered one sacrifice for sins for ever, sat down on the right hand of God. . . . For by one offering he hath perfected for ever them that are sanctified [i.e. baptized Christians]' (Heb. 10 : 12, 14).

But we his children do not have to rest content with a pious recollection of what our Redeemer once did for us. By Baptism we were made once for all members of Christ, partakers of his death and life. In the Eucharist again and again we may express our membership in the closest possible manner: by a partaking in very deed, by eating his flesh and drinking his blood (cf. John 6 : 53). No wonder the Jews and all manner of other people were and are scandalized. There is no escaping from this language: to explain that we eat and drink in a heavenly or spiritual manner does not really lessen the scandal for the unbeliever. And this eating and drinking is the culmination of what we call the Eucharistic Sacrifice.

If we speak of the Sacrifice on Calvary, our hearers will probably bring to mind a picture of the dying Christ. Yet sacrifice does not primarily signify death. By derivation the word means a making sacred or holy of something. The Eucharistic Sacrifice must be understood against the background of the Jewish sacrificial system; and for Jews the essence of sacrifice lay not in the slaughter of the victim but in the pouring out or offering of its blood, in which the life was said to reside. Sacrifice means the offering of life. The risen and ascended Christ ever lives in the glory of the Godhead as our high priest and perpetual intercessor. For he is both God and Man; as our Head he perpetually presents his Sacrifice for the whole of humanity before the throne of God, where 'he ever liveth to make intercession' for us (Heb. 7 : 25). Now as members of his Body we are admitted to a share in his heavenly high priesthood. The Church is a priestly body, whose members are joined with their Head in presenting his Sacrifice before the Father. Not of course that we can add anything to it or renew it in any manner. All we can do is to make thankful commemoration in the way Christ commanded, and unite ourselves with his perpetual intercession. What Christ commanded was that we his members should take bread and wine and do as he bid with them. So in a mysterious way the Sacrifice once offered on Calvary and eternally accepted in heaven may be re-presented on earth; not however in any sense repeated, for what the Church does in the Eucharist relates even more closely to what our Lord is now doing in heaven than to what he once did on earth. The Eucharist, though celebrated in time, is timeless, in the sense that in it eternity breaks into time. Heaven and earth meet in what we may now perhaps without fear of misunderstanding call the Sacrifice of the Mass.

The Mass or Eucharist is a sacrifice because our Lord has promised to be present there in response to the Church's prayers and offerings; present in his sacrificed glorified humanity, under the signs of bread and wine. This could never have been had he not provided for us a sign or sacrament. Calvary itself was not a sacrament. But the night before he suffered Jesus took bread and wine and made of them an efficacious sign, in other words a sacrament—something that does what it signifies. 'Do this in remembrance of me' may be fairly translated 'Do this for the recalling of me.' We recall not only his death but the whole process of his incarnation, passion, resurrection and ascension. What is made present on the altar is the Body and Blood of Jesus our Lord as our one true Sacrifice, not as it existed on earth but as it exists eternally in glory. The Church in the Eucharist makes Christ's Sacrifice her own. That is the only sacrifice God can accept from man. So sometimes we sing: 'Look, Father, look on *his* anointed face, and only look on us as found in *him*.' The Sacrifice is one, and it is Christ's. Nevertheless, if our representation of it is to have any reality, if we are indeed to make Christ's Sacrifice our own, there must first of all be some offering of what we may call our own material possessions. Certainly we have nothing of our own worthy to offer, and indeed nothing which we can truly call our own at all, for 'all things come of thee, and of thine own have we given thee' (1 Chron. 29 : 14). We bring to the altar our bread and wine, as the first-fruits of God's creation. But note that it is bread and wine, not wheat and grapes, which are brought; the material of the Church's Sacrifice may equally be called the first-fruits of man's labour on God's created gifts. Then we ask that our offering of bread and wine, representing ourselves, should be caught up into Christ's Sacrifice, now representing, nay becoming in very fact his Body and Blood, his life once offered and for ever given for us. We do what he commanded, with ritual words and gestures. The rest depends on God. We know that his promises never fail. Our offering is transformed into Christ's, and we become one with the Church on earth and in heaven, members of the Body united with their Head in presenting to the Father that only offering perfect in his eyes, the one true pure immortal Sacrifice.

Too often in the past the idea of sacrifice in connection with the central service of the Church's worship has been narrowed down into a wrong emphasis. It has consequently been misunderstood, misinterpreted, and still further misunderstood. By many it has been construed in such a way as to suggest that the mass-sacrifice is a rite performed by a priest in virtue of his ordained powers, which the layfolk passively attend, and after which they may perhaps receive holy communion. It was against this medieval aberration that our sixteenth-century reformers protested so vigorously. As always in such cases the pendulum swung too freely. In the gathering up of the tares some of the wheat was rooted up also. Thenceforth it was difficult to find the true doctrine of the eucharistic sacrifice clearly expressed in our English Communion service. Nowadays we are coming to understand it more clearly. There is little danger of a relapse into unbalanced notions, so long as we always keep in mind that our Eucharist is the holy Sacrifice of Christ *in his Church*. We may in fact describe it as the Sacrifice of the Church. 'This is the Christian sacrifice,' wrote St. Augustine long ago in the days before the doctrine had got out of focus: 'the many become one body in Christ. And it is this that the Church celebrates by means of the sacrament of the altar, where it is shown that in what she offers she herself is offered.'

One of the great objectives of the compilers of our English services was to ensure that Christian forms of worship should be common to priest and people; worship should be seen to be a common activity. Hence the original English title of our service book, *The book of the common prayer*. In our prayer of thanksgiving, towards the end of the Communion service, we give thanks to God the Father because 'we are very members incorporate in the mystical body of thy Son, which is the blessed company of all faithful people.' There is much need to re-emphasize this vital element in our eucharistic worship, a need which will have sooner or later to be met by some revision in the form and order of the whole rite. For one thing, in spite of the reformers' avowed intention, so moulded were they by their late medieval background that they made hardly any effort in practice to bring out the common or corporate idea of worship. This prayer for instance, from which a quotation has just been made, was assigned to the priest alone, the people's part being confined to an Amen at the end. But the meaning of the prayer is that all those who have just received communion are giving thanks for their fellowship in Christ, which is the same thing as their fellowship in the Church. They are, by virtue of being communicants in the Body and Blood of the Lord Jesus which they have received, themselves actual members of his Body, together with all other faithful Christians. From being a number of individuals, these men and women have become one corporate body, and that in a much closer sense than as fellow-members of a club or society. As St. Augustine puts it, when we communicate in the holy mysteries *we become what we receive;* by receiving Christ's Body from above we become his Body on earth. An immediate corollary of this statement is that it is sheer nonsense to talk of 'the Church' when what we mean is the ministerial members of it. 'Why doesn't the Church do something about it?' is a well-known gambit among the uninstructed. But the Church includes each and every one of its members, all alike responsible for its teaching and practice, each according to his own order. 'Ye are the body of Christ, and severally members thereof' (1 Cor. 12 : 27). The word 'Church' properly used by Christians does not mean its leaders, still less one of its buildings : it means the whole body of Christ's members, and never more so than when these are gathered together in the weekly or daily assembly for the Eucharist. They are gathered in different, separate buildings, of course. But they are all one in Christ. And being one in Christ they are every one members one of another (cf. Eph. 4 : 25). It is a high doctrine, and one which all are called to carry out in practice unceasingly, as well outside as inside the church building. It is for all this that we give thanks after our communion, which is the seal and completion of the Church's Sacrifice.

But thanksgiving is by no means confined to the end of the service. Indeed it is such a central feature of the whole that it has actually given its name to the rite : Holy Eucharist means Holy Thanksgiving. Unfortunately hardly any rite in use to-day brings out this emphasis, chiefly because of a wrong idea of the meaning of sacrifice or else none at all. Sacrifice is offering, and it is thanksgiving which most naturally leads to offering, even in everyday life; when we are grateful to someone, we may well offer him a present to express our gratitude in concrete form.

Nowadays we call those who come to the altar the 'communicants.' That may sound the obviously natural name for them. But it was not always so. In the first Christian centuries they were known as the 'offerers.' Those who had sinned deeply were not said to be 'excommunicated' : they were 'forbidden to offer.' This difference in terminology is symptomatic of a real and considerable difference of emphasis. If on a Sunday morning we think principally in terms of going to church to make our communion we are in fact concentrating on something we are about to receive. If however we call ourselves offerers, then it is clear that we have some idea of *giving* as the primary motive for churchgoing. And so indeed it ought to be. Of course we shall receive too, as our Lord has promised it: but it would be ungrateful, to say the least, if after all we have already received in our lives, both individual and corporate, we came to the 'holy Thanksgiving' simply with the idea of receiving more. No, we come to say the best 'thank you' that we can, and that implies that we are in a giving mood. We bring what we can, and in virtue of our membership of Christ's Body what we have brought becomes his offering, which is the same as to say the Church's offering or sacrifice.

We, the Church, Christ's members, offer our gifts (which are his) to the Father by giving of thanks. It is much to be hoped that one day the prayers of our rite will be made to express this central theme of thanksgiving a great deal more clearly. What was once a unity has been separated out far too much into component parts, which ought not to be thought of in isolation. We talk of offertory prayers, and then a consecration prayer, and communion prayers, and afterwards prayers of thanksgiving. In the earliest days there was only one prayer in the service and that was the great *Thanksgiving* or eucharistic prayer. For some time indeed it was known as *the* Prayer. In it was joined together all that we mean by both offertory and consecration as well as thanksgiving. The prayer in its earliest developed form seems to have been a Thanksgiving and no more, very possibly (though this is conjectural) concluded by the recital of the hymn of praise which we call the *Sanctus*. There was no idea of a particular moment of 'consecration.' Not that it would have occurred to any believer to doubt the reality of Christ's objective presence: but the presence was primarily 'real' in the body of worshippers who were about to receive the sacramental body of their Lord under the forms of bread and wine. It is hard to grasp the full force of this truth to-day, when for centuries Christians have been separating in their minds Christ the Head from his Body the Church. St. Augustine's 'You are what you receive' needs a deal of explaining in these days. Similarly the idea of the offertory has been pushed back in such a way that we now customarily associate it with the setting aside of the elements or 'oblations'—or even merely of the alms—before the central action begins. It is true that there must be a bringing up of our material gifts—'All that we have we offer'—but the real offering to God cannot take place unless there is something worthy to offer, and that there cannot be till something has been *done* with the gifts. What is done is that which our Lord commanded us to do 'in remembrance of me.' What happens then, and exactly how it happens is a mystery beyond human telling. We only know that now there is something worthy of God's acceptance; supremely on the altar, but, because of our vital association with it, in our persons too. 'Here we offer unto thee, O Lord, ourselves ... to be a ... lively sacrifice unto thee.' *In what she offers she herself is offered:* this is the Christian sacrifice, as St. Augustine said. No human being can offer anything acceptable to God. But in the Eucharist, the holy Thanksgiving, it is the whole Christ who is both offering and being offered, Christ the Head in the Church his Body is re-presenting on earth, as he ordained on the night before he suffered, the Sacrifice which is ever being pleaded in the heavenly sanctuary, where our King is seated 'on the right hand of the Majesty on high' (Heb. 1 : 3).

The traditional picture in Christian devotion of the altar in heaven, on which the eternal Sacrifice of the Lamb is being presented contemporaneously with the earthly Church's eucharistic offerings, belongs necessarily to the realm of imagery. There is of course no material altar in heaven, still less could Christ be thought of as located in front of it. But it is a picture which helps to bring home an important truth about the Mass, namely that it is a meeting-point of heaven and earth. In a true sense indeed there is some meeting of the two every time a single individual prayer is lifted up to God. But in the general assembly of the Church before the eucharistic altar the meeting is of an altogether more definite kind than that between the soul and her Lord in prayer. In the Eucharist the particular present moment of time is caught up into the general timelessness of eternity. Or, as it was expressed above, we may say that eternity breaks into time. Time and eternity meet in a real but incomprehensible manner. The significance of this meeting is that it guarantees the efficacy of our Eucharists—however barely celebrated, poorly attended, or half-heartedly performed. For eternity is never-varying. All that takes place on earth is subject to change and oscillation. The Church's Eucharist takes place on earth, but not on earth alone; more accurately, what happens at the Eucharist has an eternal, timeless reference. The action is not confined within the walls of the church-building nor restricted to the human participants. It is the action of the whole Christ offering himself and all his members in a relationship which, but for sin, can never be broken in time or eternity. This is the heart of the Christian mystery.

In every Mass the Church proclaims the mystery whereby all Christians, redeemed on Calvary, themselves die in order to live again. It cannot be otherwise, if we have rightly understood the doctrine of the Eucharistic Sacrifice. In this mystery we re-enact the concrete history of our redemption. 'What he never can repeat he shows forth day by day.' And it is all shown forth at once. The mystery is not a mere recollection of the past. Nor even is it a bringing into some sort of present existence each in turn of the events of our Saviour's life on earth, culminating in his death and resurrection. It is more even than that. The mystery is one. In it we partake in the one and complete action accomplished once for all by Jesus Christ on earth, and made really present by our participation in his risen life, by our membership of his Body. Every Eucharist proclaims the whole mystery: the mystery of time and eternity, of the eternal kingdom to which the Church is carrying each one of her children by means of the cross—dying to live for evermore.

How shall we realize all this in practice?

It is not likely that the average churchgoer is often occupied with thoughts such as have been outlined above. Neither is it necessary that he should be. We do not go to church to spend the time thinking out theological profundities; nor yet with the object of experiencing devotional feelings arising from such thoughts. But unless we have learnt to understand aright as much as we can of the meaning of the Christian Mystery we shall not be able to take our proper part in it. *Lex orandi, lex credendi.* It never matters what we are feeling in church, and it does not often greatly matter what we are thinking. But we must know as far as possible what we are *doing*; and that entails care beforehand to learn and assimilate the mind of the Church about what is being done. Looking at it in another way, it is only when both the clergy and the mass of the 'faithful,' as the layfolk of Christ's body in church are often called, have more fully plumbed the depths of meaning in the Eucharist—some of it long neglected or overlaid with secondary interpretations—that it will be possible for our form of service to be revised so as to express in clearer fashion what is happening at the altar and around it. First try to understand, then worship according to the ability which God may give; and right worship itself will beget deeper understanding, which in its turn should make our worship better. 'I will pray with the spirit, and I will pray with the understanding also' (1 Cor. 14: 15).

We can never put the clock back. No doubt it is true that forms of worship in the early Church were simpler, more direct and straightforward than they became later on. As time went by, so the Eucharist, and other services too, became encumbered with a number of devotional accretions of unequal merit. These too often had the effect of clouding the main outline of the action, so that in the end people could not see the wood for the trees. That is certainly the case in our English service, and to make matters worse some of the trees are not at all beautiful, being covered with somewhat rank foliage. But our service is what history has made it; and history cannot be undone. Even if it were desirable, a simple return to the primitive is impracticable. Nevertheless something must be done to counteract divergent tendencies, both before the Reformation and still more since. Our Holy Communion service in the Book of Common Prayer does not at all clearly or adequately express the doctrine of the Eucharistic Sacrifice; and largely because of deliberate dislocation in the sixteenth century it is difficult to discover any clear pattern in the rite. Sooner or later there must be some revision: our *lex credendi* must shine out more clearly in our *lex orandi*. And the opportunity is upon us in these days of universal questioning by believers and of rejection by the great and scarcely lessening mass of unbelievers.

So we return to our earlier question. Granted that conditions in this century are more like those of the early ages of Christianity than ever before—the only difference being that in primitive Christian days civilization was professedly as well as actually pagan—is it not desirable that we should try to recover something of that sense of immediate urgency which characterized the early Eucharist? And if so, how can it be done? Our concern here is not with the important question of new evangelistic techniques, but with the actual content of the service itself.

We could not, if we would, re-establish the eschatological atmosphere of the earliest days of our faith. No doubt we ought to have a more lively expectation than have most of us of the second coming of our Lord. But in the Eucharist history has by now too firmly ousted eschatology. We shall not be sincere if we pretend that every time we go to Mass we are fully prepared for the last trump to interrupt the Church's offering. There is, however, something we can learn from those far off days. For the early Christians the Eucharist embraced the whole of life. 'We cannot get on without the *Dominicum*'—the Lord's Body and Blood—was the cry of the early martyrs. Since then things have changed: too many who profess themselves Christians contrive to get along without the Sacrament at all. At the beginning of this century churchgoing was thought of as an occupation for Sundays. As for eucharistic worship, the generality of folk would not even have known what was meant by it; the Communion service, when attended, was a strictly individual affair, each communicant isolating himself, in thought if not in person, as far apart as possible from his fellow-members of the Body. To all intents and purposes the service consisted simply of a preparatory monologue by the minister, followed by the reception of communion by each individual present. The idea that here was the very heart and centre of all life must have been inconceivable to most people. Any idea of urgency simply was not there.

During this century churchmen throughout the world, and not least in our own country, have been learning a great deal more than their forebears ever understood about the meaning of the Mass and its immediate relation to every moment of our lives. What was once regarded by so many as an optional extra service early in the morning is now more and more taking that place in the centre of worship and life which by right belongs to it.

Increasingly people are being taught truly to bring their whole lives to the altar week by week, as responsible members of the Body of Christ, whose sins and shortcomings have injured their neighbours as well as themselves; for whom life on earth is purposeless except it be wholly offered in union with the Sacrifice of Christ the Head of the Body. In many churches the ceremonial, simple or elaborate as the case may be, has been adapted to make all this clearer to the participants. Before long there must be some adaptation of the ritual too—the actual wording of the eucharistic rite.

The first necessity will be to reintroduce the genuinely 'eucharistic' note into what is commonly called the prayer of consecration. Here as everywhere the main object will be not simply to restore some text from bygone days, but rather to make sure that the central prayer really does give expression to all that we mean by this service. The Eucharist, by virtue of its representation of the Sacrifice of Christ in his Church, is an offering of praise and thanksgiving for the whole of life.

At present there is hardly any thanksgiving element in the central part of our service, except it be one of the comparatively few days when a proper preface is ordered. Then the brief recital before the Father of some part of the marvellous tale of the Son's ministry does take a form similar to the old 'thanksgiving series' which seems to have made up the bulk of the eucharistic prayer long ago. What is wanted is some extension of this element. A simple suggestion has been the joining together of the themes of all the proper prefaces for the principal feasts of our Lord in such a way as to make one continuous recitation in thanksgiving form: 'We give thanks to thee, almighty Father . . . who didst send thy Son, who . . ., who . . .'; each of the relative clauses designating in turn the mysteries of Christ incarnate crucified, risen, ascended.

But though these clauses will be the kernel of the prayer, there is something else which must come before and something after.

We must first give thanks for the creation of the worlds and all that is in them, especially for rational mankind, the highest creature of all that God made and saw to be 'very good.' Our thanksgiving for creation is chiefly related to 'the Father almighty, Maker of heaven and earth.'

Then comes the centre of the prayer, as described above, relating the mighty acts of the Son (through whom all things were made) in redeeming the human race which had fallen away from God's high estate. And in the 'centre of the centre' is naturally placed what has sometimes been called the pivot of the whole prayer, the narrative of our Lord's institution of the Sacrament, the title-deeds of the whole service. So then, making remembrance of what he has done, we continue our thanksgiving by offering the Bread and the Cup, whose 'consecration' may be said to be completed by our offering, remembering that 'we' are the whole Body united with Christ our Head. At last man has a gift worthy of God's acceptance. And miraculously, by the very same means God will presently give himself to man.

Thirdly we make thanksgiving for 'the holy Spirit in the holy Church,' as they used to say long ago. Of course we cannot isolate the Spirit, for he is the Spirit of Jesus, one with the Father and the Son. Above all he informs the Church of Christ whose members we are. He inspires every baptized confirmed Christian. In particular his gifts have been poured upon the ordained members of the Church. So here we make our priestly thankoffering, each after his own order.

All of life is thus brought into the orbit of the Mass. Created by the Father, redeemed by the Son, sanctified in the Spirit, man the worshipper is about to partake of the life of that Lord in union with whom, Body with Head, he has been worshipping.

Last comes the great doxology binding all together. *Through Jesus Christ our Lord, through whom and with whom and in whom, in the unity of the holy Spirit in the holy Church, all honour glory dominion and majesty, O Father almighty, is thine for evermore, throughout all ages, world without end. Amen.*

Alternatively, we might restore the recital of the *Sanctus* hymn to its possibly earliest regular position at this point. If not here, a place will have to be found for it earlier on.

Only two essential items need to be interspersed between the great eucharistic prayer and the holy communion which is the climax of everything. The first is known as the Fraction. The sacred ministers solemnly break the Bread, in imitation of our Lord's action in the upper room before giving it to his own. And then may best come the recital by all together of the Lord's

Prayer, formerly the one and only prayer of preparation for reception. *Give us this day our daily bread. . . . As we forgive them that trespass against us.* ('Be in charity with all men,' as the Catechism directs.) By some indeed the present English position of the Lord's Prayer straight after communion is much beloved : but the earlier tradition is all the other way, and in this case there seems insufficient reason to set it aside.

There is the kernel of the rite. The actual wording of such paragraphs as have been suggested may not have the immediate effect of quickening our pulses, of producing a more 'primitive' sense of urgency in our worship. But at least it will be far clearer what exactly is being done, and the sweep of the action will carry the worshippers on unencumbered by self-regarding interruptions. The first necessity is that people should be able to understand what is happening in church and what a tremendous role each of them is playing. From that will surely come in due course, with the help of wise teaching, a true sense of the Eucharist as the all-inclusive mystery, the most vitally urgent occupation of a Christian's day or week.

On either side of the central action there must be the making ready and the giving of thanks. The latter indeed is almost otiose, as the whole essence of the rite has been thankoffering, eucharist. A short prayer of gratitude by the Church for communion with her Lord, into which each worshipper pours his own particular thanks, is all that is needed before the final dismissal : 'Go forth in peace.' Nor need the making ready be unduly prolonged. What is usually known in the West as the offertory is in the East better termed as the *prothesis,* or setting out and making ready of the elements of bread and wine, later by thanksgiving to be offered, consecrated and received. Before the eucharistic prayer there is nothing fully worthy of being offered to God. However in a lesser sense we can and shall probably contrive to say that we offer of our substance at the 'Offertory,' which then ought to be the immediate preliminary to the great Prayer of eucharistic offering.

Any other prayers in the rite, intercession for instance or prayer for the Church, must come before that. And what else remains to be said or done? Nothing. The rite is complete.

In fact for many centuries the Eucharist has been preceded by another service which is very seldom held separately. It is sometimes known as the Ante-Communion, but would be better called the Ante-Eucharist. This service is in no sense eucharistic; it is not an action at all; and it has a very definite centre of gravity elsewhere. That centre is the Bible. Shorn of its embellishments—whether of medieval ceremonial or of protestant pietism—there is presented to us a simple Bible-service, than which nothing could be more suitable as a preparation for the Eucharist. Scripture readings, interpretative psalmody, and homiletic exposition or proclamation of the faith of the Church : by these means the service of the Word prepares us for the service of the Sacrament, the Eucharist itself. Thus Word and Sacrament can never be opposed, for each has its own all-important sphere.

Is there any way in which the ordinary churchgoing man or woman can help to promote a clearer sense of the urgent immediate significance of the celebration of the Eucharist in our churches to-day? Is there anything that the man in the street can do at once? There is.

Sunday nowadays is less often than formerly thought of as the day of rest. Nowadays most people think of it as above all the day of pleasure. But both ideas would have been equally foreign to Christians of the early centuries of our era.

The idea of Sunday as a day of rest was completely absent from any early Christian's thought. Sunday for him was a working day just like any other. No one could possibly have fallen into the error of confusing it with the Jewish Sabbath, which was in any case on the seventh day, whereas the Church from the beginning held the Eucharist on the first day of the week, evidently following what was believed to be the Lord's command. (See John 20 : 1, 26; Acts 20 : 7, 11; 1 Cor. 16 : 2.) Nor was the first day singled out from any other as a day for pleasure. But so entirely separate did they think of Sunday as being from any other day—and this, remember, in spite of the fact that the outward conditions of life were precisely the same—that there was a common idea of calling it not the first but the *eighth* day; a day which signified something quite new in the whole scheme of creation. According to tradition the creation lasted six days, then came one day of rest. So now with the coming of Christ a special eighth day is added for the completion of God's work. Thus Sunday partakes of that old eschatological flavour we have before noticed. It is both in time and also in some sense outside and beyond it. Most frequently of all Sunday was called the Lord's Day, another eschatological term (cf. 'the day of the Lord' in the Old Testament). On this day in olden times it would be inconceivable that any Christian believer should not try his or her utmost, whatever the cost, to be present and assist at the Lord's Service, in other words the Holy Eucharist.

We do not feel the matter so urgently to-day. But there is some reason why we should. The twentieth century, as we have seen, has much in common with the second. In those early days no church groups or clubs or schools could have existed. The one Christian association was the Church herself, meeting once every Sunday. But this by itself provided enough inspiration for the eventual christianization of the secular state. Nowadays it is increasingly found that specifically church groups make little headway in evangelizing those who are outside. Present-day pagans must be first approached where they are, far out beyond the confines of anything to do with the Church, and only gradually and patiently encouraged to come in. But when they do come what will they find? It must be nothing less than a body of men and women on fire with love and enthusiasm for their Lord and Master, people to whom the Sunday Eucharist is no conventional parade but something which is going to mould their whole lives for the week to come. Properly prepared, it ought for a newcomer to be an overwhelming experience, an epitome of the whole meaning of Christ's religion.

The Eucharist—Thanksgiving, Offering, Communion: that is the all-inclusive Mystery.

Once every seven days for an hour or so there comes to each believer the chance to live to the full the life that is Life indeed. Starting from there, we may yet again see the world turned upside down.

CHAPTER III

FR. GEOFFREY CURTIS, C.R.

BAPTISM AND THE QUEST OF UNITY

'I acknowledge one baptism for the remission of sins' (Nicene Creed).

I

DURING recent wars various governments have tried to insist that the non-Roman Catholic denominations should be grouped together as one church. This has obvious advantages from the official point of view. Why keep a dozen files marked respectively Presbyterian, Methodist, Anglican, Baptist, etc. when one file marked Protestant will do? After the war in several parts of the East some of the unions between denominations thus achieved continued. Perhaps this was not a bad thing. It is easy for groups of Christians to go on for decade after decade in their separate ways with nothing more serious (say) than hymn-tunes and methods of psalm-singing dividing them. Where no question of principle keeps churches apart, but only social or cultural traditions, a vigorous jolt from outside may well be what God uses to shake them out of their complacent separation. At least it should startle them into thinking.

But what of divisions that are based on real theological principle? Unity enforced for political reasons by secular authority cannot obviously be a lasting thing. It cost more to redeem men's souls. Yet even here national circumstances and political action encouraging union may have beneficent effects on theological attitudes and convictions. That this has happened, and happened for our religious well-being, is part of the vindication of the Church of England as reconditioned since the Reformation. Maybe the resultant benefits should have been more substantial as well as more evident. But to this we shall return. As regards more recent history we have heard much of friendships arising in concentration camps, etc. between Roman Catholic priests, French and German and Protestant pastors whose mutual understanding before the war would have been made impossible by their denominational separations. Perhaps here too God has used outside pressures to speed on what natural prejudice or inertia in a setting of inherited hostility and suspicion tends so easily to hold up or postpone *sine die*. Some of us have been admitted to such fellowships of Protestant and Catholics bound by far more intimate understanding and brotherhood than Anglicans of different types find with one another.

If some kind of real unity in Christ, across denominational barriers, can be established at such times, does not this suggest that these barriers are of a different degree of reality or a different height than is often assumed by theologians? The Eastern Orthodox archbishop, Platon of Kiev has assured us that 'the walls that separate us do not reach up to heaven.' Perhaps we can go further and develop this pregnant orthodox reflection by pointing out that because they do not reach up to heaven where even now all Christians are raised with Christ and hidden with him in God, these barriers have on earth too a significance different to and less formidable than that attributed to them.

After all, looking earthwards with 'the mind of Christ' which is ours in the Spirit, we observe that the Church, the one body of the Word made flesh, Jesus Christ the same yesterday, to-day and forever, retains its visible unity. For there is one point at least at which the walls of separation are radically undermined. Even on the strictest doctrinal and canonical principles there is a tunnel that runs beneath them joining us together—Holy Baptism. The fact that there is a widespread carelessness, even apparent slackness, in regard both to the practice of and teaching concerning Baptism, does not destroy the importance of this as seen from heaven, for he who acts in baptism is Christ and what happens is what he willed and wills. So our unity by baptism must be taken, not in a purely formal sense, i.e. that all those validly baptized and believing will be saved or that all these, given right dispositions, are proper subjects for further sacramental grace validly administered; but in the profoundest meanings that the Bible attaches to baptism as incorporation into the one body of Christ.

II

What is the unity which according to the New Testament is given us by baptism? Or, to put it more simply, what in God's eyes does our baptism mean? The answer is given in two words. Those who have been baptized are *In Christ*.

What means this phrase repeated at least 164 times by Paul and echoed in the Petrine and Johannine letters? Scholars of many lands have laboured to decipher their meaning, and not without growing success. Thus near the beginning of this century the phrase was interpreted by a great German scholar as denoting the fellowship-mysticism of those who accept Christ as Lord. 'Just as the air of life which we breathe is *in* us and fills us and yet we at the same time live and breathe *in* this air, so it is with Paul's fellowship with Christ. Christ in him, he in Christ. The formula must be conceived as the ... expression of the most intimate fellowship of the Christian with the living Christ.' This is true as far as it goes. The formula, proving in its manifold use as supple as it is simple, is a summary expression of that mystical union of the Christian with Christ which finds such rich expression in the Pauline epistles, e.g. Rom. 6 : 1–14 or Eph. 1 and 2. But there is more at issue here than the provision of a new spiritual atmosphere.

The most decisive step forward was the discovery that the phrase connotes Baptism. This came from a most unexpected quarter, from a Lutheran modernist, Albert Schweitzer; less well-known perhaps to the public as philosopher and theologian than as a brilliant organist, organ-builder and writer on music, and as the heroic disciple of Christ who at the age of thirty turned his back on the dazzling rewards offered him by the world in order to serve the poorest of his fellow-men as a medical missionary in West Africa.

In his book *The Mysticism of St. Paul*, possibly the greatest book ever written on the apostle of the Gentiles and one which has a far greater abiding value than his more famous book, *The Quest of the Historical Jesus*, Schweitzer makes clear why it is the baptized who are described as being 'in Christ.' The meaning of the phrase is determined by the fact of the solidarity of the elect with the Messiah, the Anointed One of God. This conception is found more frequently in apocalyptic literature than in the canonical scriptures of the Old Testament. But two expressions of it are to be found in the Old Testament itself, the one in Dan. 7 and the other in Isa. 52 : 13–53 : 12. Our Lord by using the title Son of Man which is found in the former and by alluding frequently to the Suffering Servant (as for instance unmistakably in Mark 10 : 45) clearly interprets his vocation in the light of these two images which have in common a certain representative character. Christology is thus rooted in the understanding of the passion, death and resurrection of Jesus reached by a study, in combination, of these two ideas dear to Christ Himself—of the Son of Man and the Servant of the Lord. The Son of Man in Daniel is the inclusive representative of the people of God. The Servant of Deutero-Isaiah likewise incorporates within himself the whole People of God. His death is their death : his resurrection, their resurrection. His death therefore is not only vicarious but representative.

Now it is in baptism that we are identified with Messiah in his death and resurrection and are thus incorporated into his body. The theology of baptism is necessarily concerned with the two poles of this baptism of Jesus—Jordan and its fulfilment in his death, resurrection and ascension. It is our Lord himself who drew attention to the connection between the one pole and the other. Inescapably evident at the beginning of the Gospel story is the acceptance by Jesus of the baptism of John which he later spoke of as needing consummation by his death (Luke 12 : 50). The Baptist's ministry was set in an eschatological context. He was not simply a preacher of repentance in general nor was his baptism merely a symbol of that purification from sin on which he insisted in his preaching. Both his preaching and his baptism were uniquely conditioned by the eschatological situation, the drawing near of the Messianic Kingdom.

Water imagery in the Old Testament comes to have three aspects. Water is first a symbol of chaos, destruction and death. Secondly water means life and fertility. Thirdly it means cleansing. All these three aspects of water are connected with the cardinal events of the sacred history of God's People and find expression in the various rites of covenant renewal. There is the deliverance of Noah and those with him from the deluge, leading to the covenant of the rainbow (Gen. 6 : 13–9 : 13). There is God's deliverance of Israel from the Red Sea (Exod. 14; 15 : 1–21). His call for cleansing and change of garments prior to each renewal of the covenant (Gen. 35 : 1–4; Exod. 19 : 10,

14). His call to Israel through the prophets for the cleansing of its life and the promise of the renewal of that life, symbolized by sprinkling with water (Isa. 1 : 16; Jer. 4 : 14; Ezek. 36 : 25–7). In the temple, as once in the tabernacle, stood the great laver or 'sea' to hold the water in which the priests' ritual purifications were performed (Exod. 30 : 17ff.; 2 Chron. 4 : 2–6). Moreover by the time of St. John Baptist baptism by water had probably become a part of the ritual for the reception of proselytes into Judaism. We seem to have a Rabbinic justification of this in St. Paul's words: 'Our fathers were all baptized unto Moses in the cloud and in the sea' (1 Cor. 10 : 2). All these associations enriched the eschatological background of John's call to penitence and dedication for the new covenant of the Kingdom. It is not surprising therefore that he should have used such a rite to express acknowledgment by the children of Abraham of the need, even for themselves, of cleansing and entire renewal, that they may be able to stand before God's judgement in the expected Kingdom, a people ready to receive him who is coming in the name of God.

John's preaching and baptizing have but one sole aim—the preparation of a cleansed and dedicated people who are to receive the Spirit of God which was itself a mark of the age to come. Water and spirit are closely connected at crucial points in the Old Testament (Gen. 1 : 2; Ps. 33 : 6f.; Ezek. 36 : 25–7). Definite though it is in its content as a baptism of repentance for the remission of sins, John's mission is in a unique way still indefinite as looking forward essentially to him who should baptize with holy spirit. John's baptism and Christian baptism are thus closely linked, both being concerned with the last days, the New Age, the time of Messiah. John's baptism provides a purified nucleus of the former Israel awaiting the imminent arrival of the Messianic Kingdom. In Christian baptism the position is that this has already arrived; the baptized are admitted to the Spirit-endowed Kingdom and find themselves in Christ.

The request of Jesus for baptism at the hands of John is the deliberate act of one who could not and would not separate himself, as the Pharisees did, from the sinful people among whom he dwelt, yet one upon whose heart their sins lay as heavily as if they were his own. His baptism proved the solemn ritual action by which the Christ was consecrated to his death and to his resurrection. The voice and vision, which justified the action about which John had hesitated, told him that in so doing he had received his consecration to a Messiahship which is that of the 'Servant in whom' the Lord was 'well-pleased' and upon whom the Spirit was bestowed (Isa. 42 : 1). It may well have been during the forty days' fast in the desert that our Lord, pondering on the meaning of his baptism, realized the significance of the words from heaven. They recalled one of the 'Servant Songs' of Isaiah; and they thus carried with them also the implication of other words which describe the Servant's task of 'making many righteous by bearing their iniquities and pouring out his soul unto death' (Isa. 53 : 11f.). The cognate theme of our Lord's sermon in the synagogue at Nazareth on return from the wilderness is surely significant (*vide* Luke 4 : 16–19; Isa. 61 : 1f.). John must also have been pondering on the event during our Lord's absence as he names him on return as the Lamb of God (*vide* John 1 : 29, another clear allusion to Isa. 53 : 7). In the conversation which follows so soon with the ruler of the Jews in which Jesus expounds the necessity of baptism, he proclaims mysteriously his coming crucifixion and ascension (John 3 : 1–14). The 'lifting-up,' of which he speaks twice further during his ministry (John 8 : 28; 12 : 32; cf. Num. 21 : 8) as destined to draw all unto himself, finds its realization in the gathering of his people through our baptism into his body. It is surely significant that on the two occasions when according to the synoptic gospels Jesus spoke of baptism (Mark 10 : 38; Luke 12 : 50) he referred to his death. The latter words are particularly significant: 'I have a baptism to be baptized with; and how am I straitened till it be accomplished.' The baptism of Jesus, like his whole Messianic work, was to be 'accomplished' through his death on the Cross (cf. the word from the Cross 'tetelestai—it is accomplished' (John 19 : 30); the Greek word used is the same). We may be sure that his call to his disciples to take up their cross and follow him was in effect one with his promise to the sons of Zebedee that they should share his baptism (Mark 10 : 38; 8 : 34).

But the way of the Cross upon which Jesus set out at his baptism was not simply the path of suffering and death. It was also the way to resurrection and exaltation. This was made clear in the song of the suffering Servant (Isa. 52 : 13ff.) as well as in its lyric counterpart (Ps. 22) which our Lord seems to have pondered upon the cross (*vide* Mark 15 : 34). St. Paul showed his realization of this when he described our Lord as having taken 'the form of a servant . . . he humbled himself and became obedient unto death, even the death on a cross. Therefore God has highly exalted him' (Phil. 2 : 7–11). Thus the baptism of Jesus covers his whole life through its fulfilment in suffering and death, in resurrection and exaltation on to its eternal and universal fulfilment. The Messiah is the Servant, as well as the 'Son of Man' who representing and including the 'saints of the Most High' has not come 'to be served, but to serve and to give his life a ransom for many' (Dan. 7 : 13f., 18; Matt. 20 : 28; cf. Isa. 53 : 12).

At the trial of Jesus confused and garbled evidence was given against him based on a saying of his of which St. John gives the true version. 'Destroy this temple, and in three days I will raise it up' (John 2 : 19, 21 ; cf. Mark 14 : 58). Our Lord had clearly meant 'Destroy this temple (i.e. let this material house of God be destroyed as you are destroying it by greed and pride and ungodliness) and I will quickly raise up a truer—that is to say a spiritual shrine' : words looking forward to his bodily resurrection and exaltation, but also to the restoration of fallen Israel as the body of the living Christ, with himself, the risen Lord, as its Head.

The outpouring of the Spirit at Pentecost by Jesus from the Father's right hand is the counterpart of what happened to Jesus at his baptism when the Spirit descended from heaven to abide on him as the servant of God (John 1 : 32; Isa. 42 : 1). The same Spirit who abode on Jesus anointing him for his messianic ministry has ever since Pentecost dwelt in the church which is the temple of his body. For Jesus baptism meant that he was consecrated as the Messiah, the Anointed Servant of God. For us baptism means that we are consecrated as the messianic people, members of the body of the Righteous One. The most vivid realization of this life of the baptized as being life in Christ was that vouchsafed to Saul of Tarsus on the road to Damascus. 'I am Jesus whom thou persecutest.' It was because they lived in Christ and Christ lived in them that Stephen and others of his detested heresy had been empowered with transfiguring courage to resist the terrors of Jewish indignation. It was Paul who most firmly linked, as he needed to do, the forgiveness of sins in baptism with the death and resurrection of Christ.

III

The words of Christ at the Last Supper 'This is my body' may well have been the chief source of St. Paul's conception of the Church's unity through its real identity with Christ. But there were other factors. It has been well observed that he had also behind him the Hebrew way of thinking of the people of God as a single person. 'Israel is both the patriarch and all his children : the "I" of the Psalms hovers continually between individual and community: the Servant of Second Isaiah stands for the Remnant—which itself stands for the whole People. So now that Israel's destiny has fulfilled itself in the one person of the Messiah, the Church "stands for" the Messiah risen from the dead.' St. Paul has known this as perhaps none other from the moment when he heard the risen Christ saying to him, 'Saul, Saul, why persecutest thou *me?*' It is no wonder then that St. Paul shows always a striking awareness of the coinherence of Baptism and the Holy Eucharist in the mystery of Christ. There is no more striking illustration of this than that which can be found in the argument of the tenth, eleventh and twelfth chapters of the first epistle to the Corinthians. There he notes how in the experience of the children of Israel in the desert both sacraments were typified. He insists that the punishments inflicted upon the Hebrew people for their misuse of their privileges are examples which we must take to heart (10 : 1–13). We too must flee from idolatry. And then he passes to the Eucharist. We must not partake of the Lord's Table and of the table of devils, seeing that our union with Christ, the sole divine Lord, is by the one cup and the one bread proclaimed and strengthened. In our general behaviour as regards things indifferent we must have regard to our brethren, members of the same body. In Chapter 11 comes, in the course of instructions about behaviour in worship, the classical account of the primitive Eucharist and its institution by the Lord (11 : 17–34). Then in Chapter 12 it is Baptism that is once again regarded as the chief source of the solidarity of the one body of Christ as it was in 10 : 1, 2 and 4f. The focus of this unity was the one cup and the one bread of the Eucharist in 10 : 16f.; but it is baptism that functions thus in 12 : 12f. The body of Christ, the church, is identical at once with the body of Christ crucified, with his risen and glorified body and with his body given in the Eucharist.

So baptism into the death and resurrection of Christ and the eucharistic building up of his body are closely connected through the operation in both, through the Spirit, of the crucified and ascended Christ. The life of the new creation is rooted in Baptism. It is nourished, preserved, developed and uniquely expressed by the Eucharist. Without the latter there will be no growth in the divine human life in Christ, as our Lord himself made clear (John 6 : 53-8). But the source of this life is not in the Eucharist. We shall misuse the Eucharist if we ignore this or even fail continually to declare it. For this reason it is of vital importance to recover the theological and devotional focus of the New Testament, which is Baptism. Without this we cannot reveal the evangelical roots of the sacramental system nor show baptism to our protestant brethren as the Key to the door leading to Christian unity.

'In western Christianity the Holy Eucharist has so overshadowed Baptism that the nourishment of our life is presented as a gift greater than the life it sustains.' Yet 'by Baptism we receive the Christian character, the substantial gift of the indwelling Christ which is to be the vivifying and formative principle of our being. We are incapable of feeding on Christ at his supper without having received the supernatural faculty that is ours through Baptism' (Fr. R. M. Benson, S.S.J.E.).

Having had the privilege of being baptized as infants, we have not yet apprehended the necessity of *appropriating our baptism*. We have come to take it for granted that the transforming change of character that the apostle regards as effected by this sacrament can really be expected only in the age to come. Meanwhile we must do our best by 'mortification' and similar moral efforts, with the aid of regular use of sacramental means of grace, to come nearer to the state which as baptized members of the body of Christ we should ideally possess. Now it is true that many of those to whom the apostle writes are clearly far from living the new life that befits the baptized. He is frequently found enjoining them to become what as baptized members of Christ they already are. But how does he bid them to secure this? Not by any devotional means or mortifications or any other kind of efforts to do their best to attain this. It is to cleanse our conscience from such dead works that Christ's blood was shed : and in baptism unto his death and resurrection there is laid a foundation of repentance from the deadness of our former ways. Henceforth our efforts—for our will is to be more rather than less active than before—are *by faith* to appropriate or realize our baptism—the change wrought in us by the share given us, by baptism for the remission of our sins, in the victory over sin and death won by Christ on Calvary. 'Even so reckon ye also yourselves to be dead unto sin, but alive unto God in Christ Jesus' (Rom. 6: 11 and see Heb. 6: 2; 9: 14). 'If ye then be risen with Christ, seek the things that are above, where Christ is, seated on the right hand of God. Set your mind on the things that are above, not on the things that are upon the earth. For ye died, and your life is hid with Christ in God. When Christ, who is our life, shall be manifested, then shall ye also with him be manifested in glory' (Col. 3: 1–4).

The following verse in English translations runs 'Mortify therefore your members which are upon the earth; fornication, uncleanness . . .' The translation of the first word *nekro-o* by 'mortify' falsifies the sense of this passage. The word 'mortify' means in modern language as the little Oxford Dictionary indicates 'to chasten by repression.' I can reasonably be asked to mortify my indulgence in smoking, but not my fornication. The latter has got to be 'put to death' or 'kept dead.' The evil impulses are to be regarded as discarded and dead. They are the garment of the dead nature, the 'old man' put off when the Christian in baptism 'put on Christ' (Gal. 3: 27). Indeed they are no longer ours. The Greek word *humōn* translated by the word 'your' before 'members' may be a later addition to the text of St. Paul.

This regrettable translation of Col. 3: 5 is echoed in the exhortation to godparents at the close of service of Baptism in the Book of Common Prayer of 1662 and in the revised service of 1928 as well as in the collect for Easter Even. The godparents are bidden to remember always 'that Baptism doth represent unto us our profession; which is, to follow the example of our Saviour Christ, and to be made like unto him; that, as he died, and rose again for us, so should we, who are baptized, die from sin, and rise again unto righteousness: continually mortifying all our evil and corrupt affections, and daily proceeding in all virtue and godliness of living.' Pauline language is used to urge us to do continually ourselves what the apostle taught had been done once for all for us in baptism by God 'according to the working of the strength of his might which he wrought in Christ when he raised him from the dead' (Eph. 1: 19f.). When St. Paul in 1 Cor. 15: 31 observes 'I die daily' he is not speaking of self-discipline but of his daily danger of death. The grace that is ours through baptism we must realize as the apostles did by faith, not by *imitatio Christi*. The latter has its indispensable place, but as regards our baptismal death to sin and rebirth in the risen Christ Christian ethics are 'baptism-ethics,' that is to say faith-ethics. 'For ye are all sons of God, through faith, in Christ Jesus. For as many of you as were baptized into Christ did put on Christ' (Gal. 3: 26f.). We cannot endeavour hopefully to imitate the 'ensample of godly life' given us by our Saviour, save in so far as we seek to realize by faith the 'inestimable benefits' of this 'sacrifice for sin' and our cleansing incorporation through baptism into him.

IV

As the last great Anglo-Catholic Congress before the Second World War began with the solemnization of High Mass at Stamford Bridge, a tiny group of priests gathered as the guests of Fr. William of Glasshampton in his sequestered monastery. The oldest of these was the last survivor of the Christian Socialist Guild of St. Matthew, Fr. Stacy, vicar of St. Peter's, Coventry: the youngest is now bishop of that diocese. The mind of the larger gathering was intent chiefly upon the glory and significance of the Holy Eucharist. For the motto of the movement which promoted it has been from the beginning, 'It is the Mass that matters!' The smaller group, though the Eucharist was, I hope, their life, found themselves isolated by their eagerness to put the need of a fuller apprehension of Holy Baptism in the first place. Developments since those days have not convinced me that their anxiety was misplaced. The concern of this little gathering with Baptism was not merely a practical concern, though parochial experience makes ever clearer its radical and manifold practical importance. Nor was it merely doctrinal, though the whole logic of the Christian life makes clear the primacy of what Fr. Benson of Cowley even went so far once as to call 'the major sacrament.' Their impulse was what is nowadays called existential—that is to say more deeply theological—the quest of the truth of God and the discovery of his will for them and for his church in the perplexing conditions of our days. They would have called themselves 'Evangelical Catholics.' This was the result partly of upbringing—none of them, except our host, having been brought up as 'servants of the sanctuary'—partly of a certain interpretation of the Anglican Church. In so far as it was an interpretation of its more recent history, they held that the Church of England was the predestined meeting place in Western Christendom of two streams—let us call them the Sacramentalist and the Evangelical rather than the Catholic and the Protestant—which, though complementary, had flowed apart elsewhere in the west. These two streams had both been operative at the beginning in the Tractarian movement. But the former, however much indebted to the latter, had dominated, until there had been a blessed confluence of both streams through the ministry and teaching of certain great Christians, several of whom were to the fore in the famous London Mission of 1869, e.g. Bishop George Howard Wilkinson, Canon Body, Fr. R. M. Benson, Mr. Bodington and Mr. Twigg. Above all, though he was essentially a son of the Oxford Movement, it was in the teaching of the third of those mentioned, Fr. Richard Meux Benson of Cowley, Founder of the Society of St. John the Evangelist, that these streams seemed to attain the unity of a single great river.

Such a reconciliation was clearly needed. The Reformation at its best had stood for the rediscovery of something long obscured —for a new and liberating apprehension of the free grace of God over against the over-legalized Christianity of the Latin Church of the period. There is something to be learnt from the Lutheran and Calvinist traditions, as Roman theologians have come clearly and eagerly to recognize. Through Wesley and Whitefield Anglican Evangelicals had learnt vital lessons from German evangelicalism in the course of the eighteenth century. The Tractarians also, or many of them, owed a debt to the Evangelical movement of which, separated as they came to be alike in theology and in ecclesiastical practice, they were not always explicitly conscious. It was their defect that in their reaction from Protestantism, they looked exclusively to the past. Despite their great inspiration, they became 'theological archaists.' Their conception both of the Church and of Christian theology were static. Ignoring the Protestant witness they were in as much danger as the Roman Church of growing unevangelical. But the danger has been through Providence to some extent parried. Mercifully so, for the two movements rightly considered are complementary. 'The Evangelical Movement,' Mr. Gladstone remarked, 'filled men so full with the wine of the spiritual life that larger and better vessels were required to hold it.' On the other hand the Anglo-Catholic type of churchmanship has been at its best when it has been combined (as in a Canon Body or a Fr. Stanton) with a real evangelicalism. There is deep wisdom in the aphorism of the Evangelical Charles Simeon: 'Truth is not in the middle and not in one extreme, but in both extremes.' We Anglicans have never taken this lesson sufficiently to heart nor discerned theologically its full significance for ourselves: consequently 'the possibilities of synthesis within the Anglican ideal are still largely unrealized.'

Through providential convergences, such as that of which we have spoken, the convictions typical of these types of Christianity were soon realized to be by no means incompatible with one another, but rather in need of mutual completion and enrichment. And so a clear monition of the Holy Ghost was conveyed to each. To the evangelical came the call to carry his favourite principle of the givenness of grace and of man's utter need of, and utter helplessness without, his Saviour one stage farther along the road of childlike faith until he should find in Holy Baptism and Holy Communion an expression even more absolute and efficacious than he had conceived possible, of his own deepest conviction. To the sacramentalist came the challenge to provide a more faithful, a more scriptural and therefore a more inward interpretation and ministration of their heritage, in particular a worthier stewardship of the sacrament of baptism. He began to see plainly that it is disingenuous (or at best ignorant) to transfer to infant baptism a weight of doctrine and a wealth of promises which in the New Testament are associated with a responsible adult experience: that, as Dr. Pusey had said, though 'the sacrament of Baptism and the conversion of the heart are different things, both go to make up the salvation of a man.'

This twofold call had since the days of the London Mission, or so we imagined, been more faithfully responded to by evangelicals. That there had been, and still is, a real failure of comprehension on the Catholic side, I have no doubt. But how many good things have come to pass since before the Second World War. There has been the ministry of great priests and missioners from either group. The liturgical movement has been the source of an immense measure of new life at once catholic and evangelical in character. The holding of the services of the Easter Vigil even in a sadly truncated form has helped us to realize the association of baptism with the Pasch—with the mighty acts of God; with the 'exodus' of our Saviour from the world of sin and death as well as with that of Israel, his people, which prefigured it. This solemnity has carried with it the yearly renewal of baptismal vows. Again the holding of baptisms at public services has done much to make church-goers aware of what baptism means. The *Parish and People* movement, not least perhaps by its magazine during the last seven years, has powerfully helped evangelicals and catholics to understand one another, as well as the meaning of their birthright in the 'one baptism.' Several theological expositions of Christian initiation by groups of Christians as well as by individual theologians have been of great value. And now we have that for which all this has prepared the way—the fine new rites of Baptism and Confirmation in the Report of the Church of England Liturgical Commission of November 1958. There are also the rites proposed and already experimentally practised in the Northern Province. There have been valuable criticisms and counter-criticisms in the argument between the two. But one thing seems clear despite great differences as to particular theological points and as to what is liturgically practical. The Church of England catholic and evangelical is through the study of the theology and liturgy of initiation achieving a new theological maturity and unity.

In one of the reports to which we have alluded, *The Theology of Initiation* (by a theological commission set up by the archbishops of Canterbury and York and including among its signatures, Dr. A. M. Ramsey, Dr. E. G. Selwyn and Dom Gregory Dix) the following declaration is found: 'The Christian lives in two worlds. The one is the natural world order, transitory, sinful and under the judgment of God. The other is the world-to-come, the eternal world, which has broken into this world through the events of the Gospel. It is the realm of light and life, where God is supreme, sin has been overcome, and the grace of God bestows forgiveness and fellowship which are always closely bound together. . . . The rites of initiation mark this passage of the convert into this new world. It is assumed in all the New Testament language about the rites that the convert receives them with a lively faith and a renunciation of the old world. . . . In view of this, it is not to be thought that the baptism of infants (defensible though we believe this practice to be) can bear the whole weight of theological meaning which the New Testament places upon adults. The present-day counterpart to the primitive initiation is not baptism alone, but baptism together with confirmation, followed by first communion.' So the Liturgical Commission has found it necessary (in its Report of 1958) to print first as the 'archetypal service,' the baptism, confirmation and first communion of adults.

Even if it be only to aid the education of our own generations, this would seem certainly to be a wise course. To St. Paul's question so confident of an affirmative answer, 'Do you not know that all of us who have been baptized in Christ Jesus, were baptized into his death?' (Rom. 6 : 3), the honest answer of the vast majority of Western Christians would be 'No. I did not know that I had died with Christ, and been buried with him crucified, and had risen again with him in his resurrection.' But this change in us described by Paul as wrought by the mighty working of God through baptism into Christ is no figure of speech, but a fact upon the apprehension of which true progress in the Christian life depends. Yet it is still possible to hear sermons and read fresh expositions upon baptism in which the Passion and Resurrection of Jesus are scarcely mentioned. It is not long since an influential theologian, Canon Oliver Quick, expounded baptism deliberately as related particularly and primarily to the Incarnation in the same way as the Eucharist is to the Atonement. 'What he did for human nature as a whole at the moment of his holy incarnation, that he does for every individual at the moment of his baptism.' This seems to me to misrepresent seriously the teaching of the apostolic church as well as the mind of our Lord himself. According to St. Peter, St. Paul and St. John we are begotten again in baptism as a consequence of the Passion, the Death, the Burial and the Resurrection of the Incarnate Son of God who 'died for our sins and rose again for our justification.' The death to sin is as much part of the grace of baptism as is the gift of new life. Much that the adult catechumen in the primitive church learnt in the natural course of his entry to and life in the church, the Christian baptized in infancy most frequently fails to learn. He must be shown by degrees the meaning of what has been done for and in him, and his grasp of this must be more definite, vivid and profound than a knowledge of the Prayer Book catechism can ensure.

For despite the ministry of such men as Bishop George Howard Wilkinson (whose Life by A. J. Mason has done great things in the minds and souls of many priests) and of Fr. Richard Meux Benson's letters (which are full of the baptismal water of eternal life) we have not yet learnt the necessity of appropriating our baptism. It is as if the chosen people, ignoring the significance of the Divine Acts in the Passover, the exodus and the crossing of the Red Sea, had been invited forthwith to enter into the enjoyment of the land of milk and honey. It may be in our case that the diffidence of many to enter and enjoy the promised land of the Eucharistic life and the lack of spiritual fruitfulness in others who have done so, has been the result of this great omission. Is it not true that the sacramental life itself if we do not pass to it through this gateway may become a discipline of precept and practice that belongs to the old rather than to the new covenant? Does frequency in the use of the sacrament of penance really by itself ensure the realization of God's gift in baptism, the saving awareness of its crucial and inexhaustible power?

The conflict of the apostle of the Gentiles with the Nomo-catholic Judaisers of Jerusalem occupies a primary place in the New Testament. These passages constitute a God-given warning that even the most venerable codes of precepts, including those divine in origin, can interpose themselves as barriers between the soul and God; if we ignore that, coming though they do from an eternal source, God himself, they are yet secondary in character and have the nature of means rather than being themselves the end intended by God. We have in fact in the apostolic witness and victory thus described the *Magna Carta* of Christian freedom, set there to ensure that Catholicism shall never be less than evangelical; that conformity to rules and precepts shall never replace devotion to Christ himself. The Catholic rule of life has developed as an expression of Christ the Way in relation to the racial, social and cultural conditions in which his Body has had to live. We must always remember that taken by itself it has the character of the law. Its merely external observation must always engender legalism and pride in a mind insufficiently surrendered to the Redeemer himself. Martin Luther, John Wesley, William Law, Bishop Grafton of Fond du Lac and many others have found this with regard to the Catholic code of life of their time as surely as did Saul of Tarsus in relation to the Jewish law. Such a mind is characterized by emulation, restlessness, scepticism and a sense of frustration curiously compounded with complacency—the self-congratulation of one who is conscious of having conformed perfectly with all the rules. The Catholic ethical and ascetical system and code of life which we watch germinating in the later part of the New Testament, especially in the Pastoral Letters, are secondary elements in the form of the church. It is above all to the dread possibility of having a righteousness of our own that we die at baptism.

For from such snares and errors Holy Baptism scripturally interpreted holds us secure. Given its full dominical meaning, it ensures that personal devotion to our Lord Jesus Christ, saving, ruling and indwelling us comes first and controls all. This is of course the catholic temper as well as the evangelical. But we sometimes lose this or at least give it very misleading expression. Perhaps those New Testament scholars have been right who have held that it was this phenomenon in the evangelist's environment of the mistaking of forms or means for ends—of what might be called in a strict sense 'eido-latry'—which explains the elliptical character of allusions to the sacraments in the gospel and first letter of St. John. He will speak of them only where he may proclaim Christ himself as their source and substance.

The thought of St. John whose gospel provided so many lessons on baptism given to catechumens during the course of Lent in early centuries reminds us that the right understanding of baptism is of deep importance in prayer. In the life of mental prayer meditation is the process of realizing and appropriating what is ours in baptism.

No doubt this was realized by the great evangelicals. They regarded it as deriving from their experience of conversion, to the God-given reality of which they never discerned the sacramental counterpart and basis. Yet how profound, how fruitful their conversion was. 'People,' wrote Fr. Benson, 'can *study* mysticism as a thing of the past. The early evangelicals *lived* but did not study it; so, we think, they are beneath contempt.' Thank God it is not so now. We have learnt deeply to venerate and humbly to learn from them; though not without the conviction that the evangelical saints would have been even greater if they had realized the fullness and the objectivity of their sacramental heritage. It is through liturgy most of all that we have learnt from one another and through liturgy that we shall best give witness of our newly found unity in Christ. What seems needful now is to secure that liturgical expression does not outstrip the theological and religious apprehension of the people of God. We need a pause for 'stepping-back, looking at the ideas within these services—and some of them are glorious ideas, like sonship and adoption; looking at the ideas in our Prayer Book service and in the services newly proposed: discovering what we want to do, and getting it written with some freshness' (The Archbishop of York in the York convocation discussion of the 1958 Report). This must be done together through further theological study of this great theme, as well as through further liturgical experiment. And surely the time is ripe for us to find one another in Christ and go forward together. We have a new message, long awaited since our communion was nicknamed the Bridge-church, proving only, so it seemed, an impasse with a double entry; a new message for the whole Church of God as well as for our own Anglican brethren. How large, how enthusiastic would be the multitude that attended a first Anglican *Catholic-Evangelical Congress* in the Albert Hall! How clear and thankful will be the witness given there by both Catholics and Evangelicals that their concord has been made possible largely though the labours of great Christian minds which we think of as belonging rather to the Critical and Liberal movements. Through these the Church of England has been able to do for the whole Church that which Rome was not yet free to do and the need for which the East was too far from the centre of modern thinking to comprehend!

The subject of the Congress might well be 'the One Baptism for the Remission of Sins.' It was in this form that baptism found its place in the Nicene Creed, a place not accorded even to the Lord's Supper. The Oneness of Baptism was noted there for several reasons. First because it unites us with the Death of Christ which cannot be repeated. This was the teaching of Heb. 6: 4–6. Secondly there was the recognition that baptism was into the One Name of the Trinity and derived its essential unity from the One Lord. Thirdly the Oneness of baptism follows from the fact that the Church to which it is the gateway is One, being the one Body of the one Lord. Along with this goes the realization of the essentially corporate nature of baptism into Christ and into the Church which he has baptized as his bride. But these reasons for the oneness of baptism come together in another important conception: the fundamental unity of baptism and the Lord's Supper. It is significant that all the earliest accounts of baptism include also an account of the Supper of the Lord. In this light it is not difficult to see why the early church regarded baptism as 'the great mystery' and often spoke of it as simply 'redemption' or 'salvation.' St. Augustine tells us that in the Punic language of North Africa there was no other name for Baptism than simply 'salvation.' Elsewhere it had other great names—'the sacrament of unity,' 'the sacrament of the incarnation and passion.' But perhaps none represents better than the reference in the creed to the *One Baptism for the Remission of Sins* the glorious richness of the apostolic understanding of baptism, deriving from the heart and mind of our one Lord and Saviour Jesus Christ.

The baptized are already in Christ. There is, it has been noted, a constant paradox in the New Testament in the expression of their status. They are described as washed, sanctified, victorious, seated with Christ in heavenly places. They are as frequently bidden to walk worthily of their vocation and watchfully in a world where the powers of evil are everywhere active. Each side of the paradox is the expression of reality, and neither must be sacrificed to the other. But the former is grasped by faith as sovereign and ultimate and therefore of greater practical moment. It is faith that discerns that the barriers between us do not mount up to heaven, wherein we are already citizens, in whose eternal life and worship we are already eschatologically—and therefore ontologically—partakers. The deepest meaning of our baptism is this—our participation in Christ, as members of his Body, grafted in him. Thereby all who have been baptized into Christ, being one with him, are one also with one another, in a unity not constituted by men, but by God. But if this unity is already present, Christians must strive to apprehend it more fully and to express it more effectually, in the completeness of its visible form. The penitent, prayerful realization of the truth to which baptism witnesses will lead us to a clearer and more genuinely theological understanding of all the sacraments, and of the Church, their home, which forms itself (on earth) the sacrament of the mystical Body of Christ. Baptism, Eucharist, the Ministry, all the sacraments and the Church itself proceed from the same source, convey the same power and mediate the same truth—the Gospel of the saving action of Christ; his Baptism, Ministry, Passion, Burial, Resurrection, Ascension, Heavenly Session and longed-for Appearing.

Finally through baptism we find ourselves elect and predestined channels of the saving Prayer of Christ that all through consecration in the Truth may be consummated into Triune Unity of the Godhead. It is by giving free course to this Prayer and seeking this Truth that at length we shall all come to find as our Unity, both invisible and sacramentally visible, Jesus himself, the fontal Sacrament of Eternal Love, 'Supreme Head of the Church, which is his Body and which as such holds within it the fulness of him who himself receives the entire fulness of God' (Eph. 1 : 2, 3, N.E.B.).

CHAPTER IV

FR. MARK TWEEDY, C.R.

PRAYER IN THE BODY OF CHRIST

ADULTERY was her daily pastime. For two and a half Acts of a well-known play by Mr. Graham Greene, Rose Pemberton had been holding on to her charming, amoral adolescence. But her moment of truth was to come at last, with the help of an invalid priest who had gone to seed. She had been brought to see that living for the present moment by itself is not enough; something more stable is needed. Try praying, she is told by the priest, long since incapable of understanding her kind of problems. 'Prayer!' She almost spits out the word, as if the devil had thereby been called up. 'I don't believe, I don't believe,' she rages with hatred and contempt for all around her. Yet these conventional believers are her only accessible counsellors, apart from the man she is forbidden to love. In a transport of agony she makes her last appeal: 'Won't somebody help me?' There is no reply, for no one in the Living Room had learnt to care enough. Cut off, as it seemed, from every kind of love, she takes the only remedy left: the poison bottle.

But at that moment, when human love is at an end, Divine Love takes over. Just as long ago the sight of a fellow-sufferer enduring with splendour the agony of crucifixion drew the robber lifted up beside him into Paradise, so now at last, when face to face with death, this ill-used girl abandons the struggle of self-will. She looks back wistfully to her childhood's second-hand faith. She had been brought up to go to Mass, to say her prayers, and all the rest. She knows instinctively that here somewhere is her last and only hope. 'Our Father . . .' she begins, but finds she has forgotten it. But she *must* pray. And suddenly memory does a sleight-of-hand and it all comes out in a rush. 'Bless Mother, Nanny, and Sister Marie-Louise, and please God don't let school start again ever.' Then, penitent, she dies.

One of the early Fathers described prayer as that which makes the world go round. But the world of to-day appears to be going round ever faster without any assistance from prayer. Prayer by the vast majority of men and women would be dismissed as a waste of time, and certainly as incapable of effecting anything. Yet, when pressed in a crisis, some of these people will fall to 'prayer' as a kind of last resort. This 'prayer' will usually be of one sort: that which attempts to alter what looks like an imminent fate by an appeal to the Deity to overrule it—if he can. In extreme cases it may be said to be virtually a prayer that God's will may *not* be done.

Rose was not really in the worst category. She was not trying to alter God's will. She was not trying to alter anything. She simply wanted to pray. She knew she must pray somehow. She knew the Hound of Heaven was at her heels, that after all her fleeing him he had caught her up at the last moment. So, as the Lord's own Prayer will not come, she digs out of her memory the childhood words of long ago. And they, we notice, are words of request for others as well as for herself. So most of the world thinks of prayer, when it thinks at all: as asking for something we need, or want. Rose had never learnt any more about prayer than that. And yet, surely, she had prayed better than she knew. What matter words when the heart is directed straight to God? A well-known definition of prayer tells us that it is simply the lifting up of the heart, or mind, to God. Clearly that was what she was trying to do in those last moments of earthly life. The words she used were limited by her ignorance and total inexperience of any kind of adult prayer. But in the first breath of 'Our Father' she was already reaching out to God, lifting up her heart and soul as best she could. It may be too much to say that in that moment she wanted God, but at least she wanted to want him. And the answer could not be in doubt.

There must be many people who pray without knowing it. For prayer is so often presented as an 'art' or a 'science,' something at which we have to work for years before becoming proficient, if we ever do. Warnings are given—or at least have been since the sixteenth century—against our attempting to by-pass the cerebrations, by which alone a state of elementary prayer may be reached, in order to attain more quickly to the simple prayer of the heart. In all of which some real truth is expressed. But it may be doubted whether the ordinary man or woman should be faced at an early stage with these daunting prospects of 'learning to pray' at all. Indeed it has been well said that we learn to pray by praying, just as we learn to swim not by reading a textbook nor even by flexing our muscles on dry land but by jumping in and somehow becoming water-borne. Particularly may it be doubted whether the busy folk of to-day, in the headlong rush of their lives will ever start praying unless somehow they can be shown how to do it without learning, at any rate at first. Best of all if we can reveal to them the occasions when they are already on the verge of prayer without noticing it. These occasions, of course, will not necessarily coincide with the times when they 'feel good.' It is quite possible for someone to imagine himself nearer to God or approaching a state of prayer, when in fact he is in a state of purely physical euphoria. 'I feel good' is not generally synonymous with 'Thank God.' But on the other hand there are occasions when with only a little redirection the one phrase can be turned into the other. These are the times which must be isolated and identified for what they potentially are—something much nearer to real prayer than a last-resort plea to the Almighty to bring about something which is not likely to happen by ordinary means.

It might come about on top of a mountain or hill when the sun is in the right place and the view perfect. Yes, we 'feel good' : but there is more than that to it. Our feeling is not quite simple. Of course there is satisfaction in having reached our summit (great or small), and pleasure in the prospect below. But coupled with that there may often be something not unlike dissatisfaction, a bitter-sweet feeling which is hard to describe. Perhaps dissatisfaction is not the best word : *longing* might be better. Even an irreligious person may have such a longing, which is really at base nothing other than the longing of the creature for his Creator. The impression received is not a well-defined one; it is a feeling that, if (which is impracticable) we could remain just where we are and as we are, we could produce our best work, do more to justify our existence than we can in our everyday lives. This kind of experience is by no means restricted to mountain-tops. The research scientist, to take another example, uncovering more and more mysterious marvels inside the atom, will sometimes be led by his mathematics into a state of sheer wonder and almost awe; there is there a certain longing for a perfection which again and again eludes him. Or, to take one of the best examples, the sensitive listener to music will not simply 'hear' a magnificent composition: listening, he will make a response to it. Very often this response is one of enjoyment or alternatively of criticism of the actual playing of the work; sometimes it is a matter of appreciation of the greatness of the composer who conceived so wonderful a harmony of sound; but just occasionally the listener's response may go deeper. Again he would find it hard to explain. There is a kind of reaching out—*longing* is still the best word—a tumultuous desire to be identified with the music dynamically, to be carried with it, not out of control but into a deeper and fuller living of life. Above all there is under the surface a diffuse kind of thankfulness for enjoyment so rich.

None of all this is specifically Christian. None of it properly deserves the name of prayer. And yet it seems to be not so far removed from a deeper form of prayer than that represented by direct requests for favours for ourselves or others. Are these people to be told to study a manual of prayer and, having learnt how, to start 'saying their prayers' regularly at appointed times? No, that is a later stage. What is more, it is a stage which may not be reached during half a lifetime of many of our most worthy contemporaries. To plunge them straight into Chapter I of almost any book on prayer may be to kill off the only approach to prayer they have ever made and to give them in return nothing which they can 'take.' The holy writer long ago who said that 'perfect prayer is that wherein he that prays is not conscious that he is praying' may have been concerned with those who are most experienced and proficient, but his words can be used with a more elementary significance. Our task when dealing with the mass of people who have no background of faith may be first of all to help them to bring their minds to bear on what they have already, and to replace a diffused feeling of something wanted by a strong single beam of desire directed to God. Then at once may prayer begin. For we have not to wait until we have discovered and learnt the right things to say; we have not to work hard at 'getting through' to God. He is there all the time waiting for us, whether we be Christian or pagan, priest or prostitute. If we have never heard or understood anything about him, we shall have gradually to learn what he is like. But prayer of a real sort can begin before that. It matters not in what condition we come or what we say, still less what we feel. We are not aiming to make God hear what is in our minds; he knows that already. Our purpose is rather to hear something of what God has to say to us, by whatever method he may choose to express it. For that we need no knowledge, we only need attention and perseverance and, primarily, the first sparkle of faith. All else can be learnt later.

He prayeth well that loveth well. We learn to pray by praying, just as we learn to love by loving: and the two are not all that different in the end. St. Teresa of Avila, who had more claim to know than most men or women, said that prayer is 'an intimate friendship, heart to heart, with him whom we know to be our Lover.' And who is he? God the Son of God, our Lord and Saviour Jesus Christ. More than the first spark of faith will be needed before we can begin to think of him in any sense as our Lover. But the way to prayer in the end is only found in a return of love. Intimate friendship with someone of whom we have no bodily perception will not come quickly; for most people the phrase will mean little in relation to their prayer for the greater part of their lives. But in this case even to have glimpsed the truth is to be already seeking it. To want to want our Lord to-day may lead to our actually wanting him to-morrow. And just to want God is the first way in which a human being may return the Divine Love. Unlike human lovers God never changes: whatever we do about him he still continues unweariedly to love. Therefore the process of getting to know and love him which we call prayer has at least one factor less uncertain and more predictable than a human love affair; for in the latter it may take a long time for us to be sure of the permanence of the beloved's affections. A human love affair, however, may give us some pointers to the nature of prayer, the prayer of the man 'who loveth well.' People who are deeply in love can become more generous, more considerate, more forgiving than ever before. If theirs is a true, self-giving love, these qualities will not seldom extend beyond the loved one; true lovers will be more considerate to all other people. That is because any genuine human love has a tincture of divine Love in it. Also, the more intimately lovers come to know one another the more they reveal their real selves. The lover in an embrace desires to give himself as fully as he can to the woman he loves; and she the same in return. Each gives of their best. They would like in that moment to be their truest, fullest selves. Nothing less will do.

Now all this can be applied to prayer, with one vital difference: in our relationship with God the link is spiritual, not physical. Of course, so long as we are in the body, the body must have its part in all we do. Indeed in some people's prayer the feelings are actively moved. But on the whole in our approach to God we have to do without the powerful help of the feelings. In this way we are thrown back on the will, which is far more reliable than any amount of feeling or sensitivity. One of the most obvious truisms that people struggling with difficulties in prayer must often be told, to their comfort, is that you cannot feel the act of your will. It sounds so obvious but needs repeating again and again. Any idea of feeling, emotion, passion, excitement, is totally irrelevant to the progress of prayer. And yet true prayer remains more like a love-relationship than anything else we can think of with which to compare it. The secret of prayer is *longing*: longing in response to God who first loves us, longing to respond to his love, longing for union with him. We can long for God in a split second of time; during that split second we are praying. We have felt nothing, but our will has been momentarily turned to God. We have prayed . . . perhaps better than in a whole hour of mumbled words or thoughtless petitions. God does not measure prayer by the clock.

Nevertheless clocks there must be, so long as we live in time and space. The first effort of prayer may well be a short-lived hardly conscious turning of the will to God. After that comes effort. Even a human lover does not rely solely on his feelings. He sets himself to give the best of his life at all times, whatever he feels like, *for her*. To that end he and she cultivate their acquaintance, arranging to meet frequently and regularly. Moreover, if they are wise, engaged couples will make a special point of seeing each other in the most adverse conditions, enduring privations together, meeting in times of sickness or adversity. So we toil at prayer. We make regular times for it, and we try to keep them even when we are most disinclined. We may feel incapable of praying. But God does not want our prayer, he wants our selves, just as we are, elated or depressed, with good prayer or bad. We may just be bored. Then tell him so. God wants no pretence. With a casual friend we may conceal a stabbing pain we happen to have in the head, or a sorrow in the mind; but not with someone we love. With those we love we strive to be ourselves, free from pretence. Thus mutual trust is built up. It is much the same with our unseen Lover, except that he understands everything without explanation.

There seems to be an endless supply of little books which tell us how to start out on systematic prayer: of how we must first recollect God's Presence and then begin with Adoration, passing on to Contrition and Thanksgiving, and only then to Supplication, or prayer for ourselves and others. (We call this order PACTS for short.) There are also classic works by the great masters of prayer, and by their followers, on how to pursue the more advanced paths to which some are led, where God is more and more the active partner and the human soul gradually surrenders itself to become the Lord's handiwork.

But there is less evidence immediately available for that considerable number of people whose lot appears to be for most of the time to lie floundering in the mire in mid-course, unable to help themselves up and seemingly left unhelped by any supernatural agency. What are we to say to these people, or to ourselves if we belong to their number? For them vocal prayer—the reading of prayers—though sometimes helpful, more often serves to remove God even further from their recollection than he was when they first knelt down. But shutting their book only makes confusion worse confounded. They can 'picture' nothing, they can think nothing, they can do nothing. They almost envy the prophets of Baal on Mount Carmel, who at least managed to keep on calling upon their Lord from morning till noon: but in neither case is there any voice, nor any that answer. Our modern suppliant is sore tempted to get up and stand aside, mocking like Elijah. 'Cry aloud: for he is a god . . . peradventure he sleepeth, and must be awaked.' If this is the way of the Divine Lover, then he seems to have been misnamed. Father Raymond Raynes was fond of saying that people should not expect God to be reasonable; to our minds God often appears highly unreasonable, indeed downright awkward. He has his own way of wooing those whom he loves. Some earthly lovers, afraid they may lose their idols, are constantly bringing themselves to their notice, but that method often defeats its own object; the loved one apprehends that the lover is more concerned with getting and possessing than with giving. God is quite different. He wants to possess us, of course, as he knows that only thus will all joy and happiness be ours. But he will not use force, he will not unduly impinge on us, for fear we may superficially respond to the feelings we have of his near presence, while our wills remain untouched. So he leaves us to go slogging along, sweating it out by ourselves, hanging on somehow by our wills, almost believing he is no more real than the baals of old; yet still grinding through the set time, our minds pursuing and pursued by distractions in a never-ending steeplechase until perhaps (ourselves like Baal) we succumb to merciful slumber. Can this be called prayer at all? How can we justify such use of precious time?

First, a word about distractions. It has been remarked that these are of two kinds: the sort that can be turned into prayer and the sort that must be turned out of mind. A distracting thought about another person may rightly lead to a brief petition for that person's good. At the other end of the scale come evil thoughts which must be banished as quickly as may be. But there is a third kind of distracting thought which has been likened to the buzzing of flies round a garden-chair where someone is reading in summer; unless these become insupportably troublesome, we do not find it worth while to take our mind off our book in order to swat them. Even so in prayer the mind is assailed by many neutral occasions of wandering attention, which are just not worth bothering about. If we remove our attention (feeble though it be) still further from God in order to deal with these persistent distractions, only the devil gains. In the garden you can swat any number of flies, but more come. At the worst— and we may have to be content to achieve it—our prayer may still be acceptable if we can say at the end: 'Lord, you know what I meant to do, even though I failed to do it.' There is only one failure which may not be excused, and that is giving up too early.

PRAYER IN THE BODY OF CHRIST

Someone said that we should ask ourselves three questions at the end of a period of seemingly fruitless prayer. *Did I intend (or want) to pray? Have I tried to pray? Am I sorry I have not prayed better?* If we can answer yes to all three questions, then we must humbly and unscrupulously believe that we have done our best. No one can do more than their best of the moment on hand. And incidentally it is worth remembering that, as it was once put, the only thing that matters is *now*. That applies forcibly to the whole of life, but never more so than to our efforts at prayer. It does not matter in the least how nebulously (if at all) we have prayed during the last week or month or year. Nothing has been stored up against us, unless it be in our own proud hearts. All that matters is how much we are trying to give ourselves to God *now* in this particular period of prayer. Nor should we ever attempt to look ahead, wondering how we shall stick it out if things get no better in the next year or two, or twenty or fifty years. Only God knows; and he cares supremely. 'His will is our sanctification,' and we may be powerfully helped by realizing that he is working even harder than we are to effect our eternal union with himself.

So we go on as best we can, heeding all useful advice from those empowered or competent to give it, reading perhaps again and again those few books which make us want to pray, in other words make us want God more; neglecting all the other excellent treatises which have nothing to say to our own condition, and especially avoiding like the plague the kind of person who is always recommending the latest book. It seems unlikely that any 'cure' for aridity in prayer will be marketed on earth in the foreseeable future.

We may of course find our way through a different kind of prayer altogether. Just as Christianity is a corporate, not an individual religion, so the prayer of all Christians has a corporate nature or flavour. With public prayer we are not here concerned, but we may note in passing that eucharistic worship—in connection with the Holy Eucharist—should be the centre and foundation of all prayer, as there man is brought closest to his Lord by earthly means. But even our private prayers are not ours alone, for we are members of Christ, not individually but of his Body. At all times we may hitch or harness our feeble efforts to the great strong prayer of the Church—the Church which includes, beyond the vision of man to-day, all the best of those who have gone before, to say nothing of the legions of angels and the saints with the blessed Mother at their head. And if it is too difficult to realize the helping power of these, the struggler at prayer may be directed to the silent companies of enclosed Religious, for whom prayer is the very breath of life; indeed it is hard to say whether they are praying more fruitfully during their long prescribed times of devotion or at other times when at work in the house or garden or ministering to guests. One such guest, a young girl who found it hard to believe but was delighted to be a visitor at a certain convent, wrote later to a friend: 'I had a super letter from Sister. Those nuns make me feel a big heel, they're so *good* (I don't mean pious or religious).' Without pretentions, without religiosity, without perhaps special gifts of prayer, members of enclosed Orders are continuously holding up the feeble wills of those outside whose prayer is barren, and of those who can scarcely believe at all. Little as the busy world may realize, an enclosed convent is a clearing house for innumerable troubles and distresses that happen all around us. Thus all are taken to God, and the prayer of intercession merges into the prayer of reparation. Intercession at its simplest and deepest is nothing more than wanting God on behalf of other men and women. In the end there is only one kind of prayer.

Few are called to the religious life, and fewer still of these to the life of full enclosure. They are our powerful remembrancers. Most men and women have to live another kind of life altogether, in which quiet periods for prayer will be short, and even these must be fought for and jealously guarded. What of the rest of the day? Some are content to 'say their prayers' in the morning (though it is extraordinary how many practising churchmen are negligent about this all-important beginning of the day with God), then forget all about 'religion' while they become business men or farmers or housewives; and only become conscious Christians again at the evening prayer-time. What sort of a prayer-life is this? It is here that self-criticism should begin, not with questions about the quality of prayer or the standard we may or may not have attained.

'Pray without ceasing,' the Thessalonians were told. Many

would like to think that the Apostle was here indulging in hyperbole; but what evidence is there for this? The prayer of him who could elsewhere say that though still alive it would be as true to say that it was not he who lived but Christ who lived in him—how should it be anything but ceaseless? Yet we might wonder how much time he found, out of prison, for anything we are accustomed to call prayer. To pray without ceasing does not mean to kneel without ceasing (the Eastern Orthodox, by the way, very seldom kneel to pray; they regard it as a most uncomfortable posture, and believe that man should come into the presence of his Lord looking like the biped which he has been made). How to pray all through the day, or even ever at all when at our work, is something which will be different for each person. For most of us even a single remembrance of God away from church or bedside is something of an achievement. But that it can be done and has been done long after apostolic times there is abundant testimony. St. Francis de Sales, for instance, much of whose work took him into the luxurious circles of the French royal court, was once asked if he often forgot the presence of God for any length of time. In perfect simplicity he replied: 'Sometimes for a quarter of an hour.' Our modern folk will not begin by aiming so high, but that does not mean they should not aim at all. For some the sound of a factory hooter, the signature of a letter, the cry of a child, or even the chime-bell of the ice-cream vendor can be used to spark off that momentary 'arrow-prayer' which is one of the most valuable kinds of prayer that exists. The length is immaterial; as we have said, God is not clock-bound. No words are necessary, simply a direction of thought. Split-second praying, once it becomes a habit, will lead most surely on to longer efforts. But we must not succumb to any fallacy of size or quantity. Each in his or her own kind of life may think of suitable occasions for arrow-prayers. To give two instances only: the watcher by one in mortal agony may turn each groan or sigh into a moment's *Kyrie eleison;* or the man on the floor of a large industrial concern may redirect each blasphemy he hears into a glorifying of the Name. And when in turn we are bedridden with sickness we need not 'say' any prayers at all in times of pain. For the pain itself, accepted, endured, offered, can become in us a prayer which our Lord will unite with his loving Heart once pierced on Calvary.

Whether or not it be true, as the old writer put it, that it is prayer which makes the world go round, there is no doubt that the world makes prayer go round. We may like to think in fancy of our little globe spinning daily on its axis and carrying round with it countless particles and waves of prayer. There are always some, indeed the great majority, which are turned towards the sun; and the whole earth is held, by unseen gravitational forces, in its regular annual course about that sun without which we could not live at all. Even so our prayers revolve around and are directed towards Christ our Sun. As each one's prayer is speeded on its way, perchance by angels, it does not travel alone. It links up and unites with countless Christian prayers of very different kinds all round the world: the long-drawn cadences of plainsong melody in a Benedictine abbey, and the night-long contemplation of a Carmelite hermitage; the muttered masses round the tomb of St. Francis in Assisi, and the whispered longings of Orthodox pilgrims in the mosque which was once the glory of Agia Sophia in Byzantium; the hesitant courage of a Chinese priest in the face of new government regulations, and the ceaseless daily round of supplication before the shrine of St. Sergius near Moscow; the moment of recollection of a bishop before opening his synod; the wonder of a mother as she watches her new-born child; the urgent petition of an applicant for a much-sought post as he enters the room for interview; the agonized turmoil of conscience of a young employee who cannot go straight and still keep his job; the patient endurance of one in the throes of terrible suffering, and the 'Lord, how long?' of an African oppressed by white domination; the piercing second of repentance before the suicide's poison takes effect; and the flash of love directed to God himself in the midst of a lovers' embrace. All these prayers, and myriads more, are continually going up before the Throne, mingled with ours.

'The prayer of a righteous man has great power in its effects.' So wrote St. James. From time to time most wonderful results of prayer are evident. More often we shall have to persevere without expecting anything. The essence of prayer is not asking and receiving, but the deepening of a relationship of love with God our Father through his Son Jesus Christ in the Holy Spirit: Undivided Trinity to be adored for ever.

CHAPTER V

FR. HUGH BISHOP

THE CHRISTIAN ATTITUDE TO SUFFERING

'You make this world lousy,' says Doc, the drug-store owner, to some of the gang called the Jets in 'West Side Story.' 'That's the way we found it, Doc,' one of them answers.[1]

The reply is much more than an effective bit of repartee. It is a challenge which no one who professes to believe in God can ignore or evade. If there is no God, of course, there is no problem of evil. But if we affirm that the world was created by a God whose power and whose goodness are infinite, how are we to square this belief with the presence of evil in it? Whence then hath it tares? For very many people this constitutes the chief obstacle to belief. The appalling sum of all the natural disasters since time began and all the cruelty, injustice and suffering down the centuries and, in this nuclear age, the threat of worse things to come, seem to many to make nonsense of any belief in a God who is supposed to be all-powerful and all-good. If there is a God at all, they argue, the best that can be said for him is that, like Gallio, he is completely indifferent to what happens on this planet and cares for none of these things.

This is always one of the first and most pressing problems to emerge whenever unbelievers, or adolescents groping towards a faith, discuss the Christian religion; and their objections demand to be treated seriously for they represent a real problem of conscience. If mature Christians are much less troubled by these intransigent facts *as an obstacle to faith,* that is not because they are any less sensitive to the 'giant agony of the world,' or are complacent about it, but for reasons which will emerge later on in this essay.

All the same we must not exaggerate the problem. Anatole France summarized the history of the human race in the phrase, 'They were born, they suffered, they died.'[2] To most people this will seem a fantastically incomplete account of human life, for any objective consideration of the facts must lead us to recognize that there is a great deal more goodness and happiness in the world than there is pain and evil. The manic depressive finds in every experience a confirmation of his own pathological despair, but the experience of most normal men is surely nearer to that of Charles Darwin who wrote, towards the end of his long life, 'According to my judgment happiness decidedly prevails.'[3] Even for those who suffer most there is so much that is good in life that, as Bishop Jeremy Taylor wrote, 'he who hath so many forms of joy must needs be very much in love with sorrows and peevishness, who loseth all these pleasures and chooseth to sit upon his little handful of thorns.'

The very fact that pain and evil trouble us so profoundly, while the goodness and order and beauty of the world so easily pass unnoticed, itself bears powerful witness to the fact that goodness is the norm throughout the Universe. If the normal condition of life was not health but sickness and if order was the exception and chaos was the rule throughout the whole of nature, we should not be oppressed by the problem of evil. We should take evil for granted, as the people who live in the Arctic take snow for granted. The problem which would confront us then would be the problem of how to account for the presence of good in the world, and this is the problem which faces us whenever we try to explain the fact of evil by denying the existence of God or denying his goodness. I can only say that, whenever I have tried to wrestle with it, this problem of goodness proves to be even more intractable than the problem of evil.

This does not mean that there is any neat solution to the problem of evil. There are no neat solutions to any of the great ultimate questions of philosophy or theology and any theory which claimed to tie up all the issues raised by the fact of evil in a tidy package, without any loose ends, would be highly suspect for only God can expound a completely satisfying and convincing theodicy.[4] We must face these issues squarely and grapple with them with our minds as best we can, but we must not expect to have all our questions answered. There is so much that God knows and we do not. The Lord's words to Peter are often the only words that can be addressed to those who are in great trouble: 'What I do, thou knowest not now; but thou shalt understand hereafter' (John 13 : 7). There is a very large element of agnosticism in any religious faith. God has revealed to us sufficient for our needs and by these certainties we live, though even here we walk, for the present, by faith not by sight. But what remains still hidden in mystery is far more than what has been revealed. In that day when we shall know as we have been known, we shall have far more reason than the Queen of Sheba to exclaim 'Behold the half was not told me.' So we have not got 'all the answers' and nowhere more than in relation to this problem of evil and suffering do slick ready-made answers cause so much offence. Job's friends have become a by-word for obtuse complacency through their presumptuous and over-confident attempt to explain Job's sufferings with the easy answers of conventional orthodoxy, and Job's rejection of their shallow speeches represents the impatience of any deeply religious faith, when it is under severe trial, with pretentious and superficial beliefs.

This does not mean, of course, that we can ignore the intellectual problem. A full discussion of the issues which it raises is obviously far beyond the scope of this essay which is more concerned with the Christian attitude to suffering, and how it may be used creatively, than with the intellectual explanation of it. But it would be cowardly not to face the intellectual problem at all and it may be useful, as a preliminary to what I have to say later on, to state what the issues are as simply as possible, and to suggest the lines along which we may find most help in thinking of them

The problem can be very simply stated. If God is omnipotent, nothing can happen unless he wills it. If God is love, whatever he wills must be good. But a great deal that happens is plainly evil. Does this mean that God is not omnipotent after all, or that there is some flaw in his love or his goodness?

One way out of the difficulty is to abandon one of these three truths and to deny, in practice if not in word, either the omnipotence of God, or his goodness, or the existence of evil. This has led to three false theories of evil, all of which are still widely held.

The first starts from the fact of God's omnipotence but implicitly, if not explicitly, denies his goodness. God is the sole source of all that is, the argument runs, and therefore we must not shrink from making him responsible for what we call evil. Since his Sovereign will governs the Universe and everything that happens in it down to the last detail, everything we call evil must be part of his divinely ordered plan and it is useless and wrong for us to question it. This is still a widespread attitude, even among many who call themselves Christians. But to say resignedly 'God's will be done' whenever a disaster happens or an injustice is inflicted is to blaspheme his goodness. Such an attitude fails to distinguish between what God commands and what he permits and it leads ultimately to a thorough-going determinism which denies human freedom and robs both man and God of any moral responsibility. The consequences of this oversimplified logic are appalling for it ascribes all evil and suffering, including such happenings as those which have been described in the Eichmann trial, to the direct will of God.

The second proposed solution to the problem of evil is at first sight a more persuasive one. It starts from the fact of God's goodness, but defends it at the expense of his omnipotence. The Divine perfection, it argues, makes it inconceivable that God should be in any way responsible for the evil in the Universe. Whence, then, does evil come? The answer given is that it comes from the devil. God is not, in fact, omnipotent, for his will is ceaselessly being opposed by dark powers who effectively resist him. The conflict between good and evil of which we are so acutely conscious within ourselves, and which we see going on all around us, is but the out-fighting in the conflict which is perpetually being waged at the heart of the Universe.

This dualism has attracted many minds and more than one religion has been built upon it, for it corresponds to so many of the facts of our own experience. Moreover, it is obvious to any one who reads the gospels with an open mind that our Lord himself, so far from questioning the popular belief in evil spirits, attributed many of the ills of men to their agency. In the moral sphere, behind the rebel wills of men he saw an arch-rebel, 'the prince of this world' (John 12 : 31 ; 14 : 30; 16 : 11), 'he that opposeth and exalteth himself against all that is called God' (2 Thess. 2 : 4) who tempts men to choose evil instead of good. 'Deliver us from the evil one' (Matt. 6 : 13) he taught us to pray. 'An enemy hath done this' (Matt. 13 : 28) was his teaching about the presence in the wheat field of the tares, which represent 'the sons of the evil one' (Matt. 13 : 38). 'Ye are of your father the devil' (John 8 : 44) is his judgment upon the blindness and hardness of heart of the Jews who rejected him. 'He is a liar, and the father thereof' (John 8 : 44) he says of this prince of evil.

But it is no less obvious that Christ treats these demonic powers as an all-powerful Sovereign deals with his disobedient subjects. 'With authority and power he commandeth the unclean spirits and they come out' (Luke 4 : 36) was the comment of those who observed him. 'Behold I have given you authority . . . over all the power of the enemy' (Luke 10 : 19) he says to the seventy when they reported, on their return, that even the devils were subject to them in his name. There is no trace of any ultimate dualism in the New Testament. 'Hallelujah! for the Lord our God, the Almighty reigneth' (Rev. 19 : 6) is its triumphant proclamation.

So we must reject this second theory also, for dualism raises more problems than it answers. Every argument for belief in God is an argument for a belief in one God. To conceive of a god who is not omnipotent is to conceive of a being who is not God. For God is, in St. Anselm's definition, 'a Being than whom no greater can be conceived.'

The third proposed solution sounds the most improbable of all, but it has been seriously held by many people. This theory, like the last one, starts from the truth of God's goodness, which it reconciles with his omnipotence by denying the reality of evil, or at any rate explaining it away as a necessary ingredient of goodness. There cannot be anything intrinsically evil, it argues, for God's in his heaven and therefore all *must* be right with the world. If it seems otherwise, that can only be either because we suffer from the illusion that some things are evil or because we fail to recognize that what we call evil is an essential ingredient in the perfection of the whole, like the discords in a symphony which contribute to the total harmony.

To most people this will seem to be playing with words. There was nothing illusory about Auschwitz or Hiroshima or Sharpeville. The common-sense rejoinder expressed in the well-known limerick about the faith-healer of Deal is a sufficient answer to any such suggestion.

There was a faith-healer of Deal
Who said 'Although pain isn't real,
When I sit on a pin,
And it punctures my skin,
I dislike what I fancy I feel.'

The alternative explanation, that what we think of as evil is in fact a necessary ingredient of the good, is no less fundamentally at variance with the whole of human experience for it is incompatible with man's deeply rooted sense of moral responsibility. Right is right and wrong is wrong and if there is no real or ultimate distinction between them, whence comes the imperious voice of conscience speaking with its categorical imperative?

So much for these three traditional 'solutions' of the problem of evil, all unsatisfactory. It remains to complete the first part of this essay by outlining the Christian view of evil, in so far as there is any one view which can be called the Christian one.

According to this view, the clue to the enigma lies in the power to make free and responsible choices which God has given to some of his creatures, and all evil, Christians believe, is the result of the misuse of this power. If God had been content to create a universe in which everything ran like clock-work because nothing in it had any will of its own, there would have been no possibility of evil in it. The whole thing would have worked perfectly and run absolutely smoothly and very wonderful it would have been. But the actual universe which in fact exists is, potentially anyhow, far more wonderful still. For, incredible though it may seem, the fact is, Christians believe, that God has dared to create beings to whom he has given a share of his own authority and freedom. So far from detracting from his omnipotence, this belief underlines it for the creation of beings capable of resisting their creator is the most astounding of all the miracles which we attribute to divine omnipotence.

God, in his omniscience, foresaw all the evil which would result from this, but he foresaw also the remedy for it and knew that out of it an even greater good would come. So he persisted in his plan and endowed man with free-will because the fulfilment of his whole purpose in creation depended on it. For without freedom man would have been incapable of loving either God or his fellow-man, and so incapable of fulfilling the destiny for which he had been made. Man was made to love and love must be free.

But the consequences of this freedom are inescapable. We cannot have it both ways. If men are to be free to love and to obey, they must also be free to reject and to rebel. The one is not possible without the other. It is only in a world where cruelty, hatred and injustice *can* happen, that love, friendship and self-sacrifice *will* happen. Freedom is both man's greatest glory and his greatest burden.

But that is not the whole story. There is no reason to suppose that *homo sapiens* is the only created being to whom God has given intelligence and free will. According to the Christian tradition, at any rate, there are hosts of other free and intelligent beings who are pure spirits, and it was among them that the first opposition to God's purpose and will began. What the results of that pre-mundane rebellion against God were we cannot know but, if there is any truth in this belief, it means that the divine purpose met with resistance, which twisted it out of its original simplicity, before the physical universe existed. If, moreover, the angels were used by God as his agents in the work of creation, it is possible that the physical universe shows signs of acts of sabotage for which some of them may have been responsible, and this may conceivably help to account not only for natural disasters but for such phenomena as disease-bearing bacteria.

Such thoughts, of course, are purely speculative but whether there is any germ of truth in them or not, they do not imply any sort of dualism such as we have rejected already. The highest angel and the most powerful devil are as much created beings as the smallest insect. Both alike are wholly dependent upon God for their continued existence and it is only by his permission, and with power which they derive from him, that they continue to exercise the freedom which he has given them, whether for good or for ill. That is why it is so essential to distinguish between what God wills and what he permits. But the fact remains that God is ultimately responsible for everything that happens, including all the evil in the world. So far from denying it, Christians insist on this truth, but they go on to affirm that in the Incarnation of our Lord Jesus Christ we see how God accepts this responsibility and in his Passion we see how he discharges it.

Such, in brief outline, is how Christians fit evil into their mental picture of the world. Clearly it leaves many questions unanswered and much unexplained, but, so far as it goes, it helps us to fit the facts into some sort of scheme which does not involve any violent contradiction.

But how far does it go? Most people would probably answer 'Not very far.' For none of these attempted explanations really satisfy us. The human mind is so made that it must ask questions, and it is bound to try to answer them. But to many people, especially to those who have to suffer most, the answers often seem to be just words. Moreover our chief need is not for someone who will explain the problem of evil to us, but for someone who will show us how to transform the suffering which results from it from being a wasteful, negative and senseless thing into something which can be used creatively for good. This is precisely what the Christian Faith offers us. It does not attempt to explain why there is evil in the world or how it got there, beyond planting a few clues for us to follow. But it does teach us how to meet suffering and what to do with it.

Some suffering there is, and will be, in every life. It is far more important to know that it is capable of being used for good, and how this can be achieved, than it is to understand the mystery of its origin. This is the assurance which mind and heart and will alike demand, for it is only possible to reconcile the goodness and omnipotence of God with the presence of evil in the world if we can be sure that God can transform it into good. The life and death of Jesus of Nazareth provide us with this assurance beyond all doubt.

It would be wrong to think of the life of Jesus as one of unrelieved suffering, stripped of all joys. Both feast and fast are there but the feast is more characteristic of him than the fast. There is not the faintest trace in his life of any cult of suffering, or of choosing suffering for its own sake. 'Remove this cup from me', is his first reaction to it in Gethsemane, though in the same breath he adds 'howbeit not what I will but what thou wilt' (Mark 14: 36). So it need not surprise us that the first miracle which he wrought was the transformation of water into wine at the marriage feast of Cana. For, as he testified of himself, he was no John the Baptist.

'For John the Baptist is come eating no bread nor drinking wine; and ye say, He hath a devil. The Son of Man is come eating and drinking; and ye say, Behold, a gluttonous man and a winebibber, a friend of publicans and sinners' (Luke 7 : 33f.).

On the other hand suffering of every kind was woven into the texture of his life from the beginning to the end. He was born in a stable and later on he had not where to lay his head. He was misunderstood by his family and by his friends and was betrayed by one of them. Loving all men without limit, no man has ever been more venomously hated or misrepresented. He died an agonizing death in unrelieved loneliness, deserted by his friends —'they all forsook him' (Mark 14 : 50)—and, it seemed, by God—'My God, my God, why hast thou forsaken me?' (Mark 15 : 34). Never, through all the history of human suffering, has any man been able to say with better reason, 'Behold and see if there be any sorrow like unto my sorrow, which is done unto me, wherewith the Lord hath afflicted me in the day of his fierce anger' (Lam. 1 : 12).

So suffered the one man who has ever lived who 'hath done nothing amiss' (Luke 23 : 41). That is why, to those who believe in the divine status of Christ, and therefore in his divine perfection, the crucifixion of Christ is the greatest crime that has ever been committed, in which all the power of evil is focused and concentrated. Far from denying the fact of evil or trying to explain it away, the Christian Gospel reveals it to us as it is nowhere else revealed, in the full horror of its depth and range. We have not known evil at its worst until we have stood beneath the cross of Christ and seen there how perfect Love was treated. As Karl Barth has said, the problem of Judas *is* the problem of evil. Anything can happen in a world in which this can happen. But, on the other hand, it follows from this that if God can bring good out of evil here, there are no conceivable circumstances in which evil cannot be similarly transformed.

That this is so, in fact constitutes the central affirmation of the Gospel: the Good News. For it is impossible to conceive of any better news than the news that the greatest and most complete success ever won by evil has been made the occasion of evil's decisive defeat. But so it is, for when evil came face to face with goodness and love, instead of goodness becoming contaminated or love transformed into bitter cynicism, it was goodness and love which remained unchanged and evil which was neutralized and defeated. When a man is exposed to evil, more often than not he becomes infected by it, and then evil breeds further evil. If one man loses his temper with another, it is very easy for the second man to lose his temper too, or, if he has a different sort of temperament, to harbour a smouldering resentment which poisons his attitude to everything. But that is exactly what did not happen to Christ. 'When he was reviled, he reviled not again; when he suffered, he threatened not' (1 Peter 2 : 23). However men treated him, he just went on loving them, and nothing could break his love. It reached its climax when they were nailing him to the cross. The power of evil was contained and defeated at that moment of excruciating pain when instead of cursing his enemies he prayed that they might be forgiven for what they did. The bitterness of their malice only served to deepen the greatness of his love. So the resurrection of Christ is not an afterthought tacked on to the Gospel story to make a happy ending. It is its inevitable climax. But the victory proclaimed and celebrated on Easter morning was won on Good Friday afternoon. This is how God accepts and discharges his responsibility for all the evil in the world : by enduring the worst that evil can do *himself,* and doing so in such a way as to make it serve his own purposes of good. As Fr. Harry Williams has written :

'What looked like the utter defeat of goodness by evil was in reality the final defeat of evil by goodness. What looked like the weakness of a dying man was in reality the strength of the living God. What looked like tragedy was really victory. That is why, as Westcott reminded us, Jesus reigns from the tree. Not because his wounds were less severe than the spectators thought they were, not because his Passion was less bitter or terrible than the evangelists have led us to believe, not because his physical weakness was less real or his death, from the human point of view, less catastrophic than the Church has always supposed—but because precisely in and through these things the Son of Man was glorified (John 13 : 1), since by their means the power of God's love went forth to subdue and capture a rebel world.' [5]

If we believe that, we shall never complain again that suffering is wasteful or meaningless or that it defeats God's purpose, for here is concrete proof that exactly the opposite is true. If God can bring good out of evil here, he can do so everywhere always.

And so he has done, and does, and will do to the end of time, whenever men give him the chance. For though Christ's redeeming and transforming work was decisive and unique, it continues in the lives of all those who accept their sufferings, whether they are great or small, in the spirit in which he accepted his. For Christ did not suffer in order that we might be delivered from all suffering, but in order to give to our sufferings the meaning and value and transforming power of his. So all suffering can be directed and used to overcome evil with good whenever it is accepted selflessly and trustfully and in such a way that instead of breeding resentment or self-pity it bears fruit in love. So used, suffering is transformed from being sheer loss into becoming one of the most effective and productive activities open to us. St. Paul means every word he says when he writes to the Christians at Colossae:

'Now I rejoice in my sufferings for your sake, and fill up on my part that which is lacking of the afflictions of Christ in my flesh for his body's sake, which is the Church' (Col. 1 : 24).

For the doctrine of the Church as the mystical Body of Christ means that the pattern of Christ's life will be reproduced in the life of the Church in each generation and in every place, as well as in the life of each individual Christian who is faithful enough to allow him to do so. It is revealing to make a careful comparison between St. Mark's account of our Lord's Passion and Resurrection which occupies chapters 14–16 of his gospel with chapter 13 which immediately precedes it. This thirteenth chapter is a prediction of the passion of the Church, and its final deliverance, and the large number of striking parallels between this description of the future sufferings of the Church and its final vindication and the narrative of the Passion and Resurrection which immediately follows, must mean that St. Mark saw, and intended his readers to see, a close connection between the two. We read, for example, in Mark 13 : 9 : 'But take heed to yourselves: for they shall *deliver you up to councils*; and in synagogues shall ye be *beaten*; and before *governors* and kings shall ye stand for my sake, *for a testimony unto them.*'

In the Passion narrative which follows we read how Christ is *delivered* up by Judas to the Jewish *council;* how he is *beaten;* how he stands before the Roman *Governor* and *hears testimony.*

In Mark 13 : 32-3 we read : 'But of that day or that *hour* knoweth no one, not even the angels in heaven, neither the Son, but the Father. Take ye heed, *watch and pray* : for ye know not when the time is.'

There are parallels to this passage in Mark 14 : 32-42 where Christ speaks of the *hour* having come (14 : 41) and urges his disciples to *watch and pray* (14 : 35-8).

The implication of these and similar parallels is that Christ plainly warned his disciples that his own Passion would be followed by the passion of the Church down the ages and we have to expect this pattern to be reproduced in us. Like St. Peter, we recoil from the idea of a suffering Messiah—'Be it far from thee, Lord : this shall never be unto thee' (Matt. 16 : 22). But the marks of the nails are an essential part of his plan for transforming evil and redeeming evil-doers, and there must be something corresponding to them in the life of the Church, which is his body, in each generation and in the life of each faithful Christian.

And so it has been down the centuries. Those who have been closest to our Lord have been caught up into the fellowship of his sufferings and, in the transformation of evil into good which has resulted, have manifested the power of his resurrection. In some lectures which have been published under the title of *The Novelist and the Passion Story* Dr. F. W. Dillistone examines this Passion-motif in four novels by Herman Melville, William Faulkner, François Mauriac and the Greek writer Nikos Kazantzakis. In each of these novels the central character is a Christ-figure who is ready to accept suffering and death for the sake of the charity which possesses him, and though in each of these novels the story ends with what looks like a tragedy, we are left with the conviction that this apparent tragedy has made a permanent difference for good and contains the only seed of hope for the troubled situation in which the other characters are involved. Thus, to take an example, the central character in François Mauriac's novel *The Lamb* is Xavier, a young seminarian who becomes deeply involved in the lives of a married couple whose marriage was in danger of breaking down, and in the lives of those around them. He is misused and misjudged and suffers greatly physically, mentally and spiritually, and eventually is killed in an accident. But by his willingness to carry the load of their trials and sins, he helps to bring peace and hope to those with whose lives his own life has become so inextricably intertwined. Dr. Dillistone concludes:

'So we are brought back to Mauriac's central message—that whensoever and wheresoever the sufferings of Christ are reproduced in one of his servants, there salvation is being worked out: the salvation both of the sufferer and those for whom he is suffering. Christ's act is supreme, definitive, unapproachable. Yet it cannot be effective in the world to-day unless it is brought near through its re-enactment in the lives of saintly figures such as Xavier. There may, to be sure, be other ways—the whole sacramental system of the Church brings the merits of Christ to men —but Mauriac's concern is to portray the operations of the Divine Grace within the whole complex of inter-personal relationships. There it is the lamb who at all times bears the load of the sins of the world and through his passion heals and reconciles the lives of those whom he loves.' [6]

Mauriac is a Catholic Christian and so is the central figure in *The Lamb*. William Faulkner is not, presumably, an orthodox Christian nor certainly is the Corporal, the hero of *The Fable*, a novel about the 1916–18 war which follows the passion-motif very closely. For though this insight into the value and use of suffering for love's sake is derived from the Christian Gospel, it is not confined to explicitly Christian circles and the truth of it is recognized, and often acted upon, outside them. As Fr. Lionel Thornton, C.R., wrote in his book on the Atonement

'Such facts (i.e. the transformations effected by suffering) have largely become possible in the world through the Christian belief in the spiritual significance and efficacy of the sufferings and death of Christ. The supreme significance of vicarious suffering in his case has illuminated its real, though limited, significance on the widest scale elsewhere in human life. All life ultimately depends upon this principle. The unborn babe enters the world only through the sufferings of its mother. But also the supreme revelation of God's love upon the cross has shown mankind that in this world, if there can be suffering without love, there cannot be love without suffering.' [7]

This is the essence of the Christian attitude to suffering. In this world, we may, all too easily, suffer without love, but we cannot love without suffering. And such suffering, freely embraced for love's sake, has a redeeming transforming effect both on the sufferer and on those for whom he, or she, suffers, past all our reckoning.

To this conclusion I add three corollaries. First, it follows from all this that suffering, so far as the individual is concerned, is not necessarily the result of his own past sin. The temptation to say 'What have I done to deserve this?' whenever some disaster overtakes us is, for some people, a very strong one. In some non-Christian religions this idea that all suffering must be punishment for sin leads to the belief, without any shred of evidence for it, that if the sinful cause is not present in this present life, we can confidently assume its presence in some previous existence. But it is never safe to argue back in this way from suffering to sin, and each time that suggestion was put to our Lord, he emphatically rejected it. The theory that it is the wicked who suffer and the innocent who flourish like a green bay tree is notoriously untrue to the facts, and we have only to recall that our Lord suffered more than any man to expose its fallacy.

So it is often those who are nearest to our Lord who suffer most. This is what we should expect and instead of allowing it to undermine our faith when we see it happening, it ought to strengthen it. That is how Gerard Manley Hopkins interprets the death of the five Franciscan nuns who lost their lives, with all the other passengers, when the ship in which they were travelling to Canada was shipwrecked off the English coast in December 1875. In *The Wreck of the Deutschland* he says of the sister in charge of the nuns that, by accepting trustfully the terrible suffering which she could not avoid and by bearing it as Christ bore his, she 'christens her wild-worst Best.' It is when people 'christen' their 'wild-worst,' by accepting it positively and using it creatively, that the worst that can happen to us ceases to be a reason for thinking that God has rejected or deserted us, and becomes our 'best.'

Secondly, evil is always evil; always, in itself, contrary to God's will and our first duty is always to resist it and seek to remedy it. There has, at times, been something very like a cult of suffering in the Christian Church but such an attitude, so far from being Christian, is incompatible with Christian faith. The Church has always forbidden men to seek martyrdom and condemned those who did. Our first reaction to suffering, whether in ourselves or others, must always be to seek to alleviate it. But in a fallen world there will always be some suffering which we cannot alleviate, and for some people there will be a great deal. This suffering we are to see *sub specie crucis*, in the light of the cross, and accept it trustfully, confident that God can, and will, use it in order to bring good out of it both for ourselves and others. As Simone Weil wrote: 'The extreme greatness of Christianity lies in the fact that it does not seek a supernatural remedy for suffering, but a supernatural use for it.' [8]

That is why mature Christians are not troubled by the vast sum of suffering in the world in the same way as those who find it so great a 'scandal,' in the New Testament sense of the word, that it becomes for them the chief obstacle to faith. For Christians know, from the inside, how suffering can be used by God in order to achieve results which cannot, it seems, be achieved in any other way. Even God could only reconcile men to himself and to each other by suffering and dying for them.

Lastly, it is evident that suffering by itself, however great, never saved any one. It is not what we suffer but how we suffer that matters. The two criminals who were crucified on either side of our Lord both had to suffer exactly the same things. Neither of them could avoid their cross and it was no more painful for the one than for the other, but the different ways in which they suffered led to exactly opposite results. So it has been ever since. The same suffering which makes one man self-centred and selfish and breeds self-pity and bitterness and resentment in him, in another man produces courage and confidence and compassion, and a serene joy which surprises all who meet it. Such a one was the fourteenth century English saint, Mother Julian of Norwich. Miss Elizabeth Jennings writes of her:

'The sense of wholeness which is so apparent in her work springs from an undivided personality, a nature which is fulfilling itself, not denying itself. The sufferings which she depicts so vividly are an essential part of this wholeness; far from diminishing her, they completed her. She accepted suffering *as* suffering, there is not a vestige of masochism in her work, nor is there any flinching away from pain. "The problem of pain" would have meant nothing to her simply because she saw, in the Incarnation and Passion of Christ, both the explanation and the apotheosis of pain. And she recognized this not by dialectic or logic but by intuition and affinity. It is this affinity, this sympathy, in the Greek sense, that takes every trace of complacency out of her affirmation that "we shall say all with one voice: Lord blessed mayst thou be, for it is thus: it is well; and now see we verily that all-thing is done as it was then ordained before that anything was made."' [9]

That is the miracle: that not only Christ but Christians are made 'perfect through sufferings' (Heb. 2: 10). 'Ye shall be sorrowful, but your sorrow shall be turned into joy' (John 16: 20). He does not say that our sorrow will be succeeded by joy or rewarded by joy but that it will itself be transformed into joy. It is an experience which is offered to all and shared by surprisingly many. 'Suffering does not last,' wrote Leon Bloy, 'but having suffered lasts for ever.'

Meanwhile all our suffering here is shot through with the triumphant faith of the resurrection, which looks forward with confidence and hope to the time when 'there shall be no more death, neither sorrow, nor crying, neither shall there be any more pain; for the former things are passed away' (Rev. 21: 4, A.V.).

PART IV

INTRODUCTION TO PART IV

WE have suggested that Part I of this book might be called 'The Facts'; Part II 'The Reason for the Facts'; Part III 'Christian Response to the Facts.' But Christians are not the only beings affected by the coming of Christ: if they were, that coming would be very limited in its impact. 'He came into the *World*.' And so Part IV might be called 'The Cosmic Reach of the Facts.' We consider what the world is like, this world which Christ wills to redeem; the task of the Church in such a puzzling and expanding world; the nature of the 'call' that comes to each Christian included within that task of the Church; and finally the End—in the sense of 'the end-product,' and also in the common sense of 'finis'—Christ who sums up all things in himself.

CHAPTER I

✝ TREVOR HUDDLESTON, C.R.
Bishop of Masasi

THIS IS OUR WORLD

FIFTY years ago a great historian and prophet, who was also a member of the Community of the Resurrection, wrote these words—

'The scientist's world is like a government department: correct, regular and dull: the real world is coloured and changeful, gay with multitudinous laughter, and dark with many tears and appalling horrors—a world of freedom and terror, of glory and of shame unspeakable. That is the world Christ came to redeem; not the monstrous determined single being of scientific dreamers. And we cannot make the one fit the other.'[1]

No doubt when these words were written they were not only true but immensely challenging. But that was in 1909. And things have happened between then and now which make them sound strangely ambivalent. Yet—as with so much of Father Neville Figgis' writing—there is that prophetic undertone that remains, echoing on. His is the contrast between the scientist's world and the real world. The one 'correct, regular and dull': the other 'coloured . . . changeful . . . gay,' but also 'dark with many tears . . . a world of freedom and terror, of glory and of shame . . .' We know to-day that such a contrast is impossible to draw: and we know this because it is the *scientist's* world which now holds man's attention, exhilarates or depresses him, and has more real impact upon him than any other.

The world in which we Western Europeans live is, it seems to me, dominated by three concepts which are the direct consequence of scientific progress over the past fifty years; vastness, speed, complexity.

Vastness. Man to-day has been made aware of the size of the Universe not merely through reading about it in some obscure or inaccessible work. He is aware of it because his own handiwork is away out there in space: because in a little while he may himself be making that venture: because, whether he likes it or not, his own world is now recognizably only a speck of dust as tiny and as fragmentary as a million others which catch the light for a moment and then whirl on their way unseen. . . .

Speed. It is not only the consciousness of the pace of weapons of destruction which has been brought into being—though this is perhaps most obvious at the moment (wireless, TV, etc.). It is that, in our world, through scientific skills, events and ideas can be thrown at us within seconds of their emergence. There is no longer time to reflect or choose. A catastrophe on the other side of the world makes its impact more swiftly than a catastrophe in the next-door house.

Complexity. And both what is happening, and the language in which it is described, is now so complex: there is such a mass of interrelated discovery: the lines of research are so highly specialized that man is aware of his world as a world of endless and fascinating possibilities. 'The monstrous, determined single being' of Father Figgis's 'scientific dreamers' is to-day a world in which any miracle can happen and can be accepted without comment—even to the discovery of the origin of life itself—on the word of the scientist. Whereas fifty years ago, the supernatural was suspect; to-day, it is, so to say, lost in the wonders of space, time and energy.

To man, conditioned to these things as I believe him to be, what does the Christian Church look like? Where does it fit in? How would he describe it if you asked him? I think he would say: 'The *ecclesiastical* world is like a government department: correct, regular and dull . . . a monstrous, determined, single being of theological dreamers.' And he would go on to say: 'It just won't fit the world as it is.' And if that seems too depressing an assessment, it is still true enough to illustrate my point. 'Organized religion,' says a well-informed writer,[2] 'is in regular contact with a minority of some 12 per cent of the population with a minimum attendance amongst the industrial working-class.' In other words, to the vast mass of men in this country, organized religion is an irrelevance. We Christians are generally speaking only to those who are within 'organized religion.'

And yet, the very concepts which now dominate our scientist's world—its vastness, its speed, its complexity—the ideas which exhilarate and challenge; these same things create for man a profound and penetrating *loneliness*. With the preacher (Ecclesiastes) he cries: 'I applied my heart to seek and to search out by wisdom concerning all that is done under heaven: it is a sore travail that God hath given to the sons of men to be exercised therewith. I have seen all the works that are done under the sun; and, behold, all is vanity and vexation of spirit' (1 : 13f.).

In the musical, *West Side Story*—that marvellous study of contemporary youth—there are two moments of great poignancy: the first when one of two gangs, having murdered, gathers at its usual meeting-place—a drug-store. And the old man who keeps the store can contain himself no longer and flings out: 'You make this world *lousy*'—and the young leader of the gang flings back: 'We found it that way' . . . We found it that way.

The other—a dream ballet on an empty stage with a wide empty sky—to the words of a song called 'Somewhere' . . . 'Somewhere, there's a place for me. . . . Somewhere, *Somewhere*.' . . .

This note is echoed and re-echoed in our generation and in desperation at their own loss of any real community, they look for 'somewhere' to belong. A Teddy-Boy group . . . An Aldermaston March . . . A Trafalgar Square Rally: anything which will give a sense of purpose and a sense of belonging and an ideal to strive for . . . anything which will break through the frustration of living in a world which holds out together two such contrasting things—a richness of experience, full of wonder, on the one hand: a haunting fear, full of loneliness and perplexity on the other.

This is our world. It is also the world Christ came to redeem.

But this is all a picture of Europe, of what we know as 'Western Civilization,' sometimes as 'Western Christian Civilization.' There are other parts of the world which do not know this loneliness, this perplexity. The new nationalisms of India and the Far East, and of the 'Uncommitted nations,' especially Africa, show no signs of this questioning and bewilderment that characterizes the West. The hideous strength of the Inter-Continental Ballistic

Missile is a reminder to all of us that we have already moved out of one long phase of history and into another. The man-made planet now circling the moon is an indication that this new phase, the phase of inter-continental rather than inter-national relationships, may be relatively short. Assuming (perhaps rashly) that man can find a way of controlling his own weapons of total destruction and can survive the next ten years or so, inter-continental ideas will themselves be yielding to interplanetary ideas against a cosmic background. Such is the picture which is no longer phantasy but clear reality. And yet paradoxically, at the very time when we must think in terms of continents rather than nations, we find the emergence of new and exciting national groups as one of the most striking characteristics of our time.

Among these groups it is the African that is the most outstanding. The pace at which new nations have emerged and are accepting the responsibility of sovereignty on the African continent can find no parallel in history. Within the brief span of time since the end of the war sovereign states have been created or are about to be created in over two-thirds of what had been colonial territory. We have recently seen Nigeria assuming independence and becoming the largest self-governing country on the sub-continent, with a population of over thirty million and a diversity of natural wealth and culture perhaps unrivalled. We are seeing vast constitutional changes in East and Central Africa. For the first time in history a British Prime Minister has thought it necessary and wise to visit African territories officially, in order to find out for himself the meaning of events there. And then, of course, we must remember that it is not only our own but the Belgian (as we have seen in such spectacular ways), French and Portuguese colonies which are equally involved in the revolutionary changes happening, and happening so swiftly that it is impossible to keep an accurate account of them.

What is the task of the Church in all this?

Clearly the first task is to *understand*. The African giant, after centuries of what looked like slumber, is awakening, stretching his limbs, breathing the heady air of morning, *his* morning: the dawn of freedom. The Church must realize that this is what makes Africa the most exciting place on earth: that instead of having to look back in pride and self-congratulation on a long distant past, it looks forward to a future with unpredictable but fantastic possibilities, waiting to be grasped and used. It would be thrilling to be born an African to-day, and to know that one's destiny was bound up with what is so fresh and vital. We in the West with our *fin de siècle* mentality, and showing so many signs of effete civilization, can hardly begin to understand what such a moment means. Yet to try to realize the truth of what these surging tides of nationalism mean is a duty which we simply must not evade. And for the Christian Church, a right understanding *now* is essential. If we fail to understand, if, for instance, we persist in planning our missionary strategy along the lines which were valid only twenty years ago, if we are too slothful or too blind or too proud to meet Africa to-day—then it is certainly possible that we may lose our chance for centuries.

Mr. Julius Nyerere, sometime leader of the Opposition in the Tanganyika Legislative Council, and now first Minister of Tanganyika, said not very long ago:

'Political discussions in East and Central Africa become racial precisely because this racial element makes the British Government change its policy and say: "It is all right talking about democracy and universal suffrage in West Africa but we cannot talk about democracy and universal suffrage in East and Central Africa because there you have the Europeans settling." And while that is understandable, I suppose, to the British Government, we would, I hope, be forgiven if we say it is not understandable to us. There is the perpetual question of civilized standards, the civilizing influence of the European in Africa, and it is always a problem to us how it should happen that we in East and Central Africa, who are living side by side with this civilizing agent, somehow refuse to be civilized! We somehow fail to absorb this civilization, whereas our friends in Ghana, Nigeria and the Sudan absorb it quickly and get their democracy. . . . We cannot accept that, because we have white men settling within our communities, we must wait two thousand years before we get the right to vote.'

The future of Christianity in Africa may well depend on how far the Church sees the point of Mr. Nyerere's remarks. It is so hard, even for the missionary living close to the black people, to see how closely entangled with the concept of 'white superiority' is the faith he has come to preach and to share. It is sometimes obscured from the older generations of African Christians, who have been born and bred under the shadow of a benevolent paternalism on some mission compound. But, I am convinced, the rising generation of young Africans, fully informed through their reading of the newspapers and increasingly (even in 'apartheid' South Africa) made aware of what is being thought and said and done in East and West, is looking at the Church most critically. 'Christianity for us is the very expression of the dishonesty of the west,' said one of them (Mr. Ezekiel Mphahlele, the South African literary critic and English lecturer). And what he meant was that a Faith professing to be based on Love would be judged, not by the preaching of its professional priests, but by the behaviour of its believers. To preach Love and to practise Power are irreconcilables.

The challenge—to understanding, and then to disengagement—is tremendous. But if there is urgent need for repentance—repentance for the past confusion between Christian preaching and paternalism—and for rethinking—rethinking about the task of the Church in this situation—there is also much room for hope.

One day in 1960 saw, in *The Times*, statements from three leaders in different parts of 'British Africa.' They make a fascinating contrast, and at the same time a fascinating comment. Dr. Nkrumah said, in an important speech during Mr. Macmillan's visit to Ghana:

'Africa's future demands the closest unit. . . . Ghana is willing to mingle her own sovereignty with that of other countries in Africa. . . . African strength lies in our totality and union.'

Dr. Verwoerd, in a New Year interview in South Africa, said

'Tribal ways are democratic and efficient and incomparably better suited than any other to satisfy Bantu aspirations and needs.'

And the Bishop of Nyasaland, in a letter condemning a speech of Sir Roy Welensky's (of December 30th, 1959), wrote:

'The root cause of the present distress is the forcible imposition of Federation . . . against the wishes of the African population of Nyasaland clearly expressed.'

If you read these statements carefully you will see that it is the leader of Ghana, at that time the newest nation, who is thinking most clearly in terms of *continental* policy : and it is the leader of South Africa, the oldest nation, who is thinking in utterly reactionary terms. Whilst between the two stands the representative of the Central African Federation, challenged by a Christian bishop as to the very foundation principle of his country's existence. 'Forcible imposition . . . against the wishes of the African population'—this is a queer way indeed to express the idea of 'Partnership,' the declared aim of Federation itself. The bishop is entirely right : and the tragic consequences of ignoring or trying to override nationalist African aspirations are already beginning to be seen in a way that no one can now shut his eyes to, in Central Africa. Hope, then, lies with the new rather than the old. The glorious thing about Africa to-day is its vitality and freshness, its openness to ideas and to idealism, its 'uncommittedness.' With nationhood just round the corner for so many millions there, with emergence on to the world's stage a fact of to-day, not a dream of to-morrow, we have perhaps the greatest opportunity in our history to present the Christian faith as the *Catholic* faith—the faith that alone meets all Africa's needs. And we should thank God that, over the past century, so many Christian missionaries and Christian converts have by their own sacrifices laid such a strong foundation. For, in spite of all, it is still true to say that within the Christian family, where the faith in the Resurrection is preached, more than anywhere else in Africa, friendship, trust and love between men of different race have grown and flourished.

Père Voillaume, Founder and Prior of the Little Brothers of Jesus, wrote :

'National pride, racial pride, class pride, cultural pride are all ordinarily unconscious, for one breathes one's own nature in them, as it were. We *are* our families, we *are* our countries, we *are* our races, and it is all but impossible for us to judge them as if from without. . . . But the world has come to a turning-point in its history where we cannot avoid this query: either the Christians are going to comprehend what has happened and change or the Church is going to be arrested in her development. . . . The Christian communities which have been founded among the different coloured races will totter because the missionary is white and because he has come with the white official and the white business-man, and, whether he will or not, is therefore looked upon as one with them.'[3]

The only thing that can avoid this tottering of the Christian Church is supernatural love: and the condition for this is always, everywhere the same, the humility born of penitence. As Charles de Foucauld used to say 'Be little; be brothers to men and love them.' To do this on a continent swept by such storms of national and racial tension as is Africa to-day demands something more than natural qualities of mind and spirit. The ideal of 'identification,' which is the only valid one for the Christian Church at this moment in history, is, after all, the idea proclaimed by Bethlehem in that bleak and bare and wind-swept stable. And it is so costly to nature that it is unacceptable. That is why we *could* fail to hold the trust of young Africa: we *could* fail to win the allegiance of those millions who are looking for a faith to live by, but who most certainly will not accept Christianity unless its adherents are prepared to pay the price they speak about so glibly, the price of a religion whose heart and centre is the scandal of the Cross, but whose hope is the Resurrection.

And here the problems we started with—problems wider than Africa or even Africa and Asia—the problems of Vastness, Speed, and Complexity find their measure. 'This is our world': and yet more than ever this little world, a speck on the surface of a universe made up of so many worlds, shows its own inability to cope with the problems it itself creates. Christ risen is alone a match for them. To proclaim that is the Church's primary task: and here lies the greatest challenge to our faith, and perhaps the greatest opportunity for our hope; but above all, the greatest and most searching test of our supernatural and infinitely demanding love.

CHAPTER II

FR. MARTIN JARRETT-KERR, C.R.

WITNESS OF THE CHURCH IN AN EXPANDING WORLD

I

NOT long ago I heard a young African student, studying at a University in the British Isles, say 'My generation in Africa does not want Christianity. My grandfather was one of the early converts to the L.M.S. (London Missionary Society) in Bechuanaland. My father is a minister of the Congregational Church. But I have thrown all that up. When I am in trouble or in difficulties I pray to my Ancestors. Some of my colleagues laugh at me for that: they say it's sentimental, romantic. All right. It's sentimental and romantic; but it helps me. A Western religion cannot deliver Africa.' Only a month or two before that the President of the Indonesian Republic had delivered a speech at the United Nations Assembly in New York in which he referred rather scornfully to the words of wisdom coming from the Western nations: and reminded the Assembly that the Far East had a culture and a religion when the ancestors of the West were still running around painted with woad.

It is a commonplace that we in the West can no longer afford to take a Mediterranean-centred view of the world. Even our historians, usually the most conservative species of scholar, are (some of them) saying that we shall have to rewrite our history books to a world perspective.[1] And if 'secular' thought is having to revise, how much more must the Christian Church, with its commission to the whole world, rethink not merely its strategy but its sense of priorities.

That there is an increased meeting, willy-nilly, of Western and 'non-European' cultures to-day no one can deny. One of the greatest living experts on comparative mythologies, Professor Mircea Eliade of Chicago, has said this of it:

'Fortunately . . . certain great cultural movements of this century—the several revivals of religion, depth-psychology, the discovery of surrealism and of the most advanced painting, the researches of ethnology, etc.—have prepared the ground and, on the whole, have made it easier for us to understand the psychological attitudes which at first sight seem "inferior," "strange" or disconcerting. It is true that, most of the time, encounters and comparisons with non-Western cultures have not made all the "strangeness" of these cultures evident. But this is due to the fact that the encounters have been made through their more Westernized representatives, or in the mainly external spheres of economics or politics. We may say that the Western world has not yet, or not generally, met with authentic representatives of the "real" non-Western traditions. But this encounter is, in the end, inevitable. Even supposing that, one day soon, all the traditional societies now beginning to play an active part in history must end by becoming radically Westernized—in other words, assuming that the non-Western peoples are fated to lose their place in History except in so far as they become Westernized—even then the encounter and comparison with the authentic traditions of the non-Western world could not be avoided. We cannot tell what the cultural ambience of these exotic peoples will be like in the future, but only yesterday it was radically different from that of the West. . . . One day the West will have to know and to understand the existential situations of the non-Western peoples; moreover, the West will come to value them as integral with the history of the human spirit and will no longer regard them as immature episodes or as aberrations from an exemplary History of man—a History conceived, of course, only as that of Western man.' [2]

M. Eliade in several places passes judgment on the West by looking at it through the eyes of an imaginary non-European (sometimes an Asiatic, sometimes an African and sometimes a 'primitive'). This is the kind of judgment we have heard fairly often during the past twenty years or so: the 'materialism' of the West has been compared with the 'spirituality' of the East and—the conclusions to draw are obvious. It is this that has led to the popularity of western forms of neo-Buddhism, Zen, and the rest, the attempt at the popular level (as in Mr. Aldous Huxley's *Ends and Means*) to equate Eastern mysticism with the mysticism of *The Cloud of Unknowing*, St. John of the Cross, and so on. And there has been the more serious and scholarly work in this field of such writers as the late Ananda Coomeraswamy, René Guénon and Frithjov Schuon. But M. Eliade is to be listened to, not only for his encyclopaedic knowledge of the history of comparative mythology, but also for his unfaltering grasp upon the uniqueness of the Christian revelation.

He believes that this confrontation of the West with the non-West helps Western man better to understand himself, because the effort of understanding 'the others,' what is strange and foreign, 'is repaid by a considerable enrichment of consciousness.' Indeed, he suggests that, just as the discovery of exotic and primitive arts half a century ago opened up new perspectives to the European world of art, so the encounter with the non-West may lead us to reconsider some of the problems of philosophy which we have tended to disregard or to regard as closed. Such new sources of inspiration are usually unforeseeable, he suggests; and for an example he cites the contemporary German philosopher, Heidegger:

'Who,' asks Eliade, 'could have imagined, thirty years ago, that the pre-Socratics would ever be thought capable of regenerating philosophical investigation? Yet the latest researches of Heidegger are developing in that direction.'

Later in his book Eliade shows the close resemblance between Plato's theory of 'reminiscence' (according to which when we seem to be learning new things which we did not 'know' before, we are in fact 'remembering' what has been handed down in human tradition and the racial memory) and the ideas, not only of Pythagoras—from whom, as is well known, Plato derived them—but of Buddha and some of the yoga mystics.

'It is in the Platonic doctrine of the Remembrance of impersonal realities that we find the most astonishing persistence of archaic thought. The distance between Plato and the primitive world is too obvious for words; but that distance does not imply a break in continuity. In this Platonic doctrine of Ideas, Greek philosophy renewed and revalorized the archaic and universal myth of a fabulous, pleromatic *illud tempus*, which man has to remember if he is to know the truth and participate in *Being*.'

And Eliade points out the significance of the 'return to the past' in modern psycho-analytic therapeutics.

So this 'encounter' between East and West passes judgment upon the shortness of our memories in the West—even where there is a proper respect for 'tradition' on examination that tradition is often found to be quite a brash and short-lived affair. But the judgment goes deeper than that. In a brilliant last chapter to his book, a chapter he entitles 'Religious symbolism and Modern Man's anxiety,' but which he also calls, significantly, 'The Encounter—a Test-case,' M. Eliade specifically confronts the West with a non-Western view of death. He points to the passion of the modern, Western world for 'historiography'—a passion which he says is quite recent, dating from the second half of the last century, and he asks : What does this passion look like to a non-Western man?

'In many religions, and even in the folk-lore of European peoples, we have found a belief that, at the moment of death, man remembers all his past life down to the minutest details, and that he cannot die before having remembered and relived the whole of his personal history. . . . Considered from this point of view, the passion for historiography in modern culture would be a sign portending his imminent death. . . . The historiographical consciousness of Europe—which some have regarded as its highest title to lasting fame—would in fact be the supreme moment which precedes and announces death.'

True, in us modern Europeans this passion for historiography seems to be quite a neutral thing, does not seem to be connected with presentiments of disaster. But whether we like it or not, the discovery of the historicity of every human existence does in fact, if one really ponders on it, lead to the 'anxiety' or the 'anguish' of 'confronting Death and Non-being.'

'It is in trying to estimate this anguish in the face of death

... that the comparative approach begins to be instructive. Anguish before Nothingness and Death seems to be a specifically modern phenomenon. In all other, non-European cultures, that is, in the other religions, Death is never felt as an absolute end or as Nothingness: it is regarded rather as a rite of passage to another mode of being; and for that reason always referred to in relation to the symbolisms and rituals of initiation, rebirth, or resurrection. This is not to say that the non-European does not know the experience of anguish before Death; the emotion is experienced, of course, but not as something absurd or futile: on the contrary, it is accorded the highest value, as an experience indispensable to the attainment of a new level of being. Death is the Great Initiation. But in the modern world Death is emptied of its religious meaning; that is why it is assimilated to Nothingness; and before Nothingness modern man is paralysed.'

But there is one qualification to this judgment on the West:

'When we speak of "modern man," his crises and anxieties, we are thinking primarily of one who has no faith, who is no longer in any living attachment to Judaeo-Christianity. To a believer, the problem of Death presents itself in other terms: for him, too, Death is a rite of passage. But a great part of the modern world has lost faith, and for this mass of mankind anxiety in the face of Death presents itself as anguish before Nothingness.'

Since, in these traditional religions, Death is a 'rite of passage,' a sort of initiation into another mode of Life, the reverse is also true: Initiation Rites are a sort of symbolic, anticipatory experience of Death. Eliade points out that for instance, among some Bantu peoples the boy who is to be circumcised is the object of a ceremony known explicitly as 'being born anew.' And to make this sense of a 'little Death' more vivid, these Initiations always include painful ceremonies—'the initiates' mutilations . . . are charged with a symbolism of death.' Some of the tortures involved are almost unbelievable, yet they are accepted readily.

('Among the Mandan—N. American peoples—two men thrust knives into the muscles of the victim's breast and back, put their fingers deep into the wounds, passed a loop under the muscles, attached it to cords and hoisted the neophyte into the air; but before slinging him up, they inserted, through the muscles of the arms and legs, pegs to which they had tied heavy stones and buffalo heads. The way in which the young men endured this terrible torture, says an observer (George Catlin, 1867), verges on the fabulous: not a feature of their faces moved while the torturers were butchering their flesh. Once the victim was suspended in the air, a man began to make him spin like a top, faster and faster, until the wretched man lost consciousness.')

Perhaps we should not regard it as exactly a 'judgment' on the West that we have given up such hideous rites. But I remember reading the experiences [3] of a highly sophisticated, Westernized African, Mr. Tod Matchikikze, when he, in late puberty, had to return from his very modern urban life to his Xosa people to undergo the traditional rite of circumcision: and he describes it as a moving, revivifying spiritual event for which he was profoundly grateful. And I have sometimes wondered whether our rather effete, spineless adult Christianity in the West might not stand to gain from the introduction into Confirmation ritual of something a little more severely ascetic and arduous, to make it, also, a 'little death.'

II

This brings us closer to the challenge of the 'Encounter' between West and non-West to Christianity. But Christianity itself is, we must remember, a challenge to the West itself. The very presence of Christianity in the modern world, says M. Eliade, is at least a standing guarantee that the secularized views of the Cosmos or of life, characteristic of all modern Western culture and therefore radically opposed to all previous 'myths' of man, will not go unchallenged. For Christianity is at least at one level in continuity with man's permanent mythology. Indeed, there are those who believe (as, for instance, Jung does) that:

'the crisis of the modern world is in great part due to the fact that the Christian symbols and "myths" are no longer lived by the whole being; that they have been reduced to words and gestures deprived of life, fossilized, externalized and therefore no longer of any use for the deeper life of the psyche.'

In other worlds, that Christianity ceases to be a real challenge to the West when it becomes too intellectual, too rationalistic, too far sundered from the instinctive life of man. There is a leading Protestant theologian, Paul Tillich, who states this better than I can, and it is important, in view of what we shall see later, that he is a Protestant.

'Protestantism in all its forms has emphasized the conscious religious personality, his intellectual understanding, and his moral decisions. It has become a "theology of consciousness" in analogy to the Cartesian philosophy of consciousness. (He means Descartes' taking as a starting-point "I think, therefore I am.") Even religious feeling, as emphasized by pietism and romanticism, remained in the sphere of consciousness. This had a double consequence. The personality was cut off from the vital basis of its existence. Religion was reserved for the conscious centre of man. The subconscious levels remained untouched, empty, or suppressed, while the conscious side was over-burdened with the continuous ultimate decisions it had to make. It is not by chance that in Protestant countries the breakdown of the conscious personality has occurred on such a large scale that the psychoanalytic return to the unconscious became a social necessity. A religion that does not appeal to the subconscious basis of all decisions is untenable in the long run and can never become a religion for the masses.' [4]

The short-lived effect of most forms of 'revivalism' within Protestantism seems to point to the same basic defect. And this has obvious importance for the problem of the 'missionary' work of the Church, and indeed for some of the basic problems of theology itself. There has been a revival of 'Biblical Theology' of recent years, both in Great Britain and on the Continent. But one sometimes wonders whether, for instance, sufficient account is taken, even in this Biblical Theology, of the *pagan* background to Biblical religion. It is quite clear that there was no real break in the cultural history of Canaan separating the period of Hebrew occupation from the period of the earlier Canaanite rule: even local sites, and certainly sacred objects and such natural phenomena as mountains, rivers and groves, which had been sacred to the Canaanites, became (with due purification and redirection) sacred to the Hebrews too. Of course, the Hebrew prophets protested—and rightly—against reversions to 'natural religion'; but even the prophets' own teaching only became ultimately acceptable because they incorporated much of the 'paganism' to which they were formally opposed. This is made clear in the works of one Biblical Theologian who did see the point of this process, the late Dr. L. S. Thornton, C.R. He pointed out, for instance, in one of his most important later works [5] that such festivals as the Passover and Unleavened Bread were both of them originally two distinct Spring-festivals of natural religion which had nothing whatever to do with Israel's departure from Egypt; and that Jeremiah, who passionately hoped for a new Covenant ('Not according to the covenant that I made with their fathers' (Jer. 31 : 31–4)), was in fact followed by a new and yet a restored version of the old nature-religion; and that whereas the older 'writing' prophets denounced this kind of natural religion, the later prophets, from Ezekiel onwards, were its inaugurators and supporters.

'The nature-religion,' says Dr. Thornton, 'could not be suppressed. Under the fire of prophetic criticism, and after an interlude of total suspension (though perhaps not quite as "total" as has been supposed), its whole pattern is repeated in history in a form more compatible with a developed religious consciousness.'

Dr. Thornton showed how biblical tradition essentially involves, at every stage, taking up—not destroying but fulfilling—the old into the new. And he pursued this theme beyond the Old Testament into the New, and from there on to the Fathers. And don't we find the same thing happening with the spread of Christianity through Europe? We know well how Pope Gregory, for instance, wrote to Melletus—a companion of St. Augustine on his missionary visit to England, and told him that the missionaries in Great Britain need not destroy pagan temples, but should purify them and dedicate them to the true religion. Since people love public feasts, why should the old ones not be adapted? St. Boniface, we are told, used the oak of Thor to build a church, and the Irish missionaries rededicated the sacred groves of the Druids to the new religion. Many names in our Christian calendar of Feasts were adapted from the pagan mythology of Egypt or Greece (Isidore, Dionysius, Amrose); and many liturgical names (bishop, priest, deacon, church, basilica, baptism, mystery, host, sacrifice, immolate, asceticism, soul, sin, redemption, liturgy itself) were borrowed from current pagan use. And pagan feasts too, were Christianized—Yuletide became Christmas, the sun feast of the Summer solstice became a feast in honour of St. John, and the original feast now known as Candlemas was a counter-attraction to a pagan feast with similar ceremonial.[6]

These are historical facts. But can they be justified? Do they not, on the contrary, represent a reversion of the pure Christian gospel to a semi-syncretism, an accommodation of the stark and 'separatist' call of Christ to popular and superstitious demands? This will be the constant reforming cry of the protestors: and often enough it will be justified. Yet the 'pure Christian gospel' and the 'separatist call of Christ' may itself also lead to one-sidedness, to a neglect (as Professor Tillich pointed out in the significant passage quoted above) of the total human person as the object of Christ's love. And Dr. Thornton's great book is dedicated to showing how the whole process of the divine self-disclosure takes the 'form of the servant,' that is, the form of self-humiliation, coming down to our level: and so, that the condescension in using the lowly forms of natural and primitive religion is only a part of his total condescension in 'revealing' himself at all: and thus that the 'recapitulation' of all things in Christ (spoken of by St. Paul, and finely worked out by the Fathers, especially by St. Irenaeus) is something which is going on at every level.

III

This taking up, by Christianity, of the old into the new is not limited to the Old Testament, the New Testament, the Fathers, and the Christianization of Europe. For Christianity has had to 'absorb' or take into itself that mode of thought which ultimately became 'the Scientific attitude.' We can see this happening, almost like a laboratory experiment, in the later Middle Ages, when scholastic philosophy took over Muslim thought, along with Arabic mathematical knowledge. At the time of the 'Scientific Revolution' of the late fifteenth and sixteenth centuries there was a reaction against medieval thought and an emphasis on 'empirical' knowledge, i.e. observation, experiment, putting nature to the test. At first sight this might seem to be in conflict with a Christian view of the world, and in fact it did lead later to the beginnings of the perennial conflict between 'science and religion.' But there is much to be said for the view that in its early stages this scientific revolution of the Renaissance times was actually a return to a more truly Biblical view of the world. For to 'sit down humbly before the facts' is, on this view, more appropriate to man's creaturely condition than the Medieval dogmatism (which was as much Aristotelian as it was Christian) about nature, the 'deductive' or *a priori* approach to the world, which starts from certain general axioms, as if man could directly read the mind of the Creator, and tries formally to apply them to things that can be seen, measured, etc.—and often subtly twists them, in so doing, to make them fit the axioms.

Further, as Dr. Thornton has pointed out, 'science' can be said to be assimilable to Christianity in two ways. First, it is the 'scientific method' itself, applied to the Bible, archaeology, palaeography, etc., which has led to a better understanding of the Biblical view, and so, paradoxically, to the recovery of 'Biblical theology.' And second, as science has progressed it has pushed its own frontiers farther and farther away. Physics, in particular, with its discovery of radical discontinuity, of unpredictability in the behaviour of the electron and atom (or, in biology, of the chromosome), has revealed the infinite complexity of matter; it has shown the limits of measurability (since the act of measuring does, at the microscopic level, affect the thing measured); and, as Dr. Thornton puts it, 'the curious paradox results, that, whereas faith ever yearns for simplicity and clarity, it is science which now presses us back to a recognition of the mysterious.'

This possibility (to put it at the lowest) of the incorporation of modern scientific concepts and attitudes into the Christian faith is important, not merely for the survival of Christianity in the science-dominated Western world. It is also important in connection with the 'encounter' we have been considering between Europe and non-Europe. For it is often said that India, the Far East and Africa look now to the West for one thing and one thing only: technology. Where, as so often, their main problems are quite simply the problems of feeding the ever-multiplying mouths, increased production, i.e. technological advance, obviously and understandably has priority. But if that is all, then the outlook for the Christian Church is, on the world scale, bleak indeed. The nineteenth century has been called the Century of (Christian) Missionary Advance. The twentieth century can already be called—and the twenty-first century will probably also have to be called—the Century of non-Christian advance. The population-growth alone is unfavourable to Christendom. Some frank figures were given recently for the Roman Catholic Church alone. The increase of the Roman Catholic population in the world, by natural births alone, is about three million five hundred thousand per annum. The increase through conversions is, perhaps, some half million per annum. This gives a total increase of four million per annum. But the increase, again through natural births, of 'non-catholics' (which, of course includes a relatively small percentage of Christians who are not Roman Catholics, but is predominantly made up of heathens) is more than sixteen million per annum. Père Congar, who gives these figures,[7] concludes that to keep even the present ratio of Roman Catholics to non-Roman Catholics in the world, the Church would have to step up its rate of converts from half a million to six and a half million per annum. These figures would have, of course, to be altered if we were to take into account not merely Roman Catholics, but all Christian bodies, and the proportion of their total membership to the total non-Christian world; but the alterations would not be very great. And the conclusion is the same: statistically speaking, Christianity is becoming increasingly a minority religion. And if all these non-Christian nations look to the West for their scientific skill, then how this scientific skill (and the scientific outlook behind it) can be related to Christian faith is clearly of urgent importance from the missionary point of view.

IV

There is, however, another paradox we must face at this point.

Recently I heard a lecture by a highly intelligent African Christion [8] in which he asked a simple question: When, he said, Christians condemn the African witch-doctor (so-called), do they do so in the name of Christianity or in the name of modern, Western science? And he went on to say that our Western conception of medicine and health has for some centuries been profoundly materialistic—at least until the very recent invention of the word 'psycho-somatic.' The African doctor or herbalist, on the other hand, however we may dislike his methods or find them distasteful, at least had a holistic conception of health and disease. And is not this very close, in fact, to the Hebrew and Biblical notion of the body-mind-soul relationship; so may not the African, with his heathen traditions still a fresh memory, be able to recall the Christian Church to a true, more ancient, and more profoundly Christian view of life and health? The paradox is that the younger nations are looking longingly to the West for the more purely materialistic products and processes of their science, at the very time when some of the most sensitive thinkers in the West, including those working in the scientific field, are realizing the limitations of that approach and the value of the older traditions which the younger nations seem to be wanting to abandon. The paradox, however, may prove less recalcitrant than it looks if the coming together of modern science and traditional religion is a real possibility in the West and not a mere day-dream.

Concepts of health and disease are not the only ones in which traditional pagan, especially African, views are close to Biblical. The concept of 'natural justice,' for instance, is almost universal in primitive societies. The distinguished anthropologist, Professor Max Gluckman, has shown in detail that the people he studied in Northern Rhodesia (the Barotse) have, not only a concept of universal human law (they call it *milao yabutu—sc.* laws of human kind) based on divine law (*milao yaNyambe—sc.* laws of God), but even similar vocabulary, similar metaphors, for moral concepts to those used in the West. (For instance, they speak of 'crooked' people; 'straight' as = true; 'untwist' for reconcile; 'pointing to' for indication . . . etc.) Some historians of culture have even gone so far as to say that ethical concepts universally depend on theological concepts, that in every tribe and tradition the laws of right and wrong are ultimately based on that tribe's concept of God. But this is certainly untrue, for plenty of evidence has been collected [9] to show that there are several primitive cultures in which there is no such connection, and indeed in which the notions of divinity are totally amoral if not immoral.

What can safely be said is that a vague notion of a primitive, monotheistic, 'Supreme Being' is very widespread, at least in Africa: and that in many cases the ultimate sanction of the people's moral code is related to this Being. And in some cases the resemblances to Biblical views are even closer. Mgr. Walsh has pointed out the similarity between the scape-goat feast among the Ife people in Nigeria and its Hebrew counterpart.[10] Anthropologists's notebooks are full, too, of mythological correspondences between primitive and Christian experience, both sacred and secular. A recent study, for instance, of both a 'Job' and an 'Oedipus' theme in West African folk-lore [11] shows how similar, under the different dress and environment, are their notions to those we know in the West. And M. Eliade has pointed out the quaint fact that 'primitive savages' themselves have a myth of 'the primitive savage' : the Western travellers of the sixteenth to the eighteenth centuries had an idealistic notion that the 'primitive, untouched savage' was a happy, pre-Fall creature; but in fact the 'savages' they met already had a story of a paradise in which their unfallen ancestors lived, enjoying happiness and an effortless peace.

Are these 'pre-figurings' of the Christian story valid foundations on which to build, or are they tempting similarities which must be challenged, cast out, before the pure Christian faith can take root? Or, to put the same question in an aphorism : When does incorporation become syncretism? This is a perennial question which the Christian has to answer: and the answer will not be the same at every moment in history. One thing is proved, at least, from experience : that Christian missions which try to adopt the 'scorched earth' strategy always fail. A great French theologian, Père Daniélou, has pointed out, in connection with the difficult task of preaching Christianity to Moslems, that when Mustapha Kemal modernized Turkey, destroying ancient institutions (especially those concerning the place of women in society), some missionaries thought that this would prepare the way for Christianity, 'estimating that it was more valuable to have to do with free thinkers, than with Moslems, and the total absence of religion was better than a false religion.'[12] But they were proved wrong, in fact. And Père Daniélou concludes that we ought to accept the opposite view, of those who believe that since Islam has, in fact, produced souls of a profound spirituality, instead of destroying it (Islam) we ought to try to extend it into its Christian completion: 'Islam is an incomplete Christianity.' And the same principles would apply, even more clearly, to a primitive religion which has notions—e.g. of sin, of sacrifice, of sacrament, of life-beyond-death, etc.—which can easily be shown to find a fulfilment in the Christian revelation.

V

How can it be done? And in particular: what is the contribution of the Anglican Church to this particular task? How can a theology which has been so uniquely parochial as the Anglican 'version' be expected to cope with this global missionary task and this necessity for an 'incorporationist' outlook? Put bluntly: what on earth have these manic prancings of primitive religions, this remote mythological parallelism, to do with the stately tread of Cranmer's prose? What could ever be the relevance of 'our incomparable liturgy' to this planetary problem? As one thinks back to the formative Anglican names in theology, one wonders which of them had or could even have imagined, a range which could cope with the problems? Hooker? Perhaps at moments, yes: though so often limited by the immediate ecclesiological controversies of his time; and even at his best, with a conception of 'natural law' that must seem narrowly medieval to-day. F. D. Maurice? Well, his range was wider than most, but his Kingdom of Christ seems so often merely a picture of 'where the Quakers and the Romanists go wrong'; and his justifiable attack on 'notions' as no substitute for the Gospel seems sometimes based on a severely Maurician *notion* of what the Gospel is. Newman's conception of Development (so Anglican in many ways) was perhaps a pointer in the right direction, towards (as Dr. Owen Chadwick has pointed out [13]) an organic or evolutionary view, as contrasted with the static view expressed in Bossuet. But Newman's idea of the Doctrine that had to Develop was sadly moralistic and, I think, ultimately individualistic. Perhaps Dean Church was nearest to an expandable view adequate to the occasion, for he was aware of the God-given in the 'non-religious' realms of life; but his range was entirely Mediterranean-centred, and he was not, in any case, a formative theologian. Charles Gore? Too moralistic again, perhaps, though he tried to understand other faiths, and it is good to know that he had a preference, aesthetically, for pagan art, and wasn't ashamed of it.[14] One of the few living Anglican thinkers who seems to me really aware of what needs doing is Bro. George Every, s.s.m. His remark [15] that it is the primitive religions, with their rich, bloody, materialistic notions of sacrifice, that are closest to Christianity—closer than the more 'spiritual' religions of Asia—seems to me vital. And he has not been afraid to put the doctrine of the Atonement plumb into the middle of its anthropological context.[16] But it is Dr. Thornton who will, I think, in the end be seen to have done most to open up the way to a truly 'incorporationist' theology of Revelation. It is not necessary to accept some of his more fanciful excursions into 'typology' to feel that his general thought was seminal. His great theme, the 'Form of the Servant,' is that divine revelation is by self-limitation, and that this limitation includes not merely the once-for-all taking of human flesh by the Word of God, but the continuation of that as the Church accepts lowly forms (bread, wine, water, song, language, mythology) that Christ may be all in all. And thus, if it is necessary to have limitation in order to have concentration, perhaps Anglican 'parochialism' or 'provincialism' may prove to be capable of expansion. For crucial theological periods have always been short ones. The Hebrew-Hellenistic encounter was brief but fertile. The traditional Anglican appeal to 'the primitive Fathers' or 'the first five centuries' has often seemed absurd: did the Holy Ghost resign from the Committee after (say) the Council of Chalcedon? The hey-day of Anglican religion-culture lasted about a century. But in each case there was a quick ferment, followed by a slow maturing. The ferment to-day is global, and dangerously quick. We must start now to get ready for the maturing.

If it is true, as I have argued, that only an incorporationist theology (and that means also an incorporationist liturgics and pastoralia) is adequate to the task, then certain practical conclusions follow. It is significant that, so far as I know, almost all the great anthropologists have either been agnostic relativists (Frazer, Lévy-Bruhl, Malinowski, and the rest), or Catholics (either Roman Catholic, like Professor E. Evans-Pritchard, Fr. Wm. Schmidt, Professor Zaehner; or Anglican Catholic, like the late Joachim Wach, Professor E. O. James, etc.; or Orthodox, like Professor Eliade). I remember Professor Bengt Sundkler, the great Swedish Lutheran missiologist, when he visited Johannesburg in 1959, describing a recent visit to Tanganyika. He was alarmed, he said, at the growth of Islam among the Africans; and when he watched the worshippers at the Mosque at Daar-es-Salaam, and saw their prostration, rapt in the Moslem prayer-process, he understood why Islam is spreading, and wondered what resources Christianity had to meet the challenge. But then he attended Benediction at an Anglican church near Tanga, and as he saw the congregation of some thousand Africans bowing their heads to the ground before the Monstrance, he concluded —so he told us—that, foreign though this liturgical tradition was to his Swedish-Protestant up-bringing—here is the practical Christian answer to Islam.

Does this mean that we are entering the lists, to compete in the practice of magic: countering pagan *muti* with Christian? This is an easy accusation: but we should not let ourselves be bemused by this word 'magic'; it has an exact, and an inexact, use and the two are frequently confused. At least in the West we cannot afford to forget the late Professor R. G. Collingwood's remark [17] that in a world that has been atrophied by 'amusement art,' 'The more magic the better.'

And the problem goes deeper than we often realize. In the work of the modern Nigerian novelist, Chinua Achebe, *Things Fall Apart*,[18] which is written from a point of view profoundly unsympathetic to the missionary, it is suggested that the first batch of Christian converts (described in the novel) were all social misfits of one kind or another. It is hinted that for them Christianity was merely a compensation for social insecurity. No doubt things like that (*mutatis mutandis*) were said about many of the early Christians. But it is a question we must squarely face: Is our preaching a preaching of a whole faith to whole men? Of course, in another sense, without Christ none of us is a 'whole man' anyway. But we have to examine ourselves whether we, as Christian missionaries, are not sometimes cashing in on a kind of sickliness which their own pagan society could, *pro tanto,* have coped with? M. Eliade warns us against describing a religion exclusively in terms of its specific institutions and its most obvious themes. This, he says, would be like describing a man purely by his public behaviour and leaving out of account 'his secret passions, his nostalgias, his existential contradictions and the whole universe of his imagination, which are more essential to him than the ready-made opinions that he utters.' The consistent Anglican tradition has been one of reason and analogy—Joseph Butler (the one name missing from my list above) is perhaps in some ways the most formative Anglican thinker of them all. But it is our reason which tells us that reason is not all: that there is imagination, feeling, symbolizing rhythm, movement, and the rest. All this must be taken into the Christian experience, if that experience is to be universal. And it is precisely the encounter with non-Western man that may be the God-given opportunity to the Church, so hampered and narrowed by its long, Europe-centred history, to enlarge its experience—its experience, that is, of the Christ who took one nationality, spoke one language, lived in one small area, that he might become the Lord of all men, all nationalities, languages and areas. He came at a crucial moment in history: Jewish culture was just getting intermingled with Greek. The revolutionary fact of the Christ was that, as Fr. Thornton said, he raised them both above themselves: 'What made this revolution possible was not a mingling of cultures, but the new revolutionary fact of the Christ taking up that intermingling into itself.' [19]

This taking up of the (future) intermingling of cultures, Western, Asiatic, African, Polynesian, etc. into the Christ, and nothing less than that, nothing more local, more petty, more unambitious, is the task of the Church. For that is what Christ came for, 'that he might fill all things.'

CHAPTER III

✝ VICTOR SHEARBURN, C.R.
Bishop of Rangoon

VOCATION AND RESPONSE

I

OF the greatness and glory of the fundamental Christian mysteries, that which has so far been set out in this book goes far to proclaim. That they form not a great complex, but fit in utterly with God who is the altogether 'Simplex,' that also is evident on consideration. There remains one other 'complex'—man, the individual. How is it that he is not overwhelmed by all this greatness into an inevitable 'Yes'? Or perhaps it had better be put another way round—what is there in it and in him, which does enable him to say 'Yes'?

These things have often been spoken of under the terms of 'Vocation' and 'Response.' This looks simple enough—a Call from God, a Yes from man. And yet it is just here that Christian thought has moved in very different directions. Classical Protestantism as seen in John Calvin, is in revolt against the notion that there could be any merit in fallen man. Man, to him, was utterly fallen and lost; the only merits are the merits of Christ; it is on these that God looks, and for Christ's sake pardons erring and lost man. Calvin's watchword was, 'To God alone the glory.' This was a profound insight, correcting the current errors of the days just before the Reformation; of that there is no shadow of doubt. Nevertheless it has within itself the seeds of a grievous misunderstanding—it so emphasizes the 'otherness' of God, that all that is left to man is to contemplate God from afar, or rather to see what God has done for his creature, and to stir up thoughts of gratitude and awe. This is known as 'Prophetic Prayer.' It is that 'I-thou' relationship, which stresses the utter difference between Creator and creature—and there leaves it. The gulf remains between God and man—bridged only by the fact of the Cross and, while it places man in the new category of the 'saved,' yet it does not bring him into that close relationship of love with

God through Christ. The consequences are many: the Mass can be no more than a recalling of what has been done, lest there be any thought that what was done is incomplete; prayer, instead of being a growing into union with God by supernatural grace, must either find its satisfaction in one or another form of pietism, or else be chiefly concerned with 'me' and 'now'; the emphasis is on the individual, and his salvation, to the exclusion of the wholeness of the family of God, the 'Ecclesia'; attention is focused on the here and now, and relations with the mighty army of that part of the whole Church which has already passed on from earthly existence mean little. If this is a 'simplification,' a recovery of the 'simple Gospel,' then it is done only at the cost of omitting as insignificant much of the whole revelation.

Alongside this way of thinking there is another—the more traditional way, equally scriptural, and following in great measure the thinking of Augustine. Augustine taught that according to Scripture (Gen. 1 : 26) God made man in his 'image' and 'likeness'; that by the Fall the likeness was destroyed—whereas the image was permanent and indestructible—which Calvin denied. If this is so, then there is in man something, which, however heaped over by sin and its consequences, remains, and God can get to man through that enduring image. In other words, the potential link is there. Grace can enter, and lift up the life of man from the level of dead earth, as Hebrews describes it, to the level of supernatural life. Beyond this lies the possibility of a human life in union with God—eternal life beginning here and now, the newness of life, which our Lord evidenced in the Forty days after the Resurrection, and this becoming real and active in the whole life of the believer. The Resurrection of Christ is the arch, which spans the gulf between the earthly and the eternal. So the call to eternal life finds a resting-place in man, made in God's image, and now able to receive it through Jesus Christ.

God calls. Man responds—or fails to respond. Much of this book has rightly been taken up with God's side—what God has done, is doing, will do. What we are now asking is how conviction comes to man that God is in fact calling him, has a plan for him, has grace for him for the fulfilling of that plan—that the means are there—that the reward (surely a strange gift for doing no more than what we owe, and yet it is clearly there) is heaven—to be with God, and to be in love with God for ever.

Holy Scripture has one outstanding example of conviction coming to a man. It is the case of Thomas the doubter. The facts are clear: but the process or inner movement is not nearly so clear. And most of us are in like case. However transparent is the outer history, something has happened within, which we simply cannot put into adequate words.

What are the avenues along which the realization of God and his working travel into the deeps of our own selves?

They appear to be many—and to interlace. They look more like alleys than highways. We might have expected to find a sort of main trunk road leading direct from God to the soul—well marked, signposts and all. Instead we find something more like a lot of country lanes. If this is a fair picture, then to investigate the ways of what we often call 'Vocation' is a fascinating task—even if the results are still tentative.

Thomas has cried out that he must see and touch. But was that really necessary? And did he? The record does not tell us. At any rate, in so protesting, he put himself on one of the lanes of finding. For surely the senses are used by God to reveal himself to our consciousness. 'That which we have heard, that which we have seen with our eyes . . . and our hands handled . . . declare we unto you . . . and our fellowship is with the Father, and with his Son Jesus Christ' (1 John 1 : 1–3). That is how a greater than Thomas bore witness—that, he says, is how conviction came to him—and he is sure that his own testimony will bring fresh conviction to others.

But as we look into this lane, we see almost at once that there lies in it an ambiguity, when we speak of the senses as being an avenue of religious experience. Do we mean actual bodily senses? Or are we really thinking of some form of spiritual perception—with a reality of a quite different order?

One of the difficulties of language is that it provides for us no terms specially belonging to the experiences of the soul. There is no such technical terminology, so we have to make shift with borrowings from other departments, from other forms of experience—and then to use them with a meaning, which, however justifiable the analogy, is fundamentally different from their original and proper use. So we speak of seeing God, hearing his voice; and there are courageous writers who adopt all parts of the phraseology of the senses to express spiritual things. The Psalmist sings: 'How sweet are thy words unto my taste! yea, sweeter than honey to my mouth!' (Psalm 119: 103). He has consecrated the vocabulary of taste to his greater purpose. Some of the mystics speak of colours and sounds in a way that is at first strange.

Now such language of visions and voices may be literal or it may be figurative. The vision may present itself to the eye, the sound to the ear. Or else, on the contrary, that which comes may act directly on the soul. If it is this way, then the experience is only described in such terms for want of better media. And how are the two to be distinguished?

We recall the manifestation to Stephen at his martyrdom—the heavens open—Jesus standing at the right hand of God—what part of the martyr is it which SEES? We remember the conversion of Paul—and find the same difficulty. Or we come to the everyday experiences of Christian life, and ask ourselves, What is the savour of the Holy Sacrament, when we taste and see how gracious the Lord is? Or what spiritual value is there in the remembered scent of the incense? or what hearing is it with which we recognize our pardon in the words of absolution?

How difficult it is to distinguish, and yet it is not impossible. Those most rich in spiritual experience have always been the most sensitive in just this distinction. And often it has been women who have been our best teachers. Teresa laid down most delicately the lines of discrimination between sounds and sights received by the bodily senses and those presented to spiritual perception. Again, some fifty years later, there were great women in France such as Madame Acarie, who taught with security and decision, and served as guides to the great spiritual revival of their days. We truly have enough to know that the senses, both literally and figuratively, do constitute a real avenue of religious conviction.

But by saying this are we laying ourselves open to the charge of bowing to mere sentiment rather than obeying the dictate of scientific investigation? If so, that is all to the good. For we must ask what is the value of sentiment in religious experience. How can we trust a conviction which has come through the emotions? First, there is no ground for ruling out sentiment or treating emotional evidence as suspect in itself. God has given us affections —they are to serve as avenues or links with others. Why then not also with himself? For the Christian revelation shows us God as love, and shows us man as a being loved by God and, what is more, capable of loving him in return.

The way of the affections is a great way of Christian experience. Along it come some of the greatest convictions about God and things divine.

Sometimes the way of love is unobtrusive and continuous. Like the human love that grows up in the child's home, that shapes his life in the impressionable years—who can say where or when it first began to be so formative? It has been there all the time —quietly and effectively, before ever it was realized. Equally the love of God has been there all the time—in the relation between God and man—at work long before it was ever realized. 'We love him, because he first loved us.'

Along this same avenue come exeriences of the opposite character—not familiar, but novel and startling—not quiet and gentle, but passionate and stormy. For the soul is capable not only of gentle affection, but of sudden and violent 'falling in love.' Sometimes this happens when an overwhelming sense of guilt sweeps along, and awakens the sense of the need of a Saviour and Redeemer—drives home the conviction that there is such a Saviour—and his Name is Jesus—that he is even now on the threshold, knocking—and that to open to him is pardon and peace. Such a sense of guilt may come by other ways—the reproach of one whom we have injured, or even the sentence of the court. But only when it comes along the road of love has it this special value as religious experience—only then does it bring a conviction not of despair or disgrace, but of forgiveness and of God our Lover. Other emotions too have their part along this road—it may be an invasion of gratitude—all the accumulated goodness of God's fatherly love, long and persistently given, long and carelessly ignored, now realized in one great moment. Or it may be a realization of grace received in answer to prayer, and so victory over temptation—and there is stirred up a chivalrous devotion to the Lord Christ. Or the reading of some Gospel story rouses hero-worship; or a live sermon sets the sluggish heart vibrating—or the thought of the Cross calls for a wonder and love for the Crucified. We might list a great series of such experiences, highly varied, but linked by the common factor, that it is the emotional movement which brings the conviction of religious reality. It is perfectly true that emotions can be dangerous. But the danger does not lie in the fact that they exist and do move us, but in that we may stop at that point, content with the feeling and the indulgence of it. And even that danger is removed if the emotional stirring is treated as the prelude to an act of will, and the consequent strenuous, sturdy response to the stimulation of God's love.

Right at the other end of the scale from the emotions are the reflective, critical and speculative powers. Conviction can come through these also. In considering these we do well to remember that the greater part of mankind has not had its mind stretched, has not been taught to think, to weigh evidence and form conclusions. That God has given man mental powers, just as he has given affections and senses, no one will doubt. Nor shall we wisely doubt that these too can be means of communication with him. Indeed, may it not be their main purpose? And in so far as they fall short of this purpose, they are maimed and fail.

When a man verifies dispassionately and honestly the various points of the system of belief which he has hitherto held, there may well come to him a great uprising of conviction. He goes over it as an aircraft is gone over before taking flight; he finds each part secure, and is reassured. There will be elements about which he cannot make himself infallibly sure; there will always be an element of venture in the flight itself; there will be parts which can only be tested by the actual flight. But the thing is that he is satisfied that it is wise to make the venture.

Or again, there may be the force of cumulative evidence. The history of the Church since the time of our Lord is full of unsolved religious questions—and yet at the same time it is the record of a strangely persistent and irrepressible experience. Along with it, the Biblical writings raise and leave unsolved almost as many questions as they answer—but it all coheres with this continuous experience, and gives the documentary rationale of it. And if we turn to the future from the past, we see amid all that is unknown that there are dominant hopes which correspond with what we have noted in the past. And then, turning from the future to the present, we again observe a somewhat similar correspondence between the offers which religion makes us and the needs of which we ourselves are conscious. Past, future, present—separately they might be unconvincing; together they are seen to be parts of a consistent and moving whole.

Here again there is a danger. As with the emotions, we can remain content with the process, not getting beyond the critical and reflective and speculative investigation. So we become like an aircraft made and tested—remade and retested—but never taking off.

We have tried to distinguish three ways by which conviction may come. But they are separate only in theory. In practice they and others interlace. They correspond with the dominant features of the human temperament. But every man's temperament is compounded of many elements, however much one particular characteristic may dominate. And the case is the same with his available ways of access to religious experience. How compound and intricate for example are the religious experiences which come through the artistic capacities. The sense of beauty in sight and sound links us with God and reveals him to us. At first analysis it may seem that here we have to do with the senses; but again the emotional element is surely deeply involved. Nor is the intellectual element absent; for any full appreciation of beauty demands not only artistic capacity but training, hard work and discipline.

Or again when we turn to seek the meaning of worship, we find it first pictured in the Book of the Revelation—then, it is copied in our more drab way in earthly services. But how manifold are the lines along which the impressions come, and how richly diverse are the blending impressions themselves.

Conviction can come by this multiplicity of avenues, but there is an essential unity in the real conviction which comes. Along with vocation goes response, the response of the whole man. A real conviction is the action of the whole man, not of some department of his being. This does not imply that all parts of him are equally convinced—but that he as a whole is convinced. A committee may come to an unanimous vote without every member being convinced in the same degree; so the response which a man makes to God—his thankfulness, his shame, his

VOCATION AND RESPONSE 273

homage, his surrender—must be whole, and, so to speak, unanimous, though different elements in his nature share it in varying degrees.

And we have said that the ways of the coming of conviction are interlaced. If it came by one single channel alone, it might well be suspect. Pure intellectualism, pure emotionalism are alike untrustworthy. Visions and voices and the like we are bidden to test, to subject to strict spiritual verification and control, before we give them our confidence. If not, mental delusions may be held to be religious experiences; the counterfeit may discredit the real.

In actual practice, what goes deepest to the inner shrine of man's consciousness and calls for the stongest and most active response is the mixed experience. Therein the emotional element warms the cold logic of the reason, and critical work controls the data of the spiritual senses—even the least part of man's make-up contributes something to the whole effect. For this reason every man needs to have a watchful care over the less prominent parts of his individual temperament, the less frequented avenues. It is easy to be prejudiced, in favour of some, against others; in favour of some, because they are familiar; against others, because they are uncongenial. I may argue to myself, 'God has brought home to me such little knowledge of him as I possess by such and such a way—by quiet dutifulness, for example, or by unexciting, uneventful growth.' Well, thank God for that! But it does not follow that he will always do so. It may be that it came that way, because I was not expectant of or alert for any other way. I may even have missed much that I should otherwise have received, had I kept the ways open. Even if this were not so in the past, it may be the case in future, unless I take care to deal with it. My next great experience may be coming along the road of the affections, which hitherto I have been inclined to mistrust, or even to rule out. Another person might do well to meditate something like this: 'I owe my conversion to a great spiritual experience, an emotional crisis—yet it would probably be very good for me to settle down to some hard thinking. For I fancy that my weak and rather fitful hold on God would thus be strengthened; I should then be more secure in the face of the conflicting experience of other people or the criticism of those who pour cold water on what I have been through. I may even be able to help others better by so doing.' His godly motions may well come along avenues which we do not expect.

Thomas wanted the evidence of his senses. We are not told that it was in fact that way by which conviction came to him. And so it has been ever since. The vocation and the response—there is the pattern. And part at least of our care is to see that we do not prejudice our prospects by too restricted expectation—but keep all avenues open and set our will on guard, as alert and expectant as may be, at that point in us where all converge.

The manifoldness of the approaches will not alarm us; the intricate network of their ramifications need not puzzle us. The wind of the Spirit 'bloweth where it listeth,' and wafted by it along the divine channels come the great initial convictions; then the subsequent renewals of conviction and realization of God, the assurance of grace received, of salvation grasped, the secure prospect of power to amend, and of a new life in Christ begun. These —the greatest of all things—let them come to us all ways or any way, so long as they lead us, as they led Thomas, to the fullness of response, to the adoring tribute of homage, 'My Lord and my God.'

II

The coming of conviction, by whatever avenue or avenues, is the great beginning. And then? Can we deduce from Scripture and from observation the true pattern for the 'newness of life' which we have discovered?

If we start with Scripture, we find certain broad lines laid down—great principles stated—and all based on the revelation of God in the total life, death and resurrection of Christ. In this field we receive according to the measure, aim and depth of our seeking. Certainly there is no ready-made provision for every circumstance of life; rather a continual pointing away from the problem of the moment to a Person, in and from whom a new liberty is to be learnt. 'I am the way'—not 'I teach or show the way.' That is the great difference between the Christ and the other great religious teachers of the world's history. So we come to the two strands of Pauline teaching—'Christ in us' and 'we in Christ.' There can be nothing static in this, nothing acquired once for all, without growth or development. A truly personal relationship on the human level is never a fixed, static affair; at best it grows richer and deeper with time. So it is with the relationship between Christ and the soul. There is no room for complacency, for resting in our experience of yesterday or to-day. Just as in Christ everything from Bethlehem onwards had its part and place in the final effective offering of the Cross, so all that happens in and to us is a growing towards wholeness—the content of the response which we are to make to the outpouring of the love of God upon us. From the side of God it is towards a constant growth in holiness—in perception, deepening and response—that our conviction came to us. We shall expect to find along the road of earthly life souls at various stages of growth and development—and so we do.

In describing the Christian life Paul has a pleasant fancy to use again and again the language of the athlete—his training, his contest, his achievement, his prize. It is the training, the 'ascesis,' with which we are concerned at the moment. How does the newly-awakened Christian become a saint? 'Woe is me! . . . because I am a man of unclean lips.' cries the young Isaiah (6: 4): holiness and I are far apart. How can I ever be fit to stand in the Presence? Two answers are possible: either to hold that, by the merits of Christ, there will be some transformation, unknown as yet, by which such a thing will be possible; or to see in the life of the Risen Lord communicated to us by grace the beginnings of that transformation here and now. The one impossible thing is to hold that man is such that he can hoist himself to sanctity. Equally to be rejected is the thought of man as no more than the passive recipient, with nothing to do in effect than to say yes and yes and yes. If we press to its logical conclusion the thought of God the great and only Giver, and man the mere receiver, then we find ourselves with such an understanding of man as makes his great gifts of nothing worth. What then is the true balance? Is there an 'ascetic theology'—an accumulated wisdom concerning the growth of the soul and the pattern of Christian life?

In the Pauline teaching there are two lines of thought. The first emphasizes an enmity between 'sarx' and 'pneuma'—body and spirit. In this way 'body' means all that holds us down, away from God, shut up in self; 'spirit,' all that can rise to God in understanding, generosity, devotion and glad self-surrender. The saint finds in himself a warfare between these two elements to his sorrow and surprise—for these things are still there even after his surrender to his Lord and all that followed upon it. He has been accused of being the enemy of the 'body,' and so preaching a contempt of this world which is not found in the Gospels. But this is to misunderstand his aim—which is to show the urgency of the conflict and the necessity of going to war, armed with grace, against the deep-rooted forces hostile to God within human nature.

He has another line of approach in 1 Thessalonians 5 : 23, 'The God of peace himself sanctify you wholly; and may your spirit (Pneuma) and soul (Psyche) and body (Soma) be preserved entire, without blame at the coming of our Lord Jesus Christ.' That is to say, there are, not three separate parts in man, but three ways of living. Man can live like an animal (Body), like an educated and cultured person (Psyche), or, as God meant him to live, spiritually (Pneuma). In each case the higher element is to control the lower, or man goes astray. The body must not dominate the psyche, nor the psyche the spirit. This teaching was taken up by some of the greatest masters of the spiritual life; it was carefully worked out by Bernard in his sermons. And each state has its appropriate 'ascesis,' its prayer, its training, and its discipline. Nevertheless man remains ONE, not three parts wedded into one.

A slightly extended analysis of these three levels of living might be made like this : (i) There are the inferior and sensitive powers which we possess in common with the brute beasts; such are the senses, the appetites, affections, and natural passions. (ii) There is the 'psyche'—intellect or intelligence, memory and will. These are the higher or noble powers, which man shares with the angelic creation. Both (i) and (ii) have been maimed and weakened by sin, but are restored to their lost rank and dignity by our Lord. (iii) There is the 'pneuma,' sometimes called the 'nous' or apex of the soul. This is the simple and godlike basis or ground of the soul sealed with the image of God. From the psyche the three higher powers flow and re-flow into it—an analogy of the life of the Trinity. Thus man is able to know and desire: (i) according to the senses—with the appetite of the senses; (ii) according to reason and intellect—with rational and intellectual appetite and affections; (iii) with knowledge proper to the highest part of the intellect—supreme affection and a love in the highest part of the will. It follows then that, if the growth of the soul can be observed widely along these lines, there will be for each stage of growth (i) an appropriate understanding, mainly negative, of what has to be done to correct faults, in order to return and direct life Godwards; (ii) the prayer suitable to each state; (iii) the discipline suitable to each state.

It might be asked at this point, Are we attempting to systematize what should in fact be left free? The medical order of diagnosis before treatment is a real analogy. We do know much about human nature; the wise man seeks for self-knowledge. And the phenomena are all around us and within ourselves.

'Animal' man is a creature of infinite possibilities. Such were Mary Magdalene and all those afterwards who have passed on to awakening and conviction. Man living on this level is basically good-hearted and responsive to kindness and friendliness, with an amazingly sure instinct about sincerity in others. The problem is always how to convince him that any other life is conceivable. The method of the Incarnation was to get in touch by something common to both, so as to find and be found on entering in. As we have already thought, there is no main road, but many avenues by which God comes to animal man. The 'psychic' or rational man is far above the animal, but a long way off the spiritual level. He may be an ordinary, decent living person, cultured and even religious, but this last in the outward sense, for some other reason than for God's sake. He is a much more complex creature. There is a strong element of rational man in most of us; education and culture are gifts of God, but not so easy to use for his glory. What then is the 'spiritual' man?

If this is what we hope to become, how can we define it? We cannot define, but we can describe. Here is man living as God intends. 'These are they who are led by the Spirit and more fully enlightened by the Holy Ghost.' By the Spirit's leading, the downward tendency of the flesh is mastered, and man is fully grounded in love. 'He that is joined unto the Lord is one spirit'

(1 Cor. 6: 17). This does not mean pantheism; identity and individuality are preserved, but this man is drawing his life from God. In him 'spirit' (pneuma) is above all else.

There have been misleading notions about this stage of the soul's growth. The 'spiritual' man has his ups and downs; he is not 'beyond good and evil.' In him there is no formal sinlessness. But it is a state in which God has possessed the will, so that in spite of temporary aberrations that will returns to God, like a compass needle to the north. 'Love never faileth.' The scholastics defined 'caritas' or love as an 'infused virtue,' but the earlier notion of love is that of a strong habit, whose depths cannot be disturbed by what happens on the surface. Peter's denials did not destroy his love of his Lord. Paul's alternations between flesh and spirit did not ruin his apostolic life. We may think of it as God's stronghold in the Christian, which may be besieged, even put out of action, but is impregnable, and the base for all attacks on evil.

We start each with our home-made universe and, awakened, take the first step into the real, eternal, limitless universe of God—and then seek to find our place in that universe. The moment we turn and start this outwards going, the hindrances begin. First, how can I be exactly sure what is going to happen to me? That is the first enemy of faith. The next is self-will: F. D. Maurice wrote, 'to be something is man's ambition, man's sin.' It is largely based on fear—a fear of losing chances, of not doing something 'worth while'—a desire to use people and things to our own advantage. And this is easily extended to apply to God, to use God. It goes hand in hand with a wrong fear of God—that God may be wanting to change me—as indeed he does. It may go with knowledge about God, rather than trust in God, with theories about religion and the spiritual life. But knowledge has to be taught to serve, not to master, nor allowed to blind. 'No creature is sufficient,' said a dying saint.

In Ephesians 1 we have St. Paul's teaching about the universe. He speaks of the 'mystery of his will.' Man finds his true place in the universe by giving himself and leaving himself in God's care. God is faithful and perfectly capable of looking after what he has created.

In human life the most formative power is the Vision of God. We begin by catching glimpses of what we ought to be, what we ought to do. We must never go back on these. Bunyan's pilgrim caught glimpses of the Promised Land—and they were unforgettable. There was hard going before him; but the vision drew him on. Our glimpses may come in many forms—ideals, inspirations, reflections, purposes. They may be vague or precise—of loving God or of doing some particular thing. When they come, we remember the parables of the Pearl of great price and the Treasure hid in a field; the vision must be followed, with renunciation, if need be. We do not see the whole at once; that would be too much to endure. The slow movement of growth in Augustine, as shown in his 'Confessions' and in his parish sermons, is a clear example of this. One thing we cannot and dare not say, 'The heights are not for me.' Christian progress is very hard to judge. Our first ideas of the standards required are usually inadequate. It is only as we go on, that we see that its true aim is the voluntary submission to God as he is, to do his will and walk in his ways, so that the life of Christ is reproduced in us.

It is here that we see the work of the Holy Spirit most clearly; he is recreating man in the image of the Son. We might put it another way; he is working in us so as to bring about 'Christ in us'—his work is just that, as told in Genesis and the Annunciation. But man is not PRIVATELY made holy—he is incorporated into the Body of Christ. We receive the spirit of adoption; and so we are presented to the Father by the Son. Christian teaching is always trinitarian in this, never pantheistic or 'nature-mysticism.' The highest good is a common good, not an individual's good. The New Testament is emphatic about this; therein we learn that man comes to his true station only as a member of the Body of Christ. In the Confessions (viii, 4) Augustine is speaking of the joy at the conversion of Victorinus, and he says, 'When joy is shared by many, the joy of each is richer, for they warm one another.' The warmth is not in the individual progress but in the common life. That common life is the principle of the City of God, and heaven is the perfection of it.

So we come back to the question which we put earlier: How does the newly-awakened Christian become a saint? After his first awakening he has much to learn and do—even more, much to receive with heart and mind and will. As self-knowledge grows, he will see what has to be done away—and will go to it not in his own strength. Further he will see himself not in the least as a favoured individual, but in his true setting in the whole plan of God—a creature indeed, but with infinite possibilities, which are to be shared and not hoarded. Part of this sharing, if he is wise, will be the seeking of counsel; not even his study of Scripture and the wisest of the spiritual classics can take the place of this. Prayer and discipline, marching together, and appropriate to that stage of growth to which he has arrived, will be a daily duty. And, above all, his eyes will not be on himself, but on him who is the Way. We do love God, but our love is not well directed because of ignorance, but the great thing is that we know it—and are not dismayed, looking beyond that ignorance and its limitations. Love is not at our command, but we can so want it that by every means held out to us, prayer and study, sacrament and discipline, the very thing we cannot command grows in us. So 'our inward man is renewed day by day' (2 Cor. 4: 16), and our life is lived on that level which is neither animal nor cultural, but 'joined to the Lord in one spirit' (1 Cor. 6: 17).

CHAPTER IV

FR. AELRED STUBBS, C.R.

ALL IN ALL

Up till about 1940 the phrase 'The End of the World' probably seemed to most people either rather extravagant and melodramatic science-fiction, or theological poetry which you have to keep because it's in the Bible but which need not mean anything more precise than most other kinds of poetry to the ordinary person. But now we can read stories about the future, or sit through the film of the late Mr. Nevile Shute's *On the Beach*, and face this very possibility of 'The End of the World' with the usual reactions of either stoic complacency ('You can't do a thing about it') or cheerful boredom ('We've heard it all before'). Does this mean it is easier or harder for Christians to-day to talk about the traditional doctrine of 'The Last Things'? Perhaps it is both easier and harder. At any rate, let us see how one recent Christian thinker, a man of great practical scientific experience who was also a priest, envisaged these things.

The theme of P. Teilhard de Chardin's great book *The Phenomenon of Man* is that in man, and in man alone of created beings, lies the future of the cosmos. This is because in man alone has 'evolution become conscious of itself' (to quote Julian Huxley's phrase); henceforward all progress in evolution must lie in this sphere of consciousness. Moreover—and this is the source of much of modern man's fear and anguish—in this sphere evolution, in the person of man, 'becomes free to dispose of itself—it can give itself or refuse itself.'[1]

The first thing a modern man may feel when confronted with such a statement is a sense of futility. In face of the vastness of the space-time continuum how can he not feel terrified and impotent! The only remedy for this 'malady of multitude and immensity' is the fact of evolution itself: i.e. it is evolution which makes 'number' tolerable, for it uses these vast quantities in a definite process, '. . . a flux which, incredibly vast as it may be, is not only *becoming* but *genesis*, which is something quite different. Indeed time and space become humanized as soon as a definite movement appears which gives them a physiognomy.'[2]

But, even when this is perceived, even granted that the universe has up till now been in motion along these particular lines, what guarantee is there that it will continue thus in motion to-morrow? Can there ultimately be any escape from the principle of entropy? Unless a good hope can be given in answer to these questions, a real hope of achieving the infinite possibilities proposed to him, modern man is likely to go on strike, and so bring evolution to a halt. 'Ça ne vaut pas la chandelle!' Either the universe is closed —in which case thought, 'the fruit of millions of years of effort,' is still-born : or an opening exists, a way out for our souls, those personal centres of consciousness which are the peak of the evolutionary process, into what is nothing less than a new world of 'limitless psychic spaces.'

Between this absolute pessimism and absolute optimism no 'middle way,' supposedly beloved of Anglicans, exists : and man must choose! All that can help him in this choice (which, though collective, is also fundamentally personal) is the rational hope given by the history of evolution up to this present moment. With that knowledge a rational act of faith is possible. No more tangible evidence can be produced.

But, supposing that man chooses the way of optimism, there are still two false paths he may follow—that of isolation, whether as an individual or as a group (the path of a modern gnostic system such as Gurdjieff's, or of all racialist ideologies), and that of mass-movements, such as Communism. Both these paths are false because, though for different reasons, they ignore the all-important fact of the personal. The mistake of the former is to confuse individuality with personality. By isolating itself, whether as an individual or as a group, it condemns itself to sterility and to death. The error of the latter, though nobler, is no less fatal : it seeks to sink the personal in the universal and to substitute a collective for a hyper-personal goal. But the goal of ourselves is not our individuality but our person; and *according to the evolutionary structure of the world,* we can only find our person by uniting together. . . . 'There is, however, an obvious and essential proviso to be made. For the human particles to become really personalized under the creative influence of union, they must not ... join up together anyhow. Since it is a question of achieving a synthesis of centres, it is centre to centre that they must make contact and not otherwise.'[3]

Teilhard de Chardin goes on to show how love is a general property of all life. If there were no internal propensity to unite, even at a prodigiously rudimentary level—indeed in the molecule itself—it would be physically impossible for love to appear higher up, with us[4]: and to assert the *biological* necessity of universal love—the only complete and final way in which we are able to love. And as the climax of his exposition of the 'phenomenon of man' he postulates the necessary existence of 'Omega point' as the hyper-personal Centre which draws all personal centres of consciousness into union with itself and so with each other, without drowning them in an impersonal sea of collectivity. So man 'escapes from entropy by turning back to Omega.' But this hyper-personal Centre cannot itself be solely a product of evolution. To be the sufficient attractive and consistent Centre of the desires and aspirations of man it must also be right outside and altogether transcend the space-time continuum of evolution. Yet again it must be present now: we must here and now be able to be in conscious communion with it.

One final question may be put. Is the final consummation so proposed, this unification of the thinking mass of personal centres of consciousness with Omega to be an inevitable development, destined to take place in growing harmony and peace? We should like to think it—the gradual elimination of disease, hunger, hatred, war—a convergence peaceful though full of tension? Or will evil go on growing alongside good to the very end, tempting man to 'fulfil' himself along the 'cul de sacs' of isolation and collectivism? The latter hypothesis is far more like the traditional picture of the end of the world—and also, surely, truer to our actual experience of life in which evil continues to keep pace with and shadow good to the very end.

Now when we turn to the Christian revelation we find at once that at its centre is the mystery of a personal God. From the beginning of the biblical history (and, to get our perspectives right, we must remember that history, in the strict sense of the word, only begins in very modern times, say 1700 B.C.). He discloses himself as personal 'the God of Abraham, Isaac and Jacob,' 'I will be that I will be,' the very appropriate Name for the Creator of a world in evolution. From the beginning he wills to draw one particular people into personal relationship with himself, to save the many through the few. This determination is expressed in the Covenant, the external form of a personal relationship at once social and individual. The 'within' of that covenant-relationship is expressed in the Hebrew word *hesed* (translated in our English versions 'loving-kindness,' 'mercy,' 'kindness'), which includes all the qualities we expect to find in a true friendship—loyalty, truthfulness, ready sympathy, and a deep, inner affection.

The historical evolution of this People is part of the history of the evolution of the cosmos, a tale of the struggle upwards into full, personal consciousness and responsibility, a struggle certain to fail but for the presence in their midst of the redeeming God, steadfast in *hesed,* consistent, attractive, holy: a struggle which issues finally in the desired consummation, the perfect *hesed* of 'I will be that I will be' answered by the perfected response of *hesed* from the People: 'Be it unto me according to thy word.' The fruit of that union of a divine and human will is what in Christian theology we call the Incarnation, which appears in history as the human phenomenon Jesus of Nazareth, the sole justification of millions of years of evolution, with all its suffering and all its 'wastage.'

In him the difficulty of the personal and the universal is resolved. He is God and therefore he is universal. Yet God reveals himself as personal throughout the Bible, and supremely in the Person of Jesus Christ. He is man: not *a* man, but man. He took human flesh of a human girl: he took it into personal union with himself, the Second Person of the Trinity. Thus in his Person mankind is renewed: and since man, as we have seen, is from long before his historic manifestation the axis of evolution, with his coming evolution reaches its term.

But also his Incarnation is redeeming: his Name means Saviour. Evolution is not of itself an inevitably good process. In fact, as another essay has shown, evil is present in the creation almost from the beginning, and mounts in intensity and power as the universe evolves. The Incarnate comes to fulfil the creation, but by saving it from the evil which continually threatens to overwhelm and destroy it. This cosmic drama between the forces of light and darkness, which is the ruling theme of the biblical history, reaches its climax in the life, sufferings and above all death of the Incarnate. Against him all the forces which are trying to destroy man, and in man the whole creation, put forth their powers. The only weapon with which he fights is obedience to the Will of God (John 4 : 34; Luke 13 : 33, and R.V. marg. references; Mark 14 : 36, etc.). Thus his death is both the final defeat of those powers which enslave man and the way out (the 'Exodus'—see Luke 9 : 31, Greek ἐξοδος) of mankind into the final state to which the creation is from the beginning called.

Thus in the life and death of the Incarnate we see two things : God's love reaching down to save, renew and fulfil his creation; and this being done in Man, who in Christ accepts his glorious vocation to lead the cosmos through death into its final, irreversible state. The Incarnation is something wholly new, 'from above' : also it is the apex of evolution. In man evolution is free to dispose of itself—it can give itself or refuse itself. In the Incarnate it does just that : gives itself for the salvation, renewal and fulfilment of the Creation. And at the Ascension he 'returns' to the Father, bearing with him the whole Creation. 'It is done.'

Then what is the point of life? Just this, that we may 'grow up in all things into him, which is the head, even Christ' (Eph. 4 : 15), who continues to redeem and consummate the evolutionary process from within. This is the work of the Holy Spirit in the Church (not only in the visible Church, but secretly in the whole redeemed Creation), 'to sum up all things in Christ' (Eph. 1 : 10). This is the meaning of history and of our own present lives, the transformation of man from his own infected centre to the true and final Centre which is Christ. Because it is the inalienable condition of love, God waits. Besides, although the forces of evil have been decisively defeated on the Cross, until the final Day they retain a semblance of power. This means that the vocation of the Church during these last days is still supremely that of the suffering servant filling up 'that which is lacking of the afflictions of Christ' (Col. 1 : 24). We should remember this when we are tempted to be critical of her: 'when we see her, there is no beauty that we should desire her.' 'All glorious *within* is the king's daughter' : outwardly she is 'despised and rejected . . . as one from whom men hide their face, not esteemed' : 'a spectacle unto the world . . . the filth of the world, the offscouring of the world . . . always bearing about in her body the putting to death of Jesus.' 'Death worketh in us, but life in you' (Isa. 53, 2; Ps. 45 : 13; 1 Cor. 4 : 9, 13; 2 Cor. 4 : 10, 12). If this is applied first to the Ministry *vis à vis* the Church, it also applies—and must be seen to apply to the Church as a whole *vis à vis* the world. Christ did not come to condemn the world but to save it. The Church is not here to condemn the world but to save it. She only saves it by dying for it.

Therefore the sign of the end of the world will be the final Passion of the Church, accompanied by all the exterior and interior signs which marked the Passion of the Incarnate—treachery from within, an organized attack from the world without, Judas, Caiaphas, Annas, Pilate and the soldiers and the crowd all playing their parts—and not only these, but the disciples too, Peter and the rest forsaking, no one left but the very small, humble Remnant, symbolized perhaps by our Lady and the beloved disciple, and these experiencing the profound fear and desolation and abandonment of Gethsemane and Calvary. Throughout Christian history individuals have been called to follow through to the bitter end this way of the Cross: in the very last days the Church herself, or that small remnant which is the heart of the Church must undergo the Passion.

But just as there was, in the hidden depths of the Incarnate, God—'mine Holy One, thou diest not'—so in the inward heart of the Church is the Risen Christ, and all who have died in him. The Church is a visible organism. But, as with every centre of consciousness, there is that in her, her 'within,' which is not visible to the eyes of the world; and this 'within,' includes all who have died in her faith. She is one organism, indivisible, by far the greater part hidden from our eyes, living with the same divine life. This fact of faith is the ground of the Christian attitude to death and to prayers for the departed and to asking the prayers of the saints.

The decisive change of state for a Christian comes at Baptism —that is the moment of death, a death to sin, the world, the flesh and the devil, and new life in Christ, the life of charity. At this moment the centre of his being is transformed, a new principle of being is given; and the whole of the rest of life consists in becoming what we are through the gift of God in Baptism, an ever-deepening dying to self and living to God, the life of the Spirit of the Crucified and Risen Lord growing in us (or not, as the case may be: for grace is not irresistible). Thus 'physical' death is only the final moment on earth for each Christian of that process which has been going on in us ever since our Baptism. Inevitably death is a lonely experience: that is the cost of personhood. It was so for our Lord and St. Mark tells us that he was terrified at its approach (Mark 14: 33). Nevertheless he knew and said that he was not alone (John 16: 32): and what was true for him is true also for us, for even if we are called to die in complete physical loneliness and desolation we know that, if we repent of our sins, we are at one with him and his Saints in the depths of the Church, and that prayer is made for us.

Because the Church is one, and her life the Spirit of charity, we pray for the departed and ask their prayers. Prayer is charity energizing, and the prayer of intercession is 'death working in us that life may work in you.' We pray for the dead because we love them and desire their good; and this is the only way, in our present state of 'physical' separation, in which we can compass their good (though we know not how). Death cannot separate us finally: it is in fact the way to a union closer than any we can enjoy on earth. Prayer for the departed (supremely the offering of the Eucharist for their intention) is the sacrament of love which binds those who are temporarily hidden from each other.

Similarly we ask for their prayers. This is all that is meant by words which in the past have been a needless stumbling-block to many Christians, 'the invocation of Saints.' We ask for the prayers of those whom we believe to be at one with the Centre. Why do we not go direct to the Centre? We do: there is no compulsion to ask the Saints for their prayers! But once we have grasped that we have no independent existence in the Church, that we only *live* through total interdependence on each other in the Centre, that all growth in life means growth in Charity, that charity means giving and *receiving*, and that therefore to ask a favour from someone is itself—or at least can be, an act of charity and humility; and understanding that when we ask the prayers of the Saints, and supremely our Lady, we are asking the prayers of the full-grown Spirit of Christ in them—when we see all this, then the implied distinction between Christ and his Saints is seen to be unreal.[5]

Perhaps this is the place to say a word about 'purgatory,' another word that causes distress to many people, partly because of the crudity of certain Roman Catholic teaching. Only the pure in heart can see God (Matthew 5 : 8) : not all of us, to say the least, are pure in heart at the day of our death. If we have any future it can only be in a closer union with God, in a clearer vision of him—for which we need to be prepared. The Protestant objection to purgatory rests, again, on a defective doctrine of the Incarnation. It is not believed that the Incarnation affects the whole of humanity, but only the Person of Jesus Christ, who is regarded as a single individual. Once it is realized that in the mystery of that Person is contained the whole of humanity, then it is also seen how to 'grow up into Christ' means to be changed—a real, ontological and moral transformation—not a fictitious imputation of righteousness

Since the real death is the death to sin which is accomplished sacramentally in Baptism and must then be worked out in the moral order in our lives, it follows that growth in the new life of charity must be painful—a burning away of sins, actual and inherited : thus all our Christian lives are purgatorial. But most of us are pretty certain that this process will not have been completed at the day of our death : it is reasonable to assume that we shall need to be more completely purified before we are able to receive the vision of God. What we cannot know is whether that purification is accomplished in one blinding, agonizing instant through the touch of the charity of God, or whether it is a more gradual process. Neither Scripture nor the Fathers are interested in such questions : the vision of God is what matters, and their eyes are fixed on that. Catholic doctrine, however, teaches that the experience is essentially joyful. Already the will is centred on God, and the soul lies passive in his hands, willing that the fire of charity may burn away all that still obstructs the final vision. The soul suffers, not in isolation but in the redeemed and redeeming Body. She suffers for a purpose in love.

But what of those who die unbaptized, if Baptism occupies the central place in the process of transfiguration which we have given it? These may be divided into two categories: first, those who, knowing and understanding and fully accepting the truth of Baptism, yet wilfully turn away and refuse its grace (a state which it is almost impossible to conceive); and those who, for one reason or another, are unable to receive the Sacrament. The former would seem to be in danger of committing the ultimate and unforgivable sin of despair. For the latter God will provide other means of cleansing.[6] Baptism is the covenanted means of grace, compulsory for those who hear the call: but God's grace is not limited to these covenanted means.

The end of the world will be heralded by the final passion of the Church. This is foretold in Scripture in terms of a final, and to all appearances successful attack of the forces of evil. This attack continues in one form or another throughout 'these last days,' but at the very end will come to a climax of malice, cruelty and destruction in which the Church Militant will veritably die. As in the death of her Lord the forces of evil will seem to have triumphed completely. 'When the Son of man cometh, shall he find the faith on the earth?' (Luke 18: 8). The question expects the answer 'No.' This final paroxysm of evil will be accompanied by cosmic signs, paralleling those recorded at the death of the Incarnate (Mark 13: 24 and parallels), warnings of his final Coming.

This Coming will be sudden and secret: as secret and sudden (though as long and carefully prepared) as his first Coming. It will take all unawares. We do not know the time or the manner. We only know that, as the final passion of the Church is the sign of the approaching end, so the very end will be the actual Coming of the Lord himself, with his Saints; and every eye shall see him.

Then all men shall rise again (2 Cor. 5: 10; John 5: 28; Athanasian Creed), and they shall be judged in their bodies. The presence of Christ shall judge them then, as he judges all men now. At every moment we are judged by his holiness. The effect

T

of the judgment, damnation or salvation, is the absolutely infallible and just result of the particular choices of our past lives. To be human is to be loving. That love may have been misguided and twisted. But if it has in any way meant the preference of another's good to our own, then in his Presence we shall be led to cry for mercy—and no one ever cried to him in vain : for he who is our Judge is also our Saviour.

But there must remain that spark of human personality—that in me which desires something other than me. It is possible for the human spirit so to turn in upon itself that it destroys itself. This seems to be the 'second death.' All shall be raised—but it may be that some who are raised are no more like human beings than waxworks in Madame Tussaud's. In the Presence of the burning Heart of Charity they will melt like waxworks until there is nothing left. To some extent this must happen to all of us. We are so corrupted by self-love that there is a great deal of the sham, the wax-work in each of us. Divine Charity working in us has the effect of melting some of this during our lives on earth if we consent with our wills. If we do not consent the wax hardens and the human spirit withers. Then, at the end, nothing but a hard case is left, the caricature of a person. The spirit of man must choose to give itself or refuse itself. The result of refusal is death. We can only live and grow by giving ourselves away, by that losing of self in which we find our true selves. Those who fail to do this harden, fossilize and finally die : there is nothing left to give. The more we hoard, the poorer we become. This is the law of charity, the law of life. The test is something as simple as succouring the poor, visiting the prisoners, the sick and the lonely (Matthew 25 : 31ff.). Even if at the beginning one is led to do these things by the fear of hell, they are at least to some extent taking us out of ourselves.

The temptation of man is this inner refusal, which is indeed the ultimate death-wish. The only unforgivable sin is that against the Holy Ghost, and is called despair. When a man truly despairs he is denying the existence of a power that can save him from himself : he is blotting out charity. The result of that refusal is death. All other sins are forgivable. There is something which men call despair, but is really anguish, and is hope fighting against hope. The real, unforgivable despair is a hard self-sufficiency, the consummation of pride. To be wrapped in that is to be in hell. 'Hell is oneself,' writes T. S. Eliot. Hell is also, as Sartre writes, 'other people': for those who have made that ultimate refusal of Charity the presence of others is an additional torment: and the damned therefore cannot but hate and torment one another. But Charles Williams shows besides this how this damnation ultimately leads to the extinction of personhood: for the latter depends on charity. Whoever cannot love cannot live.

Hell is a possibility for all of us, and must be because of the free nature of love. By every refusal of love, whether in giving or receiving, we make the possibility a little more actual. By every movement of Charity that hard core of self is a little melted. At the Last Judgment we appear as we are, creatures willing to be consumed in love and so transfigured totally into the divine Image; or creatures doomed to be destroyed by the fire of love, which kills what it cannot cleanse. If the world is made by love, for love and of love, as we affirm, there seems no alternative. We must love or perish—not by any arbitrary decree of a 'Big Brother,' but because we are made like that, the universe is made like that: it is the condition of personhood.

This judgment men will receive in their bodies: in fact the bodies themselves will make manifest the judgment. The Bible knows nothing of the immortality of the soul. We are persons, and we need bodies to express our personalities. Even in this 'body of our humiliation' (Phil. 3: 21) the stuff of our flesh is constantly changing, so that from moment to moment we are never materially the same. Yet our bodies remain recognizable. 'You haven't changed a bit,' we say to someone we haven't met for seven years. Physically that is not true: our friend has 'changed' completely in that time. Yet he is the same: his body, the expression of his personality, remains the same. What changes a man really is sin or grace or, sometimes, extreme suffering which has temporarily overwhelmed the personality. 'I would not have recognized her, she is so changed' always refers to a spiritual alteration.

We are incarnations, a one flesh union of body and spirit. This was so evident to the Hebrews that the Old Testament as a whole has no doctrine of resurrection. Everywhere in the Old

Testament there is a tremendous vitality, springing from a belief in the living God. So great is this vitality that death could not be conceived as immediate extinction of the personality. The dead went on living, or rather existing in the 'not-land' of Sheol, for as long at least as there was any one of their name to carry on their personality on earth. When all their male descendants had died they finally ceased to exist—except in the mind of God, who knew them for ever. On earth, to live was to be in conscious communion with the living God: but death, because it meant the end of the body, separated all from him. Except in the apocryphal book of the Wisdom of Solomon, which is profoundly influenced by Hellenistic thought, there is no hint of a doctrine of the immortality of the soul—and even there that doctrine is subjected to the Hebrew conception of true life being the life of righteousness.

For Christians the doctrine of the resurrection of the body rests of course on the Resurrection of Christ. When he rose the human race rose. 'As in Adam all die, so also in Christ shall all be made alive' (1 Cor. 15: 22). Already that risen life is communicated to us in the Sacraments of the Church. In Baptism we receive that seed of Christ's new, crucified and risen life, the seed of the parables of the Kingdom, the seed of the body of charity which is to grow in us, transforming us into itself. That seed is nourished and grows by our feeding on his Body and Blood in the Eucharist. Already then we have received our resurrection bodies. Baptism is the moment of death and resurrection. We are already being changed. But this transformation, throughout our earthly life, is a hidden thing—though in exceptional people it will flash forth.

But this building up of our resurrection bodies is not automatic: because they are incarnations of charity it requires the constant co-operation of our wills. St. Paul says that we may eat the Body of the Lord to our judgment (1 Cor. 11: 27). If our wills remain centred on self, our eating of the Body defeats the purpose for which he gave it. When we eat we are entering into communion with a Person. In so far as our will is being conformed to his Will, so far is our body, the expression of our personality, being changed into his crucified and risen Body. Only by a daily dying to self in the Eucharist can we not only remain the same true person, but grow in truth and holiness. Always in this life, as in the days of his flesh, it remains 'the body of his glory' (Phil. 3 : 21) but here on earth a hidden glory, visible only through the sign of charity, the one constant.

It is only at his Coming that this glory will be revealed and we shall see him as he is—in the Body (1 John 3 : 2). At present we cannot do this through our sin-darkened vision we can only see 'in a mirror, in an enigma.' In this life we know only in part: by grace our knowledge grows; but the end of human knowledge is knowledge of our ignorance. So St. Thomas Aquinas after Mass one morning, about a year before his death, laid down his pen and wrote no more. He left his great life work unfinished. His system is incomplete. That very incompleteness is his highest wisdom. In Christ is the fullness and in him, moment by moment, we are being filled and fulfilled. But all this life long we remain fragmentary, uncompleted creatures.

'But then face to face.' In one moment of agony and joy, sweetness and bitterness inexpressible, we shall know as we have been known. All our past will be present in that moment of truth, and we shall be judged, forgiven, punished, healed, slain, made alive, our fickle *hesed* once for all taken and fixed irreversibly in his abiding *hesed*. And, even beyond that, union. 'Let him kiss me with the kisses of his mouth' (Song of Solomon 1 : 2). It is for this ultimate embrace that all of us long, whether celibates or married : for even the holiest union of married love gives only a fugitive foretaste of that abiding consummation. But this consummation is not given to us as individuals, but only as distinct persons who have wholly lost and found themselves in the divine society. So in the final vision the Apostle sees 'the holy city, new Jerusalem, coming down out of heaven from God, made ready as a bride adorned for her husband' (Rev. 21 : 2). The marriage is between 'the Lamb' (the symbol for the crucified and risen Incarnate, the Sacrifice) and his Bride the Church. Her bridal dress is the charity of the saints (Rev. 19 : 7). At that moment the whole company of the redeemed is made finally one with the Redeemer, and the evolution of the cosmos is completed. Perfect and complete vision and union, of him and with him, of one another and with one another, the summing up of all in the Incarnate.

In Heaven, according to St. Augustine, 'vacabimus et videbimus, videbimus et amabimus, amabimus et laudabimus': 'we shall rest and we shall see, we shall see and we shall love, we shall love and we shall praise.'[7] In the calm beauty of Heaven, 'where all that is not music is silence,' we shall see. 'He shall see of the travail of his soul, and shall be satisfied' (Isa. 53: 11). In terms of human justice there is no solution to the problem of evil. So far Ivan is justified in 'The Brothers Karamazov.' Only the love of God can—not solve the problem, but transcend it. In the light of the Cross Christians can at least say that if there is a problem of evil, God is at the heart of it. In 'that day' we shall know this: no cry of the inconsolable heart shall go unanswered by him who shall himself wipe away every tear from every eye. Then, and only then, shall his words to the Lady Julian be wholly fulfilled: 'All things shall be well, and thou shalt see thyself that all manner thing shall be well.'

'Except I shall see the print of the nails . . .' (John 20: 25). That is at the very heart of the vision—the precious tokens of his love, the scars of nail and spear and scourge on his holy and glorified flesh. 'We shall see and we shall love.' Those wounds are not only the pledges of God's love for us; they are the very wounds of suffering humanity, the abiding pledge of the Passion man must endure to evolve into his final state. The Passion of Christ is the Passion of the Church, of mankind. Then we, the Israel of God, Head and members, one Body, 'we shall see of the travail of our souls and be satisfied.' We shall see that which we have suffered and inflicted. In a passion of penitence and forgiveness we shall understand and adore the unfathomable goodness of God: and all our love shall be fulfilled.

'We shall love and we shall praise.' We shall praise, we shall adore. In that city wherein God and man, in the Incarnate, shall dwell, that holy city which is the glorified Body, 'I saw no temple therein: for the Lord God the Almighty, and the Lamb, are the temple thereof' (Rev. 21: 22). The end for which we were created is adoration. Beyond even union with the Incarnate lies the adoration of the Coinherent Trinity by his redeemed creation. Even here on earth we discover our vocation, in whatever sphere, only in the way of worship. When the musician is lost in his music, the scientist in his experiment, the carpenter one with his craft, the mother wholly given to her baby, the priest one with the Sacrifice he offers, then man is most himself. In that holy Jerusalem, into which all the kings of the earth, all cultures, all races shall have brought their treasures, everything says Glory. We shall live in that Trinity in Unity whom we shall adore, whose glory, refracted through the Incarnate, will penetrate us, transforming us more and more and endlessly into himself.

'For in that Trinity is the supreme source of all things, and the most perfect beauty, and the most blessed delight. Those three, therefore, do seem to be mutually determined to each other and are in themselves infinite. Now here, in corporeal things, one thing alone is not as much as three together, and two are something more than one. And in themselves they are infinite. So both each are in each, and all in each, and each in all, all in all, and all are one.' [8]

'O eternal truth, and true Charity, and lovely Eternity! Thou art my God, to thee do I sigh day and night.' [9]

NOTES

PART I. CHAPTER II

PAGE
38. 1. There are two Pauline passages at least which might seem to contradict this statement. Of these Rom. 9 : 5 is almost certainly wrongly rendered—or wrongly punctuated—in AV and RV. Some indication of this is given in the RV footnotes; and the more modern translations, as well as modern commentaries, give different renderings. As to Tit. 2 : 13, the Pastoral Epistles are of such uncertain origin and date that we must here leave them out of account; but in this passage too the RV footnote should be observed. Other passages as well as these two could be understood as dirct ascriptions of deity to Christ were it not for the fact that different modes of expression are so much more frequent and that the probability therefore is so strong against such an understanding.
44. 2. H. E. W. Turner, *The Pattern of Christian Truth* (Mowbray, 1954), p. 462f.
48. 3. John Ruskin, *Praeterita* (George Allen, 1887), vol. 2, pp. 208ff.

PART II. CHAPTER I

85. 1. Arbousset, *Missions evangéliques,* xiv, p. 57 (cit. in Lévy-Bruhl, *Primitive Mentality* (1923), p. 23).
86. 2. B. Malinowsky, *The Sexual Life of Savages* (1929), p. 359.
89. 3. B. Russell, *Enquiry into Meaning and Truth,* p. 133.
89. 4. And the Russian photograph later confirmed the Empiricist!
90. 5. *v.* Ian Crombie in *Faith and Philosophy,* ed. B. Mitchell, 1958.
92. 6. M. Brierley, *Trends in Psychoanalysis* (1951), p. 100.
93. 7. A. J. Ayer, *Pontiffs and Journeymen*—lecture to UNESCO, Sorbonne, 1946.
96. 8. Mircea Eliade, *The Myth of the Eternal Return* (1956).
97. 9. L. S. B. Leakey, *Adam's Ancestors* (Methuen, 1953), p. 218.
97. 10. Paul Tillich, *The Protestant Era* (Nisbet, 1951), p. 246.
97. 11. G. E. M. Anscombe, *An Introduction to Wittgenstein's Tractatus* (Blackwell, 1959), p. 15.

PART II. CHAPTER II

101. 1. An expression from P. Tillich, *The Shaking of the Foundations* (SCM, 1949).
102. 2. St. Augustine, *Confessions,* VII, 23.

PAGE		
103.	3.	J. Daniélou, *God and Us* (Mowbrays, 1960), Chap. III.
105.	4.	H. H. Farmer, *The World and God* (Nisbet, 1935).
108.	5.	W. Temple, in *Revelation*, ed. Baillie and Martin (Faber, 1937), p. 107.
112.	6.	J. S. Whale, *Christian Doctrine* (Fontana Ed.), p. 33.
114.	7.	L. Hodgson, *Doctrine of the Trinity* (Nisbet, 1943), p. 83.
116.	8.	L. Prestige, *Fathers and Heretics* (New Ed., S.P.C.K., 1940), p. 92.
117.	9.	J. Daniélou, *God and Us*, p. 117f.
117.	10.	L. Hodgson, *Doctrine of the Trinity*.

PART II. CHAPTER III

122.	1.	Skinner, *Genesis*, pp. 43–5.
122.	2.	Gen. 1 : 1–3, as translated by H. Wheeler Robinson, *Inspiration and Revelation in the O.T.* (Nisbet, 1946), p. 19.
124.	3.	Skinner, *Genesis*, p. 15.
124.	4.	ibid., p. 17.
125.	5.	Isa. 45 : 18, as translated in H. W. Robinson, l.c.
128.	6.	V. Lossky, *The Mystical Theology of the Eastern Church* (Clarke, 1957), pp. 94–5.
128.	7.	See A. G. Hebert, SSM, *The Throne of David* (Faber, 1941).
134.	8.	L. S. Thornton, *Revelation and the Modern World* (Black, 1950), pp. 238–43.
135.	9.	Mother Julian of Norwich, *Revelations of Divine Love*, Ch. 51.
135.	10.	N. P. Williams, *Ideas of the Fall and of Original Sin* (1927), pp. 525–30.
135.	11.	E. L. Mascall, *Christian Theology and Natural Science* (Longmans, 1956), p. 303f.

PART II. CHAPTER IV

143.	1.	W. Temple, *Readings from St. John's Gospel*, Vol. 2, p. 235.
145.	2.	B. Lindars, SSF, in *Church Quarterly Review*, Oct.–Dec., 1960.

PART III. CHAPTER II.

The author acknowledges a debt to :
Charles Gore, *The Body of Christ* (1901).
E. L. Mascall, *Corpus Christi* (Longmans, 1953).
Dom G. Dix, *The Shape of the Liturgy* (Dacre, 1945).
F. Masure, *The Christian Sacrifice* (1942).
C. Moule, *The Sacrifice of Christ* (Hodder, 1956).

The following are suitable for further reading:
M. Thurian, *The Eucharistic Memorial* (Lutterworth, 1961).
L. Bouyer, *Life and Liturgy* (Sheed & Ward, 1956).
G. Every, *A Lamb to the Slaughter* (Clarke, 1956).
G. Every, *The Baptismal Sacrifice* (SCM Press, 1959).

PART III. CHAPTER IV.
The author wishes to recommend the following books for further reading:
R. Nelson, *The End of a Golden String* (Faith Press, 1960).
W. Knox, *Meditation and Mental Prayer* (1927).
N. Grou, *How to Pray* (1927).
E. Boylan, *Difficulties in Mental Prayer* (Gill, 1946).
R. Cant, *Christian Prayer* (Faith Press, 1962).
M. Thornton, *The Purple Headed Mountain* (Faith Press, 1962).

PART III. CHAPTER V
PAGE
223. 1. Arthur Laurent, *West Side Story*, Act 2, sc. 4.
223. 2. A. France, *Les Opinions de M. Jérome Coignard*, p. 200 ('Ils naquirent, ils suffrirent, ils moururent').
224. 3. Quoted, R. W. MacKenna, MD, *The Problem of Pain*, p. 28.
224. 4. The word was coined by G. W. Leibniz to describe that part of natural theology which is concerned to defend the goodness and omnipotence of God against objections arising from the existence of evil in the world. Etymologically the word means 'the justification of God.'
232. 5. H. A. Williams, *Jesus and the Resurrection* (1951), p. 27.
235. 6. F. W. Dillistone, *The Novelist and the Passion Story* (Collins, 1960), p. 44.
236. 7. L. S. Thornton, *The Doctrine of the Atonement* (Bles, 1937), p. 131.
237. 8. Simone Weil, *Gravity and Grace* (Routledge, 1952), p. 73.
238. 9. E. Jennings, *Every Changing Shape* (Deutsch, 1961), p. 49.

PART IV. CHAPTER I
241. 1. N. Figgis, CR, reviewing Tyrell's *Christianity at the Crossroads*, in *C.R. Quarterly*, No. 28, 1909.
242. 2. In *Church Quarterly Review*.
248. 3. Père Voillaume in *Jesus Caritas*, Oct., 1958.

PART IV. CHAPTER II
249. 1. See especially G. Barraclough, *History in a Changing World* (Oxford, 1955), *passim*.

NOTES 299

PAGE
250. 2. Mircea Eliade, *Myths, Dreams and Mysteries* (Harvill, 1960), p. 8f.
254. 3. See Anthony Sampson, *Drum* (Faber, 1956).
255. 4. Paul Tillich, *The Protestant Era* (Nisbet, 1951), p. 256.
256. 5. L. S. Thornton, *Revelation in the Modern World* (Black, 1950), p. 200.
257. 6. Mgr. M. J. Walsh, in *Dublin Review*, Winter, 1959.
259. 7. J-Y. Congar, OP, *Vaste Monde Ma Paroisse* (1959), p. 18.
260. 8. Mr. T. Mohaleroe of Basutoland, lecturing at Summer School of Christian Sociology, Oxford, July, 1960.
261. 9. See esp. A. Macbeath, *Experiments in Living* (Macmillan, 1952), *passim*.
261. 10. M. J. Walsh, l.c.
261. 11. Meye Fortes, *An African Oedipus* (OUP, 1959).
262. 12. J. Daniélou, *Le Mystère du Salut des Nations* (1945), p. 48f.
262. 13. O. Chadwick, *From Bossuet to Newman* (1957).
263. 14. J. Carpenter, *Charles Gore* (Faith Press, 1960), p. 26 n.
263. 15. G. Every, SSM, *The Baptismal Sacrifice* (SCM, 1959).
263. 16. G. Every, SSM, *A Lamb to the Slaughter* (Clarke, 1956).
264. 17. R. G. Collingwood, *The Principles of Art* (OUP, 1938).
264. 18. Chinua Achebe, *Things Fall Apart* (Hutchinson, 1958).
265. 19. L. S. Thornton, l.c., p. 202.

PART IV. CHAPTER IV
281. 1. Teilhard de Chardin, *Phenomenon of Man* (Collins, 1959), p. 226.
282. 2. ibid., p. 229 (his italics).
283. 3. ibid., p. 263 (my italics).
283. 4. ibid., p. 264.
288. 5. Dislike of the invocation of Saints often springs from a defective doctrine of the Incarnation, the Person of Christ being thought of as the union of God and *a* man, instead of the taking of manhood (i.e. the whole of man) into hypostatic union with the Godhead in the Second Person of the Blessed Trinity.
289. 6. St. Gregory of Nyssa proposes a purification by fire after death for those who have not already been cleansed by the Sacrament of Baptism.
294. 7. St. Augustine, *De Civitate Dei*, XXII, xxx.
295. 8. St. Augustine, *de Trin.* VI, x, 12.
295. 9. St. Augustine, *Conf.* VII, x, 16.

INDEX OF BIBLICAL PASSAGES
(R.V. used throughout)

BIBLE REF.	PAGE
Genesis	
1 : 1	124
1 : 1–2, 4	134, 136
1 : 2	195
1 : 2–3	141
1 : 26	129, 267
1 : 31	135
2 : 4ff	134
3 : 8	34
3 : 15	35
6 : 13–9 : 13	194
12 : 1	33
12 : 3	14, 159
22 : 18	14
35 : 1–4	194
Exodus	
3 : 6	34
14	194
15 : 1–21	194
19 : 10	194
19 : 14	194
20 : 2	17
29 : 45	34
30 : 17ff	195
Leviticus	
26 : 12	34
Numbers	
11 : 24–9	151
21 : 8	196
1 Samuel	
17 : 34f	20
17 : 50	18

BIBLE REF.	PAGE
1 Kings	
18 : 21	25
18 : 39	25
1 Chronicles	
29 : 14	178
2 Chronicles	
4 : 2–6	195
Job	
4 : 15	150
7 : 12	123
26 : 12f	122
Psalms	
8 : 5	130
8 : 6	130
22	197
33 : 6f	195
45 : 13	286
51 : 6	166
51 : 11	145
74 : 13f	123
89 : 10f	122
100 : 3	111
115 : 13ff	76
119 : 103	269
139 : 1–2	106
139 : 7–8	106
Ecclesiastes	
1 : 13f	243
9 : 4f	51
Song of Songs	
1 : 2	293

INDEX

BIBLE REF.	PAGE
Isaiah	
1 : 16	195
6 : 1–5	103
6 : 4	275
11 : 6–9	47
27 : 1	123
30 : 7	123
40 : 7ff	34
40 : 25f	110
42 : 1	197
42 : 11	196
45 : 18	125
45 : 22	110
51 : 9	122
51 : 9b, 10	123
52 : 13–53 : 12	193
52 : 13ff	197
53 : 2	286
53 : 7	196
53 : 11	294
53 : 11f	196
53 : 12	197
57 : 15	34
61 : 1f	196
63 : 10, 11	145
Jeremiah	
4 : 14	195
4 : 23–6	124
31 : 31–4	256
31 : 33–4	166
Lamentations	
1 : 12	231
Ezekiel	
1 : 26	129
11 : 19–20	166
36 : 25–7	195
36 : 26–7	166

BIBLE REF.	PAGE
Daniel	
7	193
7 : 13f	197
7 : 18	197
Amos	
3 : 8	26
5 : 14f	26
5 : 24	26
7 : 14f	26
Habakkuk	
1 : 13	111
Zechariah	
9 : 9	20
Malachi	
3 : 1	35
2 Maccabees	
7 : 28	125
Matthew	
1 : 1	12
4 : 3	21
5 : 6	26
5 : 8	288
5 : 17	27
6 : 13	226
11 : 28	42
13 : 26	226
13 : 38	227
16 : 22	234
20 : 28	197
21 : 5	20
21 : 16	20
21 : 35	23
21 : 45	23
23 : 37	23
25 : 31ff	290
26 : 26	21
26 : 41	78

BIBLE REF.	PAGE	BIBLE REF.	PAGE
Matthew—(contd.)		Luke—(contd.)	
27 : 46	54	23 : 39–43	53
28 : 9	41	23 : 41	231
28 : 17	41	23 : 44	54
28 : 19	160	23 : 46	60
		24 : 21a	41
Mark		24 : 39ff	65
1 : 1f	22		
1 : 15	159	John	
8 : 29	41	1 : 1	31
8 : 34	196	1 : 14	31
10 : 38	196	1 : 29	196
10 : 45	175, 194	1 : 52	197
13 : 9	223	2 : 19	197
13 : 24	289	2 : 21	197
13 : 32–3	234	3 : 1–14	196
14 : 32–42	234	3 : 8	140, 151
14 : 33	287	3 : 34	113
14 : 35–8	234	4 : 34	114, 285
14 : 36	230, 285	5 : 19	114
14 : 38	78	5 : 28	289
14 : 41	234	6	42
14 : 50	231	6 : 53	176
14 : 58	197	6 : 53–8	199
15 : 34	54, 197, 231	8 : 28	196
15 : 39	39	8 : 33	12
		8 : 44	227
Luke		10 : 11	20
1 : 5	27	10 : 17f	79
1 : 73–4	159	10 : 30	54
2 : 49	60	11 : 25	80
4 : 16–19	196	12 : 21	38
4 : 36	227	12 : 24	72
7 : 33	231	12 : 31	226
9 : 31	285	12 : 32	196
10 : 19	227	13 : 1	232
11 : 21f	19	13 : 7	225
12 : 30	196	14 : 12	42
12 : 50	146	14 : 30	226
13 : 33	285	15 : 26	147
18 : 8	289	16 : 7	147
23 : 34	53	16 : 11	226

BIBLE REF.	PAGE
John—(contd.)	
16 : 13	147
16 : 14f	148
16 : 32	287
17 : 5	113
18 : 37	21, 22
19 : 30	196
20 : 1	189
20 : 2	67
20 : 22–4	160
20 : 25	67, 294
20 : 26	189
20 : 27	65
20 : 28	41
20 : 29	70
Acts	
9	164
10 : 2	163
13 : 32–3	159
15	161, 165
15 : 28	143
17 : 23	47
17 : 28	101
20 : 7	189
20 : 11	189
23 : 7ff	75
Romans	
1 : 3–4	40
2 : 14–15	165
6 : 1–14	193
6 : 3	205
6 : 3f	71
6 : 11	200
7 : 15	78
7 : 19	78
7 : 22–4	132
8 : 9	113
8 : 19–22	133
8 : 23	133

BIBLE REF.	PAGE
Romans—(contd.)	
8 : 26	154
8 : 38f	107
9 : 6–12	165
9 : 18–20	132
1 Corinthians	
1 : 13	166
1 : 23	41
2 : 26	62
4 : 9	286
4 : 13	286
5 : 76	175
6 : 3	130
6 : 17	277, 280
6 : 19	166
7 : 40	143
8 : 6	39
10 : 1, 2, 4f	199
10 : 1–13	198
10 : 2	195
10 : 16f	199
10 : 17	21
11 : 17–34	198
11 : 27	292
12 : 12f	199
12 : 12–27	166
12 : 27	180
14 : 15	184
15	41
15 : 1ff	40
15 : 8	38
15 : 14	66
15 : 14f	69
15 : 15	75
15 : 22	292
15 : 31	201
15 : 35	77
15 : 50	77
15 : 52	171
16 : 2	189

BIBLE REF.	PAGE	BIBLE REF.	PAGE
2 *Corinthians*		*Colossians*	
1 : 20	38	1 : 15	72
4 : 4	72	1 : 15f	39
4 : 10	286	1 : 18	166
4 : 12	286	1 : 19f	133
4 : 16	280	1 : 24	285
5 : 10	289	2 : 9	39
5 : 17	74	3 : 1–4	200
5 : 19	176	3 : 5	200
5 : 21	135	3 : 9f	130
6 : 16	34		
		1 Thessalonians	
		5 : 23	276
Galatians		*2 Thessalonians*	
1 : 1	39	2 : 4	226
1 : 17	38		
3 : 24	165	*1 Timothy*	
3 : 26f	201	2 : 14	135
3 : 27	200		
4 : 4	39	*Hebrews*	
5 : 2	114	1 : 1	22, 165
		1 : 3	182
		2 : 10	238
Ephesians		6 : 2	200
1	193	6 : 4–6	209
1 : 2, 3	210	7 : 25	177
1 : 3–14	137	9 : 14	113, 200
1 : 10	133, 285	9 : 26	175
1 : 19	201	10 : 12	175
2	193	10 : 12, 14	176
2 : 14	166	11 : 10	81
2 : 18	117	11 : 13f	81
2 : 20	24		
4 : 15	285	*1 Peter*	
4 : 25	180	1 : 3	71
5 : 14	81	1 : 3ff	40
5 : 27	152	1 : 8	70
		1 : 21	74
Philippians		2 : 23	232
2 : 5–7	39		
2 : 7–11	147	*2 Peter*	
3 : 21	291, 293	1 : 4	131, 132

BIBLE REF.	PAGE	BIBLE REF.	PAGE
1 John		Revelation—(contd.)	
1 : 1	47	1 : 18	55
1 : 1–3	268	9 : 4ff	54
1 : 3	47	19 : 6	227
3 : 2	293	19 : 7	293
		21 : 2	293
Revelation		21 : 4	238
1 : 5	55	21 : 22	294

INDEX OF PROPER NAMES

Acarie, Madame, 269
Achebe, Chinua, 264
Achilles, 51
Adonis, 72
Adoptionists, 43
Agia Sophia, 222
Alexander, 14
Amrose, 257
Anselm, St., 227
Apologists, 44
Apsu, 121, 122
Aquinas, St. Thomas, 98, 128, 293
Aristotle, 25
Athanasius, St., 44
Attis, 72
Attys, 167
Augustine, St., of Canterbury, 172, 256
Augustine, St., of Hippo, 102, 116, 128, 179–82, 267, 279, 294
Augustus, 14
Auschwitz, 227
Ayer, A. J., 93

Benson, Fr. R. M., S.S.J.E., 199, 202, 206, 208
Bernard, St., 276
Bodington, Mr., 202
Body, Canon, 202, 203
Boniface, St., 257
Bossuet, J. B., 262
Boston, 157
'Brothers Karamazov,' 294
Browning, R. B., 61
Buddha, 251
Bunyan, W., 279

Calvin, J., 266
Carton, Sidney, 64
Catlin, George, 254
Chadwick, O., 262
Chalcedon, Council of, 263
Chardin, Teilhard de, 281, 283
Charlemagne, 172
Chesterton, G. K., 163
Church of England Liturgical Commission, 204, 205
Church, R. W., 263

Cloud of Unknowing, 251
Collingwood, R. G., 264
Congar, Père, 259
Coomeraswamy, Ananda, 251
Cranmer, T., 173, 262

Daniélou, J., 261, 262
Dante, 146
Darwin, C., 224
Descartes, 94, 255
Dillistone, F. W., 234, 235
Dionysius, 257
Dix, Dom Gregory, O.S.B., 205
Duns Scotus, 129

Eliade, Mircea, 96, 249–54, 261, 264, 265
Eliot, T. S., 291
Ends and Means, 251
Euclid, 95
Evans-Pritchard, E., 264
Everlasting Man, 163
Every, Br. George, S.S.M., 263

Fable, The, 235
Farmer, H. H., 105
Faulkner, W., 234
Figgis, Fr. Neville, C.R., 241, 242
Foucauld, Charles de, 248
France, Anatole, 223
Francis, St., de Sales, 221
Frazer, Sir James, 264
Frederick the Great, 13

Gallio, 223
Gladstone, W. E., 203
Gluckman, Max, 260
Gore, C., 23, 263
Grafton, Bp., of Fond du Lac, 207
Greene, Graham, 211
Gregory, Pope, 172, 256
Guénon, René, 251
Guild of St. Matthew, 201
Gurdjieff, 282

Hamlet, 29
Harnack, A., 167
Heidegger, F., 251

INDEX

Hiroshima, 227
Hitler, A., 14
Hodgson, L., 114, 117
Homer, 51, 146
Hooker, R., 262
Hopkins, Gerard Manley, 236
Hulme, T. E., 112
Hume, D., 93
Huxley, Aldous, 251

Irenaeus, St., 44, 130, 257
Isidore, 257

James, E. O., 264
Jennings, E., 237
John, St., of the Cross, 251
Julian, Mother, of Norwich, 237, 294
Jung, C. G., 254

Kant, E., 94
Kazantzakis, Nikos, 234
Keats, J., 116
Kemal, Mustapha, 261
Kitchener of Khartoum, 14

Lamb, The, 234, 235
Law, W., 207
Leo XIII, Pope, 176
Lévy-Bruhl, 264
Luther, M., 207

Macmillan, H., 246
Malinowski, B., 86, 264
Manichaeism, 135
Marcionism, 43
Marduk, 122
Mascall, E. L., 135
Mason, A. J., 206
Matchikikze, Tod., 254
Mauriac, François, 234, 235
Melletus, 256
Melville, Herman, 234
Mithras, 167
Mphahlele, Ezekiel, 246
Mysticism of St. Paul, 193

Newman, J. H., 262
Nicaea, Council of, 43
Nkrumah, Dr., 246
Novelist and the Passion Story, 234
Nyerere, Julius, 245

On the Beach, 281

Origen, 39, 44
Osiris, 72, 167

Parish and People, 204
Pascal, B., 96, 103
Plato, 251
Platon, Abp. of Kiev, 193
Prestige, L., 115
Pusey, E. B., 204
Pythagoras, 251

Quest of the Historical Jesus, 193
Quick, O., 206

Ramsey, A. M., Abp. of Canterbury, 7, 205, 208
Raynes, Fr. Raymond, C.R., 217
Revere, Paul, 157
Ring and the Book, 61
Ruskin, J., 48
Russell, B., 88, 89

Sartre, J. P., 93, 291
Schmidt, Fr. W., 264
Schuon, Frithjov, 251
Schweitzer, A., 193
Selwyn, E. G., 205
Sergius, St., 222
Shakespeare, W., 29, 146
Sharpeville, 227
Shute, Nevile, 281
Sibelius, 76
Simeon, Charles, 203
Stacy, Fr., 201
Stanton, Fr. A. H., 203
Sundkler, Bengt, 264

Tale of Two Cities, 64
Taylor, J., 224
Temple, W., 143
Teresa, St., of Avila, 215, 269
Tertullian, 44
Theology of Initiation, 205
Things Fall Apart, 264
Thornton, Fr. Lionel, C.R., 235, 256 –8, 263, 265
Tiamat, 121, 122
Tillich, P., 97, 225, 257
Turner, H. E. W., 44
Twigg, Mr., 202

Vaihinger, H., 94
Verwoerd, Dr. H. F., 246

Victoria, Queen, 174
Voillaume, Père, 247
Voltaire, 13

Wach, J., 264
Walsh, Mgr. M. J., 261
Welensky, Sir Roy, 246
Wesley, J., 16, 203, 207
West Side Story, 223, 243

Westcott, B. F., 81, 129
Whitfield, G., 203
Whittier, J. G., 28
Wilkinson, Bp. G. H., 202, 206
William, Fr., of Glasshampton, 201
Williams, C., 291
Williams, Fr. H., 232
Williams, N. P., 135
Wreck of the Deutschland, 236

www.ingramcontent.com/pod-product-compliance
Lightning Source LLC
Chambersburg PA
CBHW071234230426
43668CB00011B/1427